to JE

Life is an ex

All best wishes to You,

Herman Haftink

BRAND NEW ME

Calgary, 10 August, 2005

DEDICATION

This Book is lovingly dedicated
to my parents
who gave me life
and who nurtured me
through war and peace:

HERMANNUS AAFTINK
(1901-1960)

JOHANNA TER HORST - AAFTINK
(1899-1948)

BRAND NEW ME

The Art of Authentic Living

Herman J. Aaftink

Cosmic Concepts

2531 Dover Lane
St. Joseph, Michigan 49085

BRAND NEW ME
The Art of Authentic Living   © Herman J. Aaftink - 1995

Library of Congress Cataloging-in-Publication Data

Aaftink, Herman J., 1933-
         Brand new me : the art of authentic living / Herman J. Aaftink.
         p.   cm.
         Includes bibliographical references.
         ISBN 0-9620507-4-1 (pbk.)
         1. Conduct of life. I. Title.
BJ1581.2.A19   1995   95-10468
158--dc20   CIP

Published by COSMIC CONCEPTS
2531 Dover Lane, St. Joseph, MI 49085

printed and bound in the United States of America

10 9 8 7 6 5 4 3 2 1

MEET THE AUTHOR

This is a "pull-up-your-chair-and-let's-talk" book. It is written as if you, the reader, and I the writer, were friends, and we carried on a personal conversation about what lifestyle and philosophy of life are the wisest choice for today's world.

My own life story begins in the tumultuous years preceding the Second World War, in Europe in a country known as The Netherlands. When the war broke out in May 1940, my homeland was overrun by the Nazis; we suffered from an incredibly brutal regime for five horrifying years. Everything we held dear was maimed or destroyed: our freedom, prosperity, health, and world of loved ones. My hometown was subjected to air raid bombardments forty-two times in five years. Thousands lost their homes, thousands of buildings were demolished. We lived in an earthly hell. Some of my relatives were active in the resistance movement. I lived in the same house with these fighters. When liberation finally came in April 1945, we were exhausted and depleted. This experience set the tone for my life's decisions and impacted my life profoundly.

My quest for the meaning of life is rooted in all of this, as yours may be if you have had to face shattering crises. It became my dream to make this quest the mission of my life, and whatever I pursued was a means toward that goal. As a young man I served in the military and trained as an accountant. I have lived in Canada for the past forty years and have worked as a bank employee, a cost accountant, an office and credit manager, a purchasing agent, a controller, a motivational speaker and a protestant minister.

For the past twenty-five years I have served as director of a self-enhancement center meeting in Calgary, Alberta, Canada. The major intent of this group has been to empower the individual, not to follow, but be in charge of one's life. Every major idea in this book has been discussed at length with dedicated friends representing all age groups. We have also tested our findings by verifying them with the "wisdom of the ages," as you will see from the running bibliography of historical and contemporary thinkers. This careful process has made the book a practical statement ready for immediate use by any reader fascinated by the challenge of living authentically....to the best of one's abilities in the service of others.

In my association with others in my field I have been privileged to conduct numerous seminars and courses, and participate in many conventions in most of the major metropolitan areas of the United States and Canada. And so, you'll notice that I have a tendency to write as I talk, in a direct and personal way. I try to involve you in what I observe and feel. I hope you'll like this approach.

Many friends have helped make this book possible and for this I am most grateful. They are so much part of it. Ah, yes, one more thing: a book like this feels to me like a "living thing". . . May it become more and more alive to you, as you proceed to make it your own. And may true authenticity be yours as a result!

INTRODUCTION

This is a LIFESTYLE book and therefore it covers not just one piece of "life's pie" but an overview of the entire living experience. The overriding intent is to empower the individual, not to follow, but to be in charge of one's own life. In this sense it is a manual for self-management. In deeper terminology, it can be described as a guide to conscious, personal evolution. Or, for those who have already begun to discover the importance of the subconscious mind, we would simply say, "Follow your dreams!"

In order to achieve these aims we enter on a voyage of discovery of truths and life-skills that have been organized, for easy reading and application, into five areas, each with a specific goal to be explored and reached:

PART ONE
The Art of Thinking — Your Key to Wellness

PART TWO
The Art of Motivation — Your Key to Success

PART THREE
The Art of Caring — Your Key to Relationships

PART FOUR
The Art of Contemplation — Your Key to Peace

PART FIVE
The Art of Reflection — Your Key to Meaning

Another way of defining our adventure is to suggest that there are five "doors" in life to be opened, in order to progressively fulfil five major needs we observe within ourselves and others. This introduction suggests the five "keys" that will enable us to open these doors.

And now these "keys" are yours; as you turn them may you find your own authentic self — in a world that needs **you**, now! Here's to YOUR "Brand New Me!"

H.J.A.
Calgary, Alberta, Canada

TABLE OF CONTENTS

THE ART OF REFLECTION — YOUR KEY TO MEANING

PART ONE

THE ART OF THINKING - YOUR KEY TO WELLNESS

"There's nothing either good or bad but thinking makes it so"

Hamlet, Act II, Scene 2
William Shakespeare (1564–1616)

CHAPTER 1

ATTITUDE IS KING

"If the power of thought is universal among mankind,
so likewise is the possession of reason, making us rational creatures"

Meditations
Marcus Aurelius (121–180)

What is the most important question you have ever asked yourself? Most likely, it has to do with improving your life: How can I change my life for the better? If you were to list this and similar questions over a period of some years you would probably be able to identify your major needs in the following five areas as they are pondered in our book:

PART ONE - **Wellness** — We all like to be healthy, energetic, with lots of vitality, get-up-and-go. We enjoy feeling good physically, mentally and emotionally. Without that wellness, it's difficult to undertake any change.

PART TWO - **Success** — We want to feel that we can achieve what we set out to do. We like to be able to seek and reach personal objectives. We wish to experience the satisfaction of creative accomplishments.

PART THREE - **Relationships** — We do not live alone on this planet and we find that at home, at work, at play and in most of our enterprises we need the ability to get along with people. Beyond this, we also seek to satisfy the deeper longings for love and intimacy. We want friendship, companionship and the sense of being really happy with other persons in our life.

PART FOUR - **Peace** — No one enjoys being nervous, upset, distressed, depressed or miserable. We seek peace of mind, we wish to be relaxed, at ease in the universe. We like to experience stillness, serenity.

PART FIVE - **Meaning** — We all wish to have a measure of understanding life and of wisdom. We believe that we can discover the meaning and purpose of our own existence. This is how we justify why we are here.

Suppose we look around the circle of people we know rather well, parents, children, close relatives, friends, colleagues, neighbors and perhaps our "significant other." We may find that, if they have expressed their needs and desires to us, (and even if they haven't) these too can be found within the general boundaries of the five concerns listed above.

To a lot of people, these things are not a matter over which they much control. Many believe the fulfillment of their needs in these areas is largely a matter of luck, chance and fate. To them what matters is the environment where you were born, the character and life-style of your parents, your genes, your education, who influenced you, whom you married, the political, economic and social circumstances of your life — the list goes on. No rational person would deny that these factors, have impacted your life. No doubt you can create your own list of specific circumstances and key people who have contributed significantly to who you are and what your life is like today.

What we are interested in, as we pursue the adventure of this book, is simply this: **WHAT CAN AN INDIVIDUAL DO** to fulfil these five needs? We are not thinking in terms of collective action, in joining a social, political, religious or other kind of movement, with the objective of improving the general human condition. Collective action does provide an important opportunity to improve the citizens' condition, but our objective here if for the empowerment of the **PERSON**. A better equipped individual will surely be a more effective participant in any organization or institution.

Where does our adventure begin? We have charted the five "oceans" of our needs, they form the five parts of this book. They are our world. Where exactly is that world? Our first answer could be "out there" — the physical world of space and time with all its forces, and organisms — including yourself. This is true, as far as it goes. Yet, as far as the individual person is concerned, this world "out there" becomes real and is experienced, interpreted and felt, only because you have an "in here." You know life by means of your mind or consciousness. The great Irish philosopher George Berkeley (1685–1753) said that we can only know our own ideas. Let's reflect on that.

There is an ancient story, or koan in the Zen tradition, that illustrates this point. Two students were arguing about a flapping banner on a windy day. One said, "I see the banner moving." The second one said, "I see the wind moving." The teacher arrived on the scene and said, "I see your minds moving," Who was right? Each one of them was right from their own point of view. But without the "minds moving" not one of them would have been aware of what was happening, let alone evaluating it or changing it. Similarly, "our world," in a real sense, does exist in our consciousness and it is by means of consciousness that we perceive and interact with "the world out there." How do we do this? We call this activity, in which we are continually engaged, *thinking*.

Let's test our line of reasoning. Ours is not an arbitrary announcement. We are not following some agreed-on authority. Let us stay with reason and do ourselves the favor of acknowledging that we are our own authority because we are "rational creatures." How do improvements occur in human society and in an individual's life? What happens if not that someone becomes aware of a failing situation and applies a better idea?

All inventions, all enrichment, technologically and culturally, are the result of thinking in new and better ways. Before the blueprint of any noble creation there exists the idea whose expression it is. Ultimately, it is ideas, thoughts, opinions and beliefs that rule our world, both "out there" and "in here." That's why thinking is the first art we are considering here. Your thinking governs your life. What we were, what we are, and what we become, is recalled, perceived and anticipated by our thinking. No wonder the literary genius Ralph Waldo Emerson (1803–1882) over and over again impressed on his readers that we are what we think about all day long.

If it's true that thinking is so vital an activity, our next question is: "How can we change our thinking and attitude, so we can create a better life for ourselves and others?" As you think these ideas through, please remember to not accept any suggestion just because you read it, but only because your own experience tells you this is worthy of your consideration. Then apply the idea and the result will be your evidence.

REALIZE THAT EVERY SITUATION MUST BE MET IN THE MIND The art of thinking recognizes that nothing and no one is outside of its realm. Consciousness is all inclusive and it is always consciousness of something. Every life's activity is its subject. If you are to meet someone tomorrow, you meet that person first in your mind. Every decision you make is made in your mind. Every reaction — be it approval or disapproval — is determined by your mind. What happens when we get upset? Our five senses report impressions of what is happening. Then our mind passes judgment and our whole being responds, we feel it. What determines this process? Your mind does. It has choices. It could choose otherwise. Who controls it? You do.

The Stoic philosopher Chrysippus of Soli (280–206 B.C.) used to compare our reaction (to events) to pushing a cylinder and a cube downhill. The same push produced different results because of the shape of the object; by the time the cylinder had rolled all the way down, the cube would only have moved a foot or two. In the same way, what happens to the way we feel in response to a person or event depends on the way we react. Experiment with this idea and discover just how much "power" you have over a given situation!

THINK FOR YOURSELF Having recognized some of the power available, we need to make it our own, to claim it. This means deciding to become responsible for our thinking. We will never develop a sturdy personality while giving others most of the responsibility for what happens to us. The art of thinking calls for taking that thinking in hand, into our own hands. This means: begin now to form your own opinions, become less dependent on what others expect you to think or feel. Stop always blaming others and start taking command of the direction of your life.

This implies two more considerations: First, open your mind to new ideas, new thoughts, new truths, new possibilities, and second, commit yourself to finding out, exploring and studying what the mind is all about. Understand yourself; it may well be the most important thing you ever do. There is much to learn because the mind, both as conscious and unconscious, is an amazingly dynamic, complex and powerful agency.

GIVE YOUR ATTENTION TO WHAT IS IMPORTANT TO YOU

Does this mean becoming more aware of arranging "quality time," through time management stopping the wasting of precious hours? Yes, but it can mean much more. Thinking can lift your life from drab meaninglessness to high significance. It can put you on the road to achieving wonderful goals. It is no surprise to add, that this will not be achieved without effort on your part.

The 20th century French philosopher and novelist Simone de Beauvoir (1908–1986) announced that each of us is "a movement toward the future — no thing is decided in advance." All this can become real for us, provided we give that future our undivided attention. For example, if you want health, you must become INTERESTED in health, not in sickness. It's like wanting a new coat — if your desire is strong enough you will SEE coats everywhere, in magazines, on people, in store windows, on billboards.

Are you constantly amazed, curious, fascinated, excited and delighted by the ever unfolding panorama of your own personal future? If not, why not? What is holding things up? Begin mastering the art of centering your attention on what is truly important to you right now. When you do, you'll soon discover an interesting principle of mind and life, for it will seem to you as if you actually ATTRACT into your life whatever you have given your attention to . . .

DO NOT LINGER OVER NEGATIVES IN YOUR LIFE This may well be the greatest challenge of all the suggestions in this opening chapter, because, "negatives" are all around us demanding our attention. But if that to which we have given our attention comes to us, we have to decide which way we want to go. You cannot expect an elevator in a highrise building to take you to the penthouse and the basement at the same time. We must choose which button it will be. So too with our mind buttons.

What happens to our consciousness when we allow it to be packed full with "news" of disasters and crime, "entertainment" of violence and horror, "conversations" of gossip and judgment? We can decide now that we will no longer tolerate negatives dominating our mind.

Does this mean following the proverbial ostrich and sticking our heads under the sand of ignorance? Of course not. No one ever helped another that way. What it does mean is: be aware of what's happening, give it your attention to the degree that it is your business to do so and to the extent that you can be of help in that situation. But don't linger over the negative and destructive, don't dwell on it, for if you do you will not only feel increasingly miserable but helpless as well. So let's change that (probably very old) habit of negative thinking. This will help: say (to yourself), "There is no need (nor necessity) for this in my life," or "This is unworthy of my attention," or "This is really none of my business."

When you start conversing with yourself in this way, you have opted on developing another interesting aspect of the art of thinking: Affirmative Self-Talk. That makes sense too, because, as you have likely already discovered, one of the best ways to get rid of a negative thought is to substitute a positive, constructive one.

USE AFFIRMATIVE SELF-TALK Affirmations are now widely used as a method to encourage and motivate people. They work as a result of the creative response of our unconscious or subconscious mind to any definite suggestion made, especially in the first person (I), present tense. The best way to prove the benefits of affirmations is to faithfully try some. Perhaps the best known affirmation is the one originated by one of the early practitioners on the subject of auto-suggestion, the French author Emile Coué (1857–1926): "Every day, in every way, I'm getting better and better." Coué obtained tremendous results in terms of self-healing and self-improvement with many thousands of persons the world over.

Affirmations work best when they are said or thought quietly, without effort, but sincerely with the expectation of the desired result. They may be repeated as often as you feel comfortable doing so. Formulate them in your own words, because it is the nature of the subconscious to respond to what it perceives as an authentic, genuine command.

What should an affirmation say? It should be a suggestion of a "desired result," applied to your own immediate need. Let's say you often feel that you are unable to "make a move" or express an opinion without the approval of certain persons in your life. Such a situation calls for a more independently thinking, assertive you. To formulate this need affirmatively you could state, "I am my own authority for everything I think and do. I will freely express my convictions at the right time and the appropriate occasion."

Statements such as this are deliberately designed to counteract negative or destructive habits of thinking. They build habits of thought and reinforce healthy self-esteem when and where the need is the greatest. When you languish too long feeling sorry for yourself, counter such thoughts saying, "I do not indulge in self-pity."

When at the start of a day, the weather looks bad, the radio reports bad news, and the folks around you declare that it's a bad day, **you** can say with enthusiasm, "This is a beautiful new day, it is filled with challenge and opportunity for me; I make the most of this day and look forward to a terrific experience. I am meeting and attracting warm, helpful, friendly and courteous people, they like me and I like them," or words to that effect. Create your own affirmations, get the feel and the drift of it and you will catch some of the spirit of life itself. Life is for living; mastering and practicing the art of affirmative thinking helps to make it so.

We will now turn to an explanation of why all this works as our adventure takes us to the doorstep of the unconscious. . .

Bibliography & Recommended Further Reading

Coué, Emile & Brooks, C. Harry: Better and Better Every Day
        London: Unwin, 1960

Peale, Norman Vincent: The Power of Positive Thinking
        Pawling, N.Y.: The Peale Center for Christian Living, 1978

Fox, Emmet: Power Through Constructive Thinking
        N.Y.: Harper & Bros., 1940

Aurelius, Marcus: Meditations, transl. Maxwell Staniforth
        Baltimore, Md., Harmondsworth, England: Penguin Books, 1967

Sandbach, F.H.: The Stoics
        N.Y., W.W. Norton & Co., 1975

Berkeley, George: The Principles of Human Knowledge.   Three
        Dialogues Between Hylas and Philonous
        London: Collins/Fontana, 1975

Zen Buddhism
        Mount Vernon, N.Y.: The Peter Pauper Press, 1959

Reps, Paul: Zen Flesh, Zen Bones - A Collection of Zen and Pre-Zen
        Garden City, N.Y.: Anchor/Doubleday & Co., Inc., 1955

Dillaway, Newton: The Gospel of Emerson
        Lee's Summit, Mo.: Unity Books, 1949

Emerson, Ralph Waldo: The Heart of Emerson's Journals
        N.Y.: Houghton Mifflin Co., 1926

De Beauvoir, Simone: The Ethics of Ambiguity, transl. B.Frechtman,
        Secaucus, N.J.: The Citadel Press, Lyle Stuart, Inc., 1975

Addington, Jack E. & Cornelia: The Perfect Power Within You
        Santa Monica, CA: De Vorss & Co., 1973

CHAPTER 2

INTO YOUR DEEPER SELF

*"My life is the story of the self-realization of the unconscious.
Everything in the unconscious seeks outward manifestation. . ."*
Memories, Dreams, Reflections
Carl Gustav Jung (1875-1961)

To a great many people, human behavior and life itself are baffling mysteries. Is there anyone who has not, at one time or another said, "I don't understand him (or her)." We wonder why people speak and act and behave in certain ways. Sometimes we are surprised at our own behavior. In addition, we find ourselves in situations where we exclaim, "Why did that happen to me?" We are unable to understand the strange pathways of our personal fate as well as that of others.

Think of all the people you know who, having lived some eighty or ninety years feel somewhat the way Christopher Columbus (1451–1506) is said to have felt in his final years. When he first left Europe, sailing west he didn't know where he was going. When he got there he didn't know where he was and when he arrived back home, he had no idea where he had been.

Columbus spoke of his discovery as an "Other World" and when you and I journey into our deeper self this too is an Other World. Knowing something about it may well be the key to understanding much of human behavior. It may provide insight into human achievement and failure and help us grasp the meaning of much of what happens to us. Let's start with what we know about the mind as awareness. With our conscious mind we are continually becoming aware of the world "out there" as well as of our world of consciousness "in here." While utilizing the five senses of seeing, hearing, smelling, tasting and touching we, reason, interpret, perceive, decide, imagine, and respond. All this is closely related to the physical organism by which conscious thinking seems to take place.

But conscious thinking does not only take place in an interrelationship with the body, it is also acted upon by an incredibly complex agency known as the Unconscious or Subconscious Mind.

How do we know all this?   We know it from observation of ourselves — what happens when we think, how we feel and what happens next. So, everything we arrive at here, as throughout this book, can be verified in your own experience; it is rational, intelligent, scientific and personal. The obvious question now is: just **what is** this Subconscious or Unconscious Mind, and if it is indeed Unconscious, how can we describe something of which we are not aware? We can because it reveals itself to us by what it does. We see, and often feel, its results. We know the cause by its effect.

These two aspects or phases of the mind have been compared to an iceberg: you see only a small part of it above the water level, but most of it is submerged. Or we may think of a modern high-rise building whose foundation and below-ground garage may be out of sight, but they form an integral part of the structure and what's observed from the outside depends on what cannot be seen.

But both these metaphors are inadequate since they do not convey the dynamic interaction that continually takes place between the two phases of the mind. A better description would be to call it a creative process. We see it at work in nature: to produce an apple on a tree, we start by planting an apple seed in healthy soil. The soil is below the surface of our viewpoint but responds creatively to the seed, eventually producing the apple tree and the fruit. We see a similar process at work in manufacturing technology: the raw materials proceed into the machinery which modifies them and eventually produces the desired product for packaging and transport. The principle we use when operating a calculator or computer is similar: we have input, reacted upon by a program, producing an output or result.

The Subconscious Mind may be compared to a "program" which responds to the Conscious Mind — what we accept as true in our thinking (consciously) is acted upon by the Subconscious which seeks to carry out the thought as if it were an order. That it has both the intelligence and the dynamics to do so, we shall discover shortly. Perhaps the best way to convey the meaning of what we say here is to use a true story.

Some years ago a lady came to see me about a problem. She was well educated, a professional in her field and well traveled. She said her problem was steps and staircases. She kept falling off various steps, bruising and hurting herself and even breaking bones. "Someday," she said, "steps will be the death of me." I tried to explain to her that this belief needed to be changed; that her mind could be re-conditioned. She welcomed this information. But a few weeks later the news reached me that she had passed away. She had suffered a fatal accident by falling down a flight of stairs!

Coincidence? There are many such "coincidences" both desirable and undesirable. We could describe these experiences as luck or fate, another way of saying we are ignorant of the cause. Let us examine the activity of our Subconscious more closely to see what we can find.

It appears to be an amazing, dynamic, highly intelligent activity. Always processing the data coming from the conscious mind and the intruding events from the "outer world," it is continually creating its own scenario of reality. It can be remarkably responsive to suggestions from the conscious mind and from the persuasion of both visual and audible advertising.

We said earlier that it is complex; yet it can be understood in terms available to all of us. There is the difficulty of describing the intangible, the non-material, and doing so in "material language." Therefore, we need to remember that the Categories of the Subconscious Mind outlined here are not an exact or complete catalogue of the subject. We also need to be aware that the dynamics of each category know no strict borderlines — the entire process is interrelated and one activity cannot be isolated from another.

While no descriptions of the relationship between the Conscious and Subconscious will totally and accurately describe this amazing, complex phenomenon, it will help our understanding to consider five basic Categories of their functioning. The first three are personal, related to each unique individual, and the last two, while beyond the personal, include it just the same.

MEMORY — We know we have memory because we are able to recall or remember a person, an event, a feeling and an experience. The English word "mind" is derived form the gothic old English "gamunds" which means "memory." For centuries, that area of our consciousness which we call the subconscious was thought of only as memory, a storehouse of past experiences. Today we may describe memory as an intangible videotape of everything we have thought and felt, both "out there" (the events of our lives) and inside us (what we have experienced within, the world of inner reaction).

Even when we do not remember, the memory may well "be there" but not immediately available. How often when meeting someone and unable to remember their name have you found it, "popping into your head" at a later time. Apparently all kinds of stresses affect our ability to recall. There are techniques of association and remembering which can help us recall.

What is important to us is how we deal with what we experience and subsequently remember. Memory contains all our beliefs and opinions both true and false. These don't just lie there as if deposited in a filing cabinet. Suppose you had an unpleasant experience in a relationship with another person. You have "forgotten" that person or so you think. You do not think of that person consciously anymore. Then you walk into a restaurant and you spot that same person. Now it's ten years later, but time doesn't seem to matter for up come the same emotions, perhaps anger or resentment and you realize in MEMORY the videotape is still playing.

The consequences of what we believe an experience means to us on occasion will go far beyond unpleasant feelings. They may affect our health, our success, our relations and our peace of mind. What causes some memories to be deeply retained? Are their interpretations fixed forever? No, they are not. The marvelous good news about the subconscious is that no matter how "repressed" or "depressing" an experience may have been, its character and climate can be replaced and improved by new, positive, healing experiences and memories. Both our personality and health can look forward to vastly improved quality of life.

INVOLUNTARY FUNCTIONS — It is quite obvious that there is some intelligence at work within us. There are many functions and processes that are carried on throughout the vast empire of our physical and mental-emotional being. Let's stop and think for a moment. Without conscious direction there takes place within us the processes of respiration, digestion, assimilation, circulation, elimination and all the other activities including those of the subconscious "chemist." Your heart keeps beating and your lungs keep breathing. In addition, our subconscious makes it possible for us to learn, and upon practice, to automatically respond and repeat what we have learned.

This is how we form and re-form habits, establish and re-shape what we call our conditioning. One well known pioneer researcher of "conditioned reflexes" was the Russian physiologist Ivan Petrovich Pavlov (1849–1936). He discovered that if you ring a bell before feeding a dog, the animal will salivate, as usual, at the sight of the food. Repeat this often enough and the dog will salivate when the bell is rung even if there is no food present. Everything we have learned to do is accomplished by means of this subconscious ability to remember and respond. We walk, talk, type, drive a car by the same process. We are conditioned beings and that's why we do not have to learn, every day, all over again what we acquired before. We need not re-invent the wheel daily.

The involuntary functioning of our Subconscious also includes the experience called sleep, when we consciously "fall" into unconsciousness. During sleep our physical, mental and emotional being keeps functioning by means of the Subconscious and this same intelligence also produces DREAMS. We may well ask: who is it that writes the script, directs the actors and action of these inner movies? And what is their meaning? We'll explore this fascinating topic in Chapter 5.

PERSONALITY — We all seem to come into this world already endowed with a unique personality — a fact which can be readily observed in newborn babies. Where did our personality come from? Perhaps most of us can point to qualities (both physical and mental emotional) which we appear to have inherited from our parents, grandparents and other ancestors. What do we find in our personality which of course "shows up" in our behavior? We think of it as our "self" (some would say as our "soul"), our identity, but perhaps even more as that part of us where we feel our emotions, our moods, our desires and our motivations. How much of what we do and say is governed by our prevailing emotion. How differently we act when, for example, LOVE is our dominant emotion as compared to FEAR.

Our personality and character are in a constant state of change. When someone says,"I'm this way or that because of my personality," (I'm shy, I'm outgoing, I'm always talking before I think) that is of course quite true. But it is also true that one's personality can be changed. A new belief or opinion can change it for better or worse.

The subconscious is not fixed or static, it is alive and subject to suggestion. This is why the affirmative thinking techniques described in Chapter 1 work. Nothing is fixed, all is open to improvement, growth and enlightenment. But when beliefs and opinions are damaging and we continue to hold on to them, their destructive effects also continue. They not only mark and mold our personality but also interfere with the natural, healthy functioning of our body. Beyond these personal categories, there is much more to be seen in our ever-changing pictorial mental underworld.

THE COLLECTIVE UNCONSCIOUS — Our individual being has much in common with the entire human race of today and of countless generations before us. Carl Jung wrote that our consciousness began its evolution from an animal-like state which seemed unconscious and that this same process is repeated in every child. That is why we are already equipped with specifically human INSTINCTS as well as the potential for higher functions, before the "upbringing" or conditioning process begins. A pre-history of millions of years is already within us, part of us.

Jung referred to the motivations and their symbols which we have in common with humanity as a whole as **Archetypes**. The same symbols occur in the dreams of people of very different cultural background. These images and sounds are evident in the literature, myth, poetry, art and music of varied civilizations, current and ancient, even though there was no known direct communication among them.

The collective unconscious, sometimes called the race mind, also makes possible the communication between the subconscious of one individual and another. We speak of this experience as telepathy. There is an empathic bond between certain individuals, which, when cultivated, may result in one person being able to "read" the mind of another. We are all alive with the same life, energy and intelligence. Knowing that we actively participate in the collective unconscious, gives us access to a vast world of experience we wouldn't know, if we thought of ourselves only as separate individuals, limited by a personal lifespan.

THE INDWELLING SPIRIT — Beyond the history of the developing, evolving human organism there is also the presence of what we may call "that which makes life possible" or the divine Spirit or Infinite Wisdom, Intelligence and Energy of life itself. How do we know that we are also spiritual beings, linked up to a higher intelligence, a Universal Spirit? We know it because of the function of intuition and guidance in our lives. We also know it because of what we feel in the states of contemplation and meditation. There is that within us which responds to our natural desire to feel "at home" in the Universe. Reaching the highest level of perception, this is known as a mystical experience or cosmic consciousness. We'll explore the wonderful awareness of the "deepest layer" of our deeper self in The Art of Contemplation.

We become more aware of Cosmic Mind when we consider the source of the greatest breakthroughs in the field of invention and technology. Where did the great composers, the artistic geniuses, the spiritual giants, the profound philosophers obtain their inspiration other than from some inner wellspring of wisdom?

We too have access to the Divine Source, the Infinite Presence without limits to love and wisdom. We can think beyond time, space and circumstance; we can "break through" to true creativity, as we become unconditioned and authentic. Here we have immediate application, helpful and practical, of our study. The Subconscious is an agency of absolutely marvelous creativity able to change your whole life, and the lives of everyone you know, for the better!

Bibliography & Recommended Further Reading

Jung, Carl Gustav: Memories, Dreams, Reflections (autobiography)   ed: Jaffe, A.,
    N.Y.: Vintage, Random House, 1963

Murphy, Joseph: The Power of Your Subconscious Mind
    Englewood Cliffs, N.J.: Prentice Hall, Inc., 1970

Troward, Thomas: The Doré Lectures
    N.Y.: Dodd, Mead, & Co., 1960

Troward, Thomas: The Edinburgh Lectures on Mental Science
    N.Y.: Dodd, Mead & Co., 1909

Cuny, Hilaire: Ivan Pavlov, the Man and His Theories
    London: Souvenir Press, 1964

Gray, Jeffrey A.: Ivan Pavlov
    N.Y.: Viking Press, 1980

Babkin, B.P.: Pavlov, a Biography
    Chicago: University of Chicago Press, 1974

Gay, Peter: Freud - A Life for Our Time
    N.Y.: W.W. Norton & Co., 1988

Clark, Ronald W.: Freud, the Man and the Cause
    N.Y.: Random House, 1980

Fine, Reuben: A History of Psychoanalysis
    N.Y.: Columbia University Press, 1979

Wehr, Gerhard: Jung. A Biography
    Boston: Shambhala, 1988

Hannah, Barbara: Jung, His Life and Work. A Biographical Memoir N.Y.: G.P.
    Putnam's Sons, 1976

Teutsch, Joel Marie & Champion, K.: From Here to Happiness
    N.Y.: Cornerstone Library, 1967

ABC's of the Human Mind
    ed: Guinness, Alma E., Pleasantville, N.Y.: Reader's Digest, 1990

Sagan, Carl & Druyan, Ann: Shadows of Forgotten Ancestors — A Search for Who
    We Are   N.Y.: Random House, 1992

CHAPTER 3

HEALING FROM WITHIN

*"The body being subject to the mind, . . . when the mind is
corrected of its error, the truth is established, which is its health."*

The Complete Writings, Volume I
Phineas Parkhurst Quimby (1802-1866)

If you wake up in the morning not feeling well, it affects everything
you are trying to do. Aches and pains make us miserable and difficult to
get along with. Physical discomforts interfere directly with our efforts to
be successful, to excel, to be serene, to think rationally and to
communicate.

The cost of health care is a major concern to individuals and
societies the world over as is evident from any daily newspaper you may
pick up. On what does our health and wellness depend? Most thinking
people today would respond in terms of these five areas of influence:

NATURAL ENVIRONMENT — We are all becoming increasingly
aware of the importance of a sound ecology for our planet and of the
dangers of pollution of air, water and soil. It is now part of good
citizenship to help protect and improve our environment.

GOOD NUTRITION — It has been said that "you are what you
eat." The terrible fact of hunger is still one of the major challenges of the
world's nations. To those of us who have access to plenty, wise choices
must be made to maintain and enhance correct standards of physical
health and there are now vast resources of information available to help
us do that.

PHYSICAL ACTIVITY — The recently developed weight control
industry is but one sign of the advisability of physical exercise. Activity
stimulates — "use it or lose it" is a truism.

PROPER HYGIENE — Now one of the "musts" of a civilized society. Cleanliness and sanitation are among the first virtues parents teach their children.

These first four areas are well known, there is excellent literature available covering each of these; detailed comments lie outside the scope of this book. There are in today's society radical propagandists in each area claiming the supreme importance of their chosen interest. But balanced living is achieved by being both informed and applying the available knowledge from all these resources for health.

HEALTHY-MINDEDNESS — This term was made famous by the great American psychologist and philosopher William James (1842-1910) in his Gifford Lectures at Edinburgh, Scotland in 1901-02. Describing the answer to the question, "What is human life's chief concern?" James answered . . "how to gain, how to keep, how to recover HAPPINESS." The beginning of the 20th Century was the time when substantial public awareness and academic attention developed examining the relationship between a person's state of mind and their health.

As we have noted in Chapter 2, our conscious and subconscious mind is intrinsically involved and dynamically active in the maintenance of all aspects of our health. Now, let's see how this knowledge translates into the working principles of **self-healing** which you and I can use on a daily basis. To utilize the ideas presented here with effectiveness, requires, before all else, an attitude of **honesty**. We must be completely and totally honest with ourselves in order to obtain the desired results. Self-knowledge includes detecting self-delusion.

As we direct our attention to the five fields of self-healing, please remember that whatever we say here is not to be interpreted as either replacing or opposing any other therapeutic or healing method. Also we wish to make it clear that the examples used to illustrate the processes described are not fictional or "anecdotal" (a term used to deny evidence obviously based on fact). Rather, the events stated are — as are the cases throughout this book — real events that happened to real people, even though the persons mentioned are not identified.

It may seem strange that after a period of more than one hundred and fifty years of the effective practice of self-healing the above statement needs to be made. Yet, our culture as a whole considers the ideas explored here as off-beat, weird or unreliable, hence to be avoided. The truth is, that "healthy-mindedness" is a proven, vital factor in promoting our physical health.

As all of us have had times of when abuse of our bodies has left us in pain, unable to achieve our minds' desires, we will now look forward to learning the the secrets of good health as we explore our **FIELDS OF SELF-HEALING**.

THE POWER OF SUGGESTION AND BELIEF on the cure and healing of illness. We may not be aware of it, but everything we do, and much of what we experience, is the result of having first believed a suggestion. Just how dramatically beneficial the application of this statement can be, was clearly brought home to me when I witnessed the following incident:

The parents of three young children, after attending one of my lectures on self-healing approached me with the news that their oldest daughter, age three, was suffering from a tumor in her head and had been "given up" by the doctors in the hospital where she was confined.

The little girl was no longer interested in eating or playing and had difficulty sleeping. The mother appeared to be filled with fear and worry, so it was easy to see how unlikely it would be for her daughter to be cheerful and optimistic. Both parents were of a traditional religious persuasion and expressed beliefs in "God's will" if their little girl were to die; yet they also wished there were some miracle cure they could obtain.

My intuition told me to ask them whom their daughter really trusted. They replied it was themselves, her mother especially. I then asked them to tell their daughter they were going to take her to a special person who would tell her how she would get well again, and that this was sure to happen. This was a total reversal of what the girl had been told up to now, namely the medical opinion of certain death.

The parents did exactly what I had suggested and the next day, having been given a pass by the hospital administration to leave with their daughter for a few hours, I had the opportunity to talk with the little girl, in the presence of her parents. I told her that she would soon be well again because that night, after she fell asleep, two invisible hands belonging to a wonderful but invisible friend would go inside her head and without hurting her, would take away, piece by piece, the lump that had made her so sick.

She looked at me in amazement but understood what I said, smiled and said she was expecting this to happen, as was confirmed by her parents. I had also asked the parents not to contradict this expectation in her presence, and to refrain from discussion with the medical staff who, after all were doing the best they knew. Also they should keep our experiment a secret from their friends and relatives. Above all, they were not to worry but simply relax and focus on imagining their daughter well and happy.

The next morning the mother telephoned me, her voice filled with wild excitement: her daughter had not only had a good night's sleep but when she woke up had asked for breakfast, wanted to play with her toys and told everyone the pain in her head was "much less!" Imagine the joy these folks felt!

We carefully agreed to continue with our plan and had a couple more meetings similar to the first one. The little girl was well enough to leave the hospital some ten days later, her formerly white cheeks apple red again, laughing, having fun and interested in everything in her world.

At this writing, the incident happened about fifteen years ago and the trouble never recurred; monitoring at the hospital was maintained for several years, the medical doctors declaring the case an "unexplained remission." To my knowledge they never enquired into possible alternate causes of this astounding recovery.

This is not an isolated incident. I have witnessed many similar healings and know of many more reliable persons who have experienced or witnessed such cures. The key to effective healing through suggestions seems to be the belief of the person seeking the healing in the **authority** of the resource person offering the suggestion. The belief can not be faked and the suggestion cannot be doubtful or conditioned.

A trusted friend of mine was for many years active in assisting people to understand and apply the hidden powers of the subconscious mind. He told me of an elderly Irishman, devoutly Catholic, who had been declared "terminal" by his doctors, much to the dismay of his son who loved him dearly. The son decided to have an ordinary splinter of wood encased in crystal by a jeweler. He presented it to his father with the message that he had obtained a splinter from "the true cross," courtesy of the archbishop. Anyone who prayed holding the splinter would be healed.

The father believed his son, and (having his entire subconscious belief system or mind in complete harmony) prayed as was suggested and subsequently was completely healed. It was noted that he was never told the truth of the matter. Perhaps this is the secret of many of the so-called miracles of faith healing. But there's more which must be said.

RECOGNITION AND REMOVAL OF PAYOFFS. We have, up to now, tacitly assumed that everyone **wants** to be well and healthy, but is this assumption justified? It would seem natural for a normal person to wish for health, yet there are many who prefer other "pay-offs" or benefits (apparent to themselves) instead of good health. We could be thinking of smoking, overeating, addictions to alcohol and other drugs — these are obvious. The more unconsciously motivated choices belong to those who appear to use physical discomfort to solicit love and attention from others. Look around the circle of your acquaintances, and see if there isn't someone you know who resembles the lady in the following illustration:

She's "retired," not because she's physically too old to be productive, but having outlived her husband who always had to do everything for her, she's now counting on her relatives and friends to provide all the services that require some work, because she's always "in pain" and discomfort.

Her doctors — and there is an impressive list of them,

are baffled, no one seems to know exactly what's wrong with her, "yes it is a rare case indeed." If you phone or meet her, she's always full of vaguely defined complaints, "Oh yes, some day things will get better and today is not as bad as yesterday." To be sure, she puts on an optimistic face.

In the meantime a relative mows the lawn, cleans the house and takes her shopping. A kind neighbor clears the snow in winter and other dear friends cook meals for her and take her places. She is completely self-centered — does not even care for a dog, cat or bird. When she has her regular bouts of more serious set-backs there are the flowers and cards, the phone calls and visits. "Get well, soon," they say, but she never does. It simply would be an unbearable shock to her (subconscious) system if she ever did!

Of course, having once "sacrificed" her life for her children, it is now their turn to look after her. Should not children love and obey their parents? And don't you feel sorry for her? Don't you suggest any solutions though — if you do, she'll drop you. . .

If all this sounds familiar, so do the reports of army recruits who suddenly take ill when a demanding platoon maneuvre is about to take place. Or the drudgery of inventory taking at year's end can be easily avoided by developing a convenient cold. It takes genuine human honesty to face our "pay-offs," become responsible and choose health, instead.

"THE EXPLANATION IS THE CURE" - is in quotation marks because this phrase was coined by Phineas Parkhurst Quimby (1802–1866). He is considered by many the first practical psychosomatic healer of modern times. Quimby developed an astoundingly successful practice in the U.S. State of Maine in the 1840's – 1860's. During a period of over twenty years he acquired the faculty of "tuning in" to the people who came to him for help.

His methods were highly unusual. Instead of asking the "patient" to tell him what the trouble was, he would sit for awhile in silence with the suffering individual, becoming aware of that person's pains or discomfort, then of the causal factor behind them, the "videotape" of memory we referred to the Chapter 2. Thus Quimby was literally "reading" that person's subconscious; this may seem unbelievable, but the historical record of his work verifies the truth of his methods. Perhaps it can be best understood when we realize that we are all more or less sensitive to another person's "vibes" and the more sensitive we are, the more aware we become of what she or he is all about.

Here's a brief description of what "Park Quimby" once experienced: A lady came to see him who was suffering from dropsy, an earlier term for edema, an abnormal accumulation of fluid in body tissues. Quimby held her hand and it seemed to him as if they were both travelling toward the ocean, then on it, witnessing a fierce storm. In the storm was a fishing vessel with a man aboard who was desperately attempting to save his boat, but to no avail. The vessel and fisherman disappeared under the waves.

When the lady heard Quimby's description of this "reading of her mind" she confirmed that she had lost a close friend at sea in the manner he described FIVE YEARS EARLIER! Quimby comments that to cure the lady was "to bring her from the scene of her troubles." This he was able to do; she overcame her feelings of bereavement and recovered. This is one of hundreds of cases documented by Quimby where emotional shock had induced a physical disease. That is why it is so important to pursue balanced emotions and healthy-mindedness.

Perhaps the best known similar case is the healing of journalist-editor Norman Cousins (1915–1990). While suffering from a very painful, life threatening condition he realized his life had for too many years been too serious. So, he started watching "funny" movies and comedians' performances, and began really laughing again. It was his way of "coming back" to a healthy consciousness and eventually to recovery. Ask yourself what kind of video program is getting first billing in your subconscious mind? Worthy of our attention? You bet your good health it is.

CONSTRUCTIVE VISUALIZATION — What can a "patient" do when some "experts" who are ignorant of the mind as healer make a pronouncement of doom on a vulnerable human being? One thing being practiced with encouraging results is getting into the habit of imagining oneself as being completely healthy. Too many suffering persons see themselves as sick, weak, falling apart, a victim of some evil fate.

Our imagination has been called the workshop of the mind because we do much of our thinking there in pictures. Just as a videocamera records what's "out there," our imagination records what we give it to produce "in here." To illustrate, a lady who was suffering from a tumor at the back of her neck and had been given three months to live, went to visit a renowned medical clinic. This facility was using a technique, considered controversial at that time, now widely known as visualization.

She was instructed to imagine the tumor as a dragon on her back; she saw her white blood cells as knights attacking the tumor with swords. Within a year of faithful practicing of this imaging technique the tumor had shrunk so she could function normally again. A few months later she was in total remission and has remained so for several years.

Can constructive thoughts and moods fight disease and heal the body? There are signs everywhere that people are waking up to their own healing potential. Wouldn't it be exciting if research efforts were to be directed toward a better, scientifically defined, understanding of our imagination and the still largely unknown abilities of our healer within?

SELF-HEALING MEDITATION — Is there an easy way to apply the principles of self-healing so that if you feel "something coming on" you can immediately counteract that feeling and free yourself? Some have used a method we call self-healing meditation. This starts with the simple realization that the moment we decide to relax and direct our thinking to a higher awareness, the subconscious response of feeling better is inevitable. Since our lives are so often filled with stress, just the decision to stop, relax and think affirmatively, is already helpful.

One way of doing this is to definitely take time, perhaps at the end of the day, when there are no more "deadlines" to be met, to be by yourself: turn off the television set or radio, put your telephone on answering, and don't let any other activity interfere with your privacy.

To stop the possible stream of images "pushing through" your consciousness, decide to give your attention to a favorite affirmation, poem or inspired prose that appeals to you and moves you. Keep your train of thought affirmative. If you are easily influenced by audio material, use peaceful background music and perhaps a pre-recorded message that is helpful to you. Better yet, formulate your own statement of affirmation of life giving it the highest philosophical and spiritual content of which you are capable, then read it aloud, or record it and play it back to yourself.

Remember that your subconscious mind not only listens to your consciously accepted suggestions but responds to them creatively. When you pronounce, with feeling, words to the effect that "the perfect healing activity of Infinite Intelligence is now being activated, doing what needs to be done to regenerate and create the healthy person I am meant to be," something happens that only those who have felt and experienced it will sincerely appreciate.

It eludes the cynic because the thinker actually is the process. The observer cannot grasp it anymore than an outsider can taste the affection that is felt by two lovers.

Relax and contemplate in your own way. Let your meditation be really you, not an adopted procedure from an outside source. Keep it secret in the way that those who do not understand it do not have an opportunity to discourage you.

I have found after more than thirty years of privately practicing self-healing meditation and philosophical contemplation that the ancient Roman emperor-philosopher Marcus Aurelius (121–180) was right when he wrote: "At any moment you choose you can retire within yourself. Nowhere can you find a quieter or more untroubled retreat than in your own soul. . ."

This is your invitation to experience your healing from within...

Bibliography & Recommended Further Reading

Quimby, Phineas Parkhurst: The Complete Writings (ed.: Seale, E.,
    contrib. ed.: Aaftink, H.J.), Vols. I, II & III
    Marina Del Rey, CA: DeVorss & Co., 1988

Cousins, Norman: Anatomy of an Illness as Perceived by the Patient
    N.Y., London: W.W. Norton & Co., 1979

Siegel, Bernie S.: Love, Medicine & Miracles
    N.Y.: Harper & Row, 1988

Siegel, Bernie S.: Peace, Love & Healing
    N.Y.: Harper & Row, 1989

Evans, Warren Felt: The Mental Cure, Illustrating the Influence of Mind
    on the Body
    Boston: Banner of Light Publ., 1869

Addington, Jack Ensign: The Secret of Healing
    N.Y.: Dodd, Mead & Co., 1979

James, William: The Varieties of Religious Experience. A Study in
    Human Nature
    N.Y.: Random House, 1929

Seale, Ervin: Mingling Minds, Some Commentary on the Philosophy and
    Practice of Phineas Parkhurst Quimby
    Linden, N.J.: Tide Press, 1986

Collie, Errol Stafford: Quimby's Science of Happiness. A Non-Medical
    Scientific Explanation of the Cause and Cure of Disease
    Marina del Rey, CA: DeVorss & Co., 1980

Goldsmith, Joel S.: The Art of Spiritual Healing
    N.Y.: Harper & Row, 1959

Simonton, O. Carl: Getting Well Again
    N.Y.: St. Martin's Press, 1978

Moyers, Bill: Healing and the Mind
    N.Y.: Doubleday, 1993

Anderson, C. Alan: Healing Hypotheses. Horatio W. Dresser and the
    Philosophy of New Thought
    N.Y.: Garland Publ., 1993

CHAPTER 4
THE STRESS SOLUTION

Nothing can bring you peace but yourself

Self-Reliance
Ralph Waldo Emerson (1803-1882)

Too much stress is now widely considered the number one personal problem of our time and culture. It is the cause of much emotional and physical suffering. No one will be able to enjoy real wellness without mastering the art of significantly reducing the degree of unwanted stress in their daily life.

The consequences of this fact were made clear to me by the head of a hospital emergency ward, a young, informed (and keen observer) medical doctor. He said: "There's no disease that couldn't be caused by stress."

The physical stress symptoms include lowered resistance to illness, headaches, allergies, infections, hardening of arteries, high blood pressure, indigestion, back pain and muscular aches. The psychological and behavioral stress symptoms include insomnia, edginess, depression, indecision, impatience, moodiness, overeating, abuse of alcohol and drugs. Stress will be characterized by dissatisfaction, feeling guilty when inactive and feeling like you're about to explode. Surely we all wish to avoid this suffering of being captive to these enemies of wellness.

Here we are in the most technologically advanced and sophisticated society in recorded history and still we have this terrible monster depriving us of the fruits for which we have worked so hard! So we ask, what CAUSES this monster in our midst?

In ancient Greek mythology there's a many-headed monster called Cerberus, who lived in Hades, the underworld, symbolic of the unconscious mind. Hercules' mission: to pull it (Cerberus) out of Hades and render it harmless. Hercules represents the spiritual "hero" in all of us, who has the ability to conquer whatever emotional monster may wreak havoc below the surface of our consciousness. Famed mythologist Joseph Campbell (1904–1987) pointed out that "the hero with a thousand faces" is known to every civilization by such names as Krishna, Buddha and Christ, the divine self within the individual.

But how is mythology to become practical reality? How shall we be able to conquer the monster of distress? A good place to start in this adventurous enterprise is to take a closer look at the enemy. If you have observed stress in yourself and in others, your picture of the monster will likely have five heads — each head representing one of the major sources of distress in modern society:

LACK OF TIME or perhaps we should say *PERCEIVED* lack of time. What productive, ambitious person has not felt overburdened, pressured by the inability to meet obligations and expectations. We feel overworked, worn-out and tired. Not just at the end of the day but at any time. Since we cannot meet the demands of our responsibilities and duties, we're often late, taking work home. People call us "workaholic."

Soon we won't take days off, refuse to enjoy a vacation, we're irritated by traffic, we answer folks who ask us how we are with "I need more days in the week." We're always in a hurry, everything we ask for has a *RUSH* stamp on it; we feel out of control our life going downhill.

FEAR OF REJECTION. To many people, the primary motivation for living seems to be to please everyone else in their lives, to seek to obtain everyone's approval and if possible, their love as well. Since this is impossible, tension sets in. If we did not succeed in pleasing everyone, well then "I'm to blame, I'm the guilty party." The thoughts running through our minds will be along these lines: "I should have _ _ _ If only I had said or done this _ _ _ How could I have _ _ _ I must never make a mistake _ _ _ What are they 'spreading' about me now _ _ _ I'm going to be left out _ _ _ "

This fear of rejection is rooted in the need for acceptance, and is closely related to the fear of loneliness. This in turn is related to shyness and ultimately can be traced back to a lack of self-esteem. The distress inside a person so afflicted is a virtual hell.

WORRY about what's ahead, in the immediate future, or even years ahead. This is the result of our response to what we fear for ourselves and our loved ones, and humanity of our planet. Much of this fear originates with the media (TV, radio, newspapers, journals, etc.). There is a universal response of anxiety to the continuous bombardment of negative and destructive "news." If we were to hear nothing else about life we might believe that the world contains only scenarios of war, violence, crime, corruption, disasters and their resulting misery.

Knowing what we know now about the power of suggestion and the creativity of the subconscious, is it any wonder that the public is stressed out of their wits with fear of the future. We are led to believe that future will only see a worsening of our already dire conditions. Who would not worry thinking that "the whole world is evil?"

Since most persons feel powerless in the face of all this, their self-image becomes one of helplessness and hopelessness. Added to this will be one's personal fear of misfortune: fear of failure, loss of job and income, ill health, old age with increasing inability to look after oneself, and finally of dying. A modern monster indeed.

ANGER. How do you react when people do not behave in the way you expect? What do you do when those you trust or admire do not live up to your expectations? What's your response when "things" don't work out the way they are supposed to?

Is there anyone who has not felt anger rising from within? Who has not been upset, felt "hot under the collar?" This kind of distress is familiar to all who have experienced the end of a relationship (separation, divorce, death of a loved one, problem of the "ex," the tug-of-war over children). In these situations our emotions run high with our desire for justice, resentment toward those who hurt us, sometimes spiced with a craving for revenge.

Tension due to relationship problems is the topic of much daily conversation: tales about relatives, hell at home, violence between people who vowed everlasting love. At our place of work the air will often be filled with tales of deceit, lying, jealousy, envy, injustice and sexual harassment.

In addition there is the enormous stress of being passed over on the job by others whom we feel are less qualified. One's ability to cope becomes consumed under negative thoughts about inefficiency, bureaucracy, laziness of others, and the existential feeling that life is unfair and not worth pursuing. Are there any who escape this distress trap?

POVERTY or the inability to "make ends meet." The fear of loss of prosperity, of becoming poor and destitute, is always there for those who are too deep in financial debt or living on too tight a budget. There are people everywhere who when called upon to share with those in need would like to do so but are afraid to be generous.

Older generations experienced by the economic depression of the 1930's and the lean fearful years of the early 1940's, have never quite forgotten what those lean years were like. That deep feeling of insecurity and distress, "where is our next meal coming from," visions of ending their days in the "poor house," remain as vivid memories. So strong have these desperate thoughts been that often these fears have infected children and grandchildren.

Fear of the future in terms of lack and shortage translate into anger about taxation, thinking others are so much better off and hence luckier, mind sets that cause us to be less productive. Dickens' Scrooge lives on in many of us: looking for that bargain, hunting for hours for a "better deal," shopping in the cheapest stores. All of which causes our minds to be centered on poverty consciousness which means a mind filled with the fear of lack. This results in personal distress which never seems to leave since life is consciousness and one simply cannot get outside or away from one's own consciousness.

If this description of the five-headed monster seems a rather lengthy, perhaps even tedious one, let's not for one moment forget that much of our distress is unconscious, that is, we suffer unknowingly. By bringing the monster to our awareness, to the surface of our consciousness, we can finally have a good look at it, recognize it for what it is, and DO SOMETHING ABOUT IT!

All informed persons in the self-help field know that the very first step, and an absolutely essential one toward solving "the problem," is to admit and recognize that there **IS** a problem and to become aware of the true nature of that problem. Having said that...can we pin the monster down (so to speak) and discover its essence?

There is a quite common misunderstanding about this subject, namely that *any* kind of stress is harmful and should be avoided. One way of looking at stress in a realistic perspective is to think of "the metaphor of the elastic band" imagining that an elastic band could think and feel:

> We could see our little friend in three situations, first, not "doing" anything, just lying on a desk, in a box. It would think: "Isn't life terrible. I feel useless, nobody wants me, no one cares if I'm here or if I'm not, life is an incredible bore."

> But presently, a human being comes along and puts our elastic band around a bunch of files. It now thinks: "Wow! Look how important I am now, I'm holding these important papers in place, do I feel useful, this is what I was trained to do, my life has meaning."

> Now imagine a third scene where a human being once more appears, now pushing more and more files inside our elastic friend, stretching it to the point of breaking. Can we imagine our little friend thinking (and if it could — screaming!) "Don't do that, I cannot handle that much? I can't hold out any longer, please take some of the load off, if not I'm going to burst and then you won't have any of my services left. . . !"

Stress plays much the same role in our lives. Not enough of it makes our lives dull and we're left trying to cope with boredom. This is the no-stress condition, which in turn, if sustained, produces distress also. The right amount of challenge and creative pursuit provide us with a healthy, balanced amount of stress — this is the natural tension we feel just before we're about to perform — write an exam, skate in a hockey game, or immediately prior to taking the platform as a public speaker.

The most skilled and creative artists of any highly challenging enterprise feel this kind of healthy stress and mature. Self-actualized individuals seek and welcome it. But distress, as described above, means we are unable to cope with the situation, we need help, we need answers, we need solutions. There are many solutions offered by numerous contemporary books and seminars on stress. Let's proceed with an answer offered by the Art of Thinking: how can our THINKING help reduce the degree of distress we as individuals experience?

Let's ask ourselves the fundamental question back of all the various manifestations of the distress monster: WHERE DOES THE MONSTER LIVE, in what locale will we "tackle" it? Now that we have pulled it out of the underworld of our subconscious where is it?

There is but one answer: IT IS IN OUR CONSCIOUSNESS, it is in our world of perception, our imagination, our awareness, in short, OUR THOUGHTS. How did it get there? The monster, like weeds in a garden, was seeded, planted and nourished there by but one culprit: SUGGESTION. It is through the contemplation of, acceptance of and belief in the suggestion offered to our mind, that the monster, politely called distress, gets a hold on us.

Shouldn't it make perfect sense then that we can get rid of the monster by reversing the process? That is, by withdrawing our consent to the unwanted (though invited) tenant? How is this done? It is done through conscious, directed thinking in terms of withdrawing or denying power to the negative suggestion.

DENY THE POWER OF INHERITED DISEASE: When dealing with serious illness, our doctors customarily ask if parents, grandparents or siblings have manifested this disease. Being reminded of this disease, and its fatal effect on someone close to us, we may (warranted or not) accept this as our death sentence. While there can be certain genetic weaknesses in family lines, by no means do these always occur in every child of the line. However, simply accepting the idea that we are fated for the worst, without any the personal proof of the insidious inheritance, can wreck enormous damage on our to body as well as mind.

How can such a person pull the monster out of their underworld? By defining and repeating until it becomes a belief — an affirmative suggestion such as this: "I deny that what happened to my ancestors has any power over me — I inherit only health, strength, and limitless good from my Infinite Parent, Nature (or whatever universal concept of ultimate good is acceptable and comfortable to you)."

DENY THE NECESSITY OF LACK AND POVERTY In an authentic sense, what we have produced in our lives in terms of self-generated circumstances and conditions, is our harvest. If we're not happy with our harvest we can learn from those who every fall (or harvest season) gather in a harvest of grain. One vital key to a good harvest is to sow the best seeds of the previous harvest.

So let's not be afraid to GIVE. And that includes giving the highest and best thoughts we have to our subconscious: "I refuse to believe in disasters and depression in my future. I deny the necessity of lack and poverty and realize that my personal prosperity begins with thinking thoughts of abundance, opportunity and plenty. The media or any other source of destructive thoughts have NO POWER over me."

DENY THAT YOU ARE A WEAK, SECOND RATE OR FLAWED PERSON Realize right here and now that no matter where the suggestion that you are an inferior human being may have come from, (parents, school, religion, peers, institution) you have the right and power to deny the authority of that suggestion. Holding a low opinion of yourself is not a virtue, it is, on the contrary, a vice and it is the root soil of the distress monster within. So, start thinking and affirming that you are a worthwhile, important and growing individual, who has access to all the intelligence, sophistication, wit and wisdom there is.

Whenever that poor self-image rears its ugly monster-head, deny that it has any influence over you. You used to believe that nonsense, but not any more. You've changed, you are a new, confident person now.

DENY THAT ANY OTHER PERSON CAN HOLD YOU BACK OR DESTROY YOU How often have you heard someone say: "She or he ruined my life." Perhaps, but no matter how awful the behavior of that person may be or have been, ruining one's life completely seldom takes place without the victim's own consent. Too frequently we allow another person to upset us or block our progress. An illustration:

A woman attends inspirational self-help lectures and finds herself solving many personal problems and meeting new, interesting friends. Her husband wants her home, doesn't believe in "that weird stuff" and is afraid to lose his domineering power over her. He insists she stop attending. She reluctantly complies, gradually turning herself into a brooding, distressed woman.

The truth is that NO ONE has the power or the right to stop her or you from growing, but your rightful place in life has to be claimed. Say to yourself: "No person has the power to upset me, destroy my happiness or prevent my progress." Use your own words in defining your affirmation and repeat "until done," as recipes state.

DENY THAT ANY EMOTION HAS POWER OVER YOU

We hear it daily; "I'm depressed; don't bother me, I'm in a bad mood. Am I angry or what, I'm livid, you'd better believe it! Boy am I upset," etc. etc. The varieties on this theme are almost endless. Why do we let destructive emotions hurt us and drive our present and potential friends away, spoiling our opportunities for success and fun? Don't we realize it is only because we have not taken our thinking and feeling in hand. We have foolishly let a phony mental monster take over the driver's seat for a wild, dangerous ride.

Distress due to "bad moods" and emotions can be immediately reversed by affirming: "This mood that I sense is coming over me has no place in my consciousness, so I am canceling it right now. I have executive power and control over how I will feel, therefore, I declare a state of joy, optimism and rational thinking right here and right now." Break through the distress barrier, take the monster by the tail and throw it where it belongs, into its native nothingness. This liberation is within your grasp and power. Use your power of affirmation and you've taken a major step toward authentic living.

Bibliography & Recommended Further Reading

Campbell, Joseph: Myths to Live By
      N.Y.: Bantam, 1988
Campbell, Joseph: The Hero With a Thousand Faces
      N.Y. Princeton University Press, 1973
Selye, Hans: Stress Without Distress
      N.Y.: Signet, 1975
Selye, Hans: The Stress of Life
      N.Y.: McGraw-Hill,1978
Selye, Hans: The Stress of My Life, A Scientist's Memoirs
      N.Y.: VanNostrand Reinhold Co., 1979
Addington, Jack and Cornelia: The Joy of Meditation
      Marina del Rey, CA: DeVorss & Co., 1979
Dickens, Charles: A Christmas Carol 1843
      N.Y.: Bantam, 1983
Carnegie, Dale: How to Stop Worrying and Start Living
      N.Y.: Simon & Schuster, 1951
Goodloe, Alfred: Managing Yourself: How To Control Emotion, Stress
      and Time
      N.Y.: Franklin Watts, 1984
Hanson, Peter G.: Stress for Success, Thriving on Stress at Work
      Toronto: Collins Publ., 1989
Lewinsohn, Peter M. e.o.: Control Your Depression
      Englewood Cliffs, N.J.: Prentice-Hall, Inc., 1978

CHAPTER 5
OUR SECRET NIGHT LIFE: DREAMS

"We may expect that the analysis of dreams will lead us to a knowledge of man's archaic heritage, of what is psychically innate in him. . . According to Aristotle . . . a dream is thinking that persists. . . in the state of sleep"

The Interpretation of Dreams
Sigmund Freud (1856–1939)

Dreams — we all "have" them. What are they, what do they mean, if anything? How can we benefit from the knowledge and study of our dreams? Do our dreams have anything to do with our wellness, the way we feel, the way our lives turn out, the quality of our experience, the nature of our destiny?

We have seen, on our journey that by mastering the art of thinking we affect, to a significant degree, our state of health and wellness, for the better. We have also seen that our thoughts cannot be considered separate from our unconscious, that we interact with, are supported by and literally live by our unconscious.

To consider the art of thinking without paying attention to the messages we nightly receive from our unconscious, would be to ignore one of the most important activities of our own being. Refusal to attempt to understand our dreams would mean to agree that "ignorance is bliss" which is the opposite of every principle of human progress.

Nevertheless, most of us pay little or no attention to what dreams may tell us. Once awakened by a desire to understand ourselves, we face an adventure into unknown territory. We have the feeling that this may be one of the "last frontiers," this inner space of dreamland and sleep. We are not entirely without guides. The profound and scholarly work done by Sigmund Freud and Carl Jung as well as others, is no doubt helpful, but, the journey is, beyond the general ideas, an intensely personal one.

So, here we are; supposing we wish to add to our art of thinking a practical understanding of our dreams, how shall we proceed?

Recognizing that the following is only a brief and incomplete introduction, let us look at five aspects of our subject that will at least open the door sufficiently to encourage us to continue our exploration into our own mysterious but fascinating dreamland.

DREAMS ARE A PRODUCT OF UNCONSCIOUS ACTIVITY

Defining, in simple terms, what dreams are, is not easy. How would you explain it to someone who has never dreamed? (Which has never been the case, as far as we know. Dreaming appears to be so vital to our health that research into sleep habits shows that when people are not allowed to dream, they become disoriented and unable to function).

We say we "fall asleep," which we don't consciously do, but we "let it happen," somewhat like we "fall in love." Our conscious awareness of ourselves in our time-space environment diminishes and our "consciousness" moves into what can only be described as another dimension where we are part of an entirely different world. Which seems real to us "at the time," even though dream time and space are of a different quality.

In fact, the nature of the dream experience is unlike anything we experience in our waking state. We might say that it is like watching a video cassette, although we are often part of the action. Which raises an interesting question: who is the script writer, producer and director of the video? Who decides what the contents shall be and is there a meaning or purpose included? Or is the question irrelevant — is it some automatic response activity without design? But when we look at the highly intelligent nature of some of our dreams, we have to consider that some intelligence is at work. . .

Jung says that "the dream is a little hidden door in the innermost and most secret recesses of the psyche, opening into that cosmic night which was psyche long before there was any ego-consciousness." From our own observation we know that dreams occur involuntarily, spontaneously, communicating a message from some level of our unconscious. This message is sometimes clear, as when we are presented with the solution to a problem, and sometimes obscure, because it presents itself in symbols and pictures with which we are not familiar.

The esoteric symbols will require deciphering, even as scholars of early languages unveil the meanings of some ancient Dead Sea scroll.

In the early years of the 20th Century some researchers, baffled by what seemed to be so many absurd images, believed that there is an invisible clown within us, a trickster who attempts to fool or deceive us. Study your dreams carefully and you'll find, much that you may not understand, but no evidence of "something playing games." The deeper we dig, the more sense and integrity we shall discover.

THE FIRST KEY TO UNDERSTANDING DREAMS IS CONTEXT   Assuming we remember a dream accurately, our greatest challenge is the attempt to understand the **meaning** of the message since many symbols are frequently unclear. The key to comprehending the symbols is finding out what these symbols mean to the **dreamer** under ordinary, waking circumstances. Personal dreams are personal to THAT DREAMER, so interpretation requires knowledge of the dreamer's scenario of contexts.

When I was a very small boy, I would sometimes go to my grandmother for advice and comfort; she was most kind and loving but also full of wisdom and insight, people would seek her out for counsel. Now, suppose my grandmother appears in my dream. She would (likely but not necessarily) represent a source of wisdom or prudent advice to me.

To another person, who may have had an estranged or hostile relationship with her or his grandmother, the symbol of her appearance in that person's dream would mean anything but friendly, helpful information. A father figure could mean: love, care, protection, comradeship, bonding; but it could also signify anger, domination, dictatorship, violence and enmity. To discover the meaning we must know something about the context or the consciousness of the dreamer.

All this will not surprise us when we consider where we have come from. Going back even a few generations we have huge number of ancestors each one with unique qualities. Many persons find themselves dreaming about their ancestors, even those they hardly knew. They seemed like real people, usually giving advice in a puzzling situation. This is part of our inheritance, there is much to be learned here. Call it genes, or call it telepathy, let us not be discouraged by semantics. The fact is ancestral wisdom is being communicated; the unconscious, being unconscious, is breaking through, in order to help us in some way, into our awareness.

It is clear then that it is hardly advisable to try to understand the symbology of your dreams by a short-cut method such as a dream-symbol dictionary. We are not trying to translate a foreign language. Rather, we are trying to comprehend the communication(s) of our consciousness.

WHAT TO LOOK FOR IN OUR DREAM EXPERIENCE

Interpretation of symbolic material. As with exploring the meaning of all symbolic material such as ancient scriptures, myths, legends, etc., there are two approaches and the choice, upon reflection, is ours: **Objectively:** The person, thing or situation in the dream **is** the person, thing or situation in "real life." Your old friend appearing means it is your old friend as a spokesperson (but of course not as an incarnation) in an actual situation.

Subjectively: The person represents a principle; as mentioned, a grandmother symbolizes wisdom or needed advice.

Repetition of dreams. People who have developed an understanding of their dream life report that series of dreams, if on the same topic, are significant. Look closely also at repeated dreams. One counsellor I know reported that a young man came to him with the complaint that he experienced the same dream night after night until it became a terrible nightmare and he was afraid to go to sleep.

In his dream, the dreamer found himself in the backyard of his home, surrounded by a white picket fence. Perched high on the fence posts were a collection of his relatives, parents, uncles and aunts, all staring at him. No sound, no movement, just silent staring.

"What should I do?" the dreamer asked the counselor. "Well," said he, "I suggest you sharpen the points of the fence!" This was not just a quip.

The young man was suffering from poor self-esteem due to a domineering father and equally demanding mother, while other relatives were of the same stripe. So our young friend tried, without success, to please them all, to live up to their impossible expectations. Being unable to do so turned him into a procrastinator and a person who dared not express his own opinions. He had to free himself from his relatives' domination and authority and become his own, independent self. The dream, although most uncomfortable, was an important message that helped him make the necessary decisions for a better life.

Another significant happening to watch for is a dream that continues, like a hidden soap opera, to unfold, night after night. Also, become aware of dreams that occur to more than one person at around the same time, such as two lovers or a parent and child.

"Filing Cabinet" Dreams. These are common, but not as simple and insignificant as they may look at first. What we mean is, and almost all aware persons have noticed this, that our dream is a re-enactment of an event, usually somewhat traumatic or stressful, that happened the day before.

Close and careful comparison between actual event and dream usually reveals that the dream is, however, NOT AN EXACT repetition of the experienced event: something has been added or changed. So, pay attention to this video version, there may be a message that interprets, adds meaning to or explains the event itself.

We call these "filing cabinet" dreams here because it seems that what happened is this: we have just filed an experience into memory when "something" in our unconscious pulls the drawer (of memory) open and an underground wind blows the papers out into open awareness again.

The puzzle of out-of-character behavior. Jung told of a young man whose strict, religious and domineering father appears as a drunk and disorderly man in his dream. Jung's interpretation: Your father may appear perfect but he's not, nobody is. So don't feel so inferior, you're O.K. and it's all right to be yourself. When we dream that a person acts out of character, our unconscious may be revealing an aspect of that person or situation of which we had not been aware or had not sufficiently taken into account.

Wish fulfilment. Freud and other scholars have emphasized that many dreams are projections of hidden wishes. The theory is that if we cannot have a wished-for experience here and now, our dream gives us our wish fulfilment or substitute. This relieves pressure and the distress of unsatisfied desires. Hungry people dream about food, lonely and unloved people dream of intimacy and sexual experiences.

As is well known, Sigmund Freud placed great emphasis on sexual symbols in dreams; Jung believed this phenomenon to be present but only as part of what is still a most complex activity. When we recognize the element of wish fulfilment in our dreams, it may be time to take a closer look at our inner desires and our latent potential, all unconscious, which may now be knocking at the door of consciousness to be given recognition. Perhaps the time has come to master the fine art of motivation — see the next section of this book. . .

VERY SPECIAL DREAMS. There are occasions in the dreamlife of aware, observant persons who have a degree of self-actualization, when a dream literally WAKES US UP, that is, it has such an impact on our consciousness that upon waking we can, unlike most dreams, simply not shake it off, nor do we want to. These are the dreams that hold some vitally important, sometimes life-saving message for us which we are not to ignore except at our peril.

The nature of such a dream may be "collective" seemingly arising from the collective unconscious referred to in Chapter 2; the symbology frequently occurs in the dream reports of many and varied cultures all over the world, and over a vast period of recorded history. The message is always of primary significance to the life of the dreamer at the moment but also has universal value to all persons in similar circumstances.

I experienced such a dream on a visit to New York City some years ago. At the time, I was faced with several personal challenges with which I had to come to grips but was reluctant to resolve. The continuing tension was at the cost of my health and wellness.

In this dream I found myself in an unkempt garden, grown wild with weeds and very tall grasses. The garden appeared to be the backyard of a large house, where many of my relatives, colleagues and friends had gathered. They were engaged in animated conversation, not with me, but with each other. Suddenly, out of the tall grass a huge snake appeared which shot up straight in front of me, lifting its presumably poisonous head with tongue directly in front of my face, hissing dangerously. I was terrified and immediately screamed for help.

The persons in the house paid no attention however — either because they did not hear me or they did not care, but I felt I was definitely "on my own." Then an intuitive thought came to me. It said: "just pick up the snake by the tail and shove it into its mouth." I did so without hesitation and, much to my surprise, it worked and, as if by magic, the snake was transformed into a wheel, which, with a slight push of my hand, simply rolled away until it was no longer visible.

I then awoke. I discussed this vivid dream with a close friend, the late Dr. Ervin Seale (1909–1990) who was familiar with Jungian dream analysis. We decided the meaning of this dream was that I was not to look for solutions to my problems outside of myself (relatives and friends did not come to my rescue). The message was: become responsible for your own life and look for the answer in the question.

It was true that the solution to my problems was in the situation itself and what was required was my decision and action. These I proceeded to carry out in my life and the dream turned out to be the key to a life transforming experience for me. In retrospect it also became apparent to me that the (identified) persons in the large house "were themselves" and not only would have been unreliable sources of advice but they could care less, being interested only in their own pursuits.

Therefore, pay special attention to high impact, collective dreams. No doubt, some knowledge of mythology is helpful here, but we can often sense intuitively what the meaning is. In addition to the personal meaning, the message is usually universally applicable; in this case, to take responsibility for one's own life and to be open to and act upon one's intuition, and to recognize that the solution is contained in the problem.

Often, such dreams offer help far beyond a personal need. Inventions have been revealed in dreams. A friend who works in computer programming solves problems frequently by expecting the answer to come to her in a dream and this has become her experience. We can aid the process by affirming to ourselves (our subconscious) before going to sleep that we anticipate the desired answer or information to be conveyed to us in our dream. The power of suggestion once more, when activated, is our faithful servant, seemingly having access to infinite intelligence!

CHECK-IT-OUT: HELPFUL HINTS ON HOW YOU MAY BENEFIT FROM YOUR DREAMS. If dreams have not played an important part in your life up to now, this is probably due to the fact that we grew up in an environment where dreams were looked upon as so much nonsense and we were taught not to pay any attention to them. Thus conditioned, our subconscious, while containing all this valuable information, and "wishing" to convey it to us, has nevertheless no choice but to forget and ignore its own products because it was ordered to do so by the captain of the ship, the conscious mind. But all this can be changed, and at once, too. Here's what we can do to benefit more from our dreamlife, already active within us:

Decide to make dreams part of your life — Change the conditioning by changing your evaluation: instead of being nonsense, tell yourself and your unconscious: dreams are vitally important in my life and I am now treating my dreamlife as an indispensable asset of my being. Remember Jung's advice: "Meditate on it long enough (the dream that is) and almost always something comes of it."

The scriptures of world religions and the texts of great philosophers and sages endorse this view. In the Bible, Joseph's dream interpretation saves a whole generation from starvation, the Wise Men at the first Christmas are guided to avoid the evil Herod, Pilate's wife is shown Jesus' innocence. All of which signifies that ancient wisdom recognizes and applies the helpful messages of dreams.

Keep a journal or notebook of your dreams; think, ponder, reflect and meditate on their meaning. What do your dreams tell you over an extended period of time about you and your life and your destiny?

To remember your dreams. This seems to be the greatest difficulty most people have in this area: they dream but don't remember their dreams. We can do the following:

first: Have a pad of paper or taperecorder next to you while asleep, so when you wake up you can "record" your dream at once. Wait and you will likely lose or forget valuable imagery and details.

second: Gently affirm, before going to sleep: "I am remembering my dreams" or "I will remember my dreams" or your own words to that effect.

Study further. Familiarize yourself with the valuable and serious study and research done in this field, especially by Sigmund Freud, Carl Jung and Jung's followers and associates. Their work contains extensive details on dream analysis and interpretation based on thousands of actual dreams, researched in context. It is a fascinating enterprise well worth your time, effort and attention.

The art of thinking is the key to wellness. The more we know about our thinking processes, and our consciousness, the better our chances for health and happiness. Next, we naturally ask ourselves: equipped with this marvellous skill of right, rational thinking, how can I I make my accomplishments match my thinking? So now is the time to take up The Art of Motivation, because nothing gets done until someone is motivated!

Bibliography & Recommended Further Reading

Jung, Carl Gustav: The Structure and Dynamic of the Psyche
    N.J.: Princeton University Press, Bollingen Series,The Collected
    Works of C.G. Jung, Volume 8, 1978
Jung, Carl Gustav: Memories, Dreams, Reflections (autobiography),
    Aniela Jaffe, editor
    N.Y.: Vintage, Random House, 1963
Jung, Carl Gustav: Man and His Symbols
    N.Y.: Dell Publ., 1964
Jung, Carl Gustav: The Portable Jung, ed. Joseph Campbell
    N.Y., London: Penguin, 1988
Jung, Carl Gustav: Modern Man in Search of a Soul
    N.Y.: Harcourt, Brace & Co., 1933
Jung, Carl Gustav: On the Nature of Dreams
    N.Y.: Analytical Psychology Club of N.Y., Inc., 1948
Freud, Sigmund: The Interpretation of Dreams
    N.Y., Harmondsworth: Penguin, 1977
Von Franz, Marie-Louise: On Dreams and Death, Jungian Interpretation
    Emmanuel Xipolitas Kennedy & Vernon Brooks, transl.
    Boston & London: Shambhala, 1987
Progoff, Ira: At a Journal Workshop, Chapter 16
    N.Y.: Dialogue House Library, 1975
Jastrow, Joseph: Freud, His Dream and Sex Theories
    N.Y.: Pocket Books, Cardinal, 1955
Fromm, Erich: Greatness and Limitations of Freud's Thought
    N.Y.: Mentor, 1980

PART TWO

THE ART OF MOTIVATION - YOUR KEY TO SUCCESS

"It is quite true that man lives by bread alone - when there is no bread. But what happens to man's desires when there is plenty of bread...?"

Motivation and Personality
Abraham H. Maslow (1908-1970)

CHAPTER 6

SELF-ESTEEM: FEELING GOOD ABOUT YOURSELF

"...I have discovered that with sound self-esteem, success and happiness are inevitable."

Essays on Self-Esteem
Lilburn S. Barksdale (1908–1987)

The mind is our most precious asset. It contains tremendous and mysterious hidden powers which both affect and facilitate our wellness and everything else that is happening to and through us. Therefore it is natural to ask: Equipped as I am with this marvelous ability to be and to do and to become: what goals will I choose, and I how will I become empowered to attain them? We must look into **motivation**, because nothing happens, in personal human achievement or collective action, until one is motivated. Without sufficient motivation we will not act on our desires. Thoughtful and careful observers of human behavior would agree with Napoleon Hill, a 20th Century researcher of human personal success, that the starting point of all achievement is desire.

You can easily prove this to yourself. Suppose you have invited a friend to a concert or sports event, but in response are receiving nothing but various excuses not to join you. Now suppose you said to your friend: "If you come, there will be a certified check for $10,000 waiting for you." Suddenly, the response changes to a most receptive, "Of course I'll come!" What happened? Your friend became motivated, the desire to join you which was insufficient to move her or him, is now activated, vitally alive and waiting to be translated into enthusiastic action!

What then is our problem? Doesn't everyone want to be successful, to be prosperous, to achieve one's potential? We would say yes, of course. Why then do comparatively few pursue an achievement plan for success? We may ask this question simply because we care about people and would like to see them deriving happiness from being of service in their community. Or we may ask this question because we are concerned over the enormous cost of government services looking after those who demonstrate no desire to become "tax-paying citizens." Social problems in modern societies the world over contain at their base precisely this problem. Still, we find ourselves asking,"Why do so many persons give up? Why do so few really try?"

If we do not believe in ourselves, we cannot succeed. From what we now know about the life-governing activity of our subconscious, this should not come as a surprise. Do we proceed with anything when we are firmly convinced it cannot be done? The answer is clearly negative. That is why, in our investigation of the secrets of personal achievement, we must start with the attitude by which we view our SELF.

We're in good company here, for Abraham Maslow, the recognized master in the field of human motivation research in the 20th Century, comments that all people in our society have a need for a worthwhile evaluation of themselves to attain any self-esteem. When this need is satisfied, we then have the foundation from which to proceed, with a self-confidence equal to the size of our tasks.

Where in the world will we find self-esteem adequate for our goals? From whence did our current sense of self-identity come? Our thoughts naturally go back to childhood. French 17th Century philosopher René Descartes said that our problem is that we have first been a child. Sigmund Freud agreed. Why? What happened? When we look around us and listen to people we find that their conversation and actions easily reveal the source of their self-identity. Here are some examples of self-image derived from beliefs "swallowed" when we were quite young:

Background (in the animal world: breeding) — Nationality, clan, caste. "I'm a daughter of the Empire," "I'm a real McCoy," "I'm a French Canadian."

Education — "In grade 1 I felt like a nobody, but look at me now." People identify with the "fancy piece of paper" on the wall: certificates, diplomas, degrees. This is followed by making one's profession the central self, "I'm a teacher," "I'm an engineer," "I'm a nurse."

Habits and Behavior — We accept ourselves to the degree that we conform to the behavior expected by the society around us. Although of declining importance, not long ago if you were divorced you were an outcast. A child born of parents who were not married had a tough start. How often do you hear: "I'm a bum," "I'm a misfit?"

Physical Image — People identify with their appearance: "I'm too fat, so . . ." "I'm too young so I can't get a job," "I'm too old to start this . . " "I'm only a woman . . " And we let gender or sexual preference limit us.

Accomplishments — We value power and prestige and prop ourselves up with them. We have great self-esteem when supposedly successful and applauded by others but sink low when our projects don't work, we lose our job, or people criticize us, etc.

Values and Beliefs — Here religion plays a role for many: how can one have healthy self-esteem while believing that one is a miserable sinner, incapable of any good deed?

Money and Assets — In a culture where people who are wealthy count and are respected, the poor and persons who don't pursue materialism receive little esteem.

Family Status — A woman may feel that her "self" all her life belongs to someone else: she's somebody's daughter, somebody else's wife, then somebody's mother and grandmother, but what's her real self?

Membership — We make sure we belong to the right church, lodge, club, association and are properly initiated through the approved ritual. We wear insignia, medals and rings to re-enforce that self-image as a member, in "good standing" of course.

Opinion of Others — Think about this one. How much of what you were told about yourself as a child and teenager is still part of your self-belief? Were you accepted, praised, appreciated or not? How often do we hear parents say to their child in a shopping mall: "You're stupid, you'll never amount to anything. If you do this once more, I won't love you anymore or I'll kick you out . . .?" But we don't have to return to childhood to suffer from deflated self-esteem due to other people's opinions. Destructive criticism has ruined many promising careers that could have enriched our global community; sensitive artists and other creative persons become discouraged and bitter.

Why are so many people seemingly so mean-spirited? According to L.S.Barksdale, one of this century's prominent self-esteem teachers, fierce competitive drives, greed, selfishness, jealousy and envy are all symptoms of insecurity and low self-esteem. The incredible need some people seem to have to condemn, tear apart, dominate, possess and control is rooted in poor self-esteem; for persons who genuinely love themselves do not act in this way. Other symptoms of low self-esteem are drinking, eating and smoking excessively, lack of close friends, value-judging, masking one's feelings, pride, arrogance, procrastination, timidity and resentment. All these negative attitudes are attempts to compensate for a lack of self-worth, wanting to feel "more than" by making others out to be "less than."

How do we build mature, healthy self-esteem repairing the damage that has been done to the belief-system of so many people? I had the privilege of having known and worked with Dr. Maxwell Maltz, the famous plastic surgeon and author of Psycho-Cybernetics. He makes a key observation, based on his work with thousands of persons, ranging from young students to senior citizens: The self-image can be changed!!

How do we go about altering deep-seated opinions? Is it possible to crack open an ingrained mind-set? My own experience with many individuals over a long period of time has taught me to believe it can be done. But permanent self-change requires sustained effort.

We have a problem here: the person who knows that poor self-esteem lies at the bottom of his or her unsatisfactory living experience has to be motivated to rise above it and this motivation must come from within. We, as friends, can suggest, challenge and encourage, but the individual has to WANT to do it. Something has to "click" inside. This must become more than a surface motivation for personal popularity and prosperity. Any truly worthwhile, lasting change involves a breakthrough from the deepest spiritual layer of that person's unconscious. That is why this aspect is listed first of the five steps to feeling better about yourself or building mature self-esteem.

1. **CONTEMPLATION**— Awareness of yourself as a spiritual being is often described as a recognition that "comes" to you from what Jung called the archetype of perfection within you. But that does not mean we

cannot approach such an awareness rationally and philosophically. We can become relaxed (perhaps with the aid of an inspirational, mystical book) and reflect on our source.

Where did we, as an individual consciousness really come from? While this may be a profound mystery, we can say that an intelligence and presence greater than we are preceded us, or thought us into being. Is not all of life a gift? Does not a blueprint precede the creation and the idea the blueprint? Is not everyone and everything we know an idea in our mind and could we know anyone or anything if that were not so?

Does it make sense that the Universe we observe also has within itself a consciousness that expresses itself and creates as anyone or anything else is created in our own personal experience? Is the blueprint and the original idea called "myself" contained within that infinite vastness of the Universal consciousness? What if I identified with THIS presence? Is this, perhaps, the meaning of Jesus' statement "I and the Father are one" and might this well be an explanation of his power and divine self-esteem?

What happens, what do we feel, when we put all our activities on hold for half an hour or so and meditate on Ralph Waldo Emerson's inspired sentence: "We lie in the lap of immense intelligence which makes us receivers of its truth and organs of its activity?" Read, study and contemplate Emerson's essay entitled "Self-Reliance" and in so doing allow yourself another opinion on which to base your self-esteem; not one of ignorance, but of cosmic wisdom. By virtue of that truth, can you see yourself as a precious spiritual being, of infinite worth and potential?

2.   **SELF-DIRECTION** — Can we acquire a healthy personal self-concept and at the same time be completely controlled, dominated by another or others? Not likely? You cannot be yourself until you become yourself. This requires taking the firm stand: "I am responsible for myself and I take this self-responsibility seriously." This will stop the blaming tendency toward all those whom you perceive as having sold you a poor bill-of-goods that resulted in less-than-adequate self-esteem. It may have happened, but you are withdrawing your consent to holding those beliefs right now, because from now on YOU and you only will decide what you

believe about yourself.

In mythology, consciousness is sometimes compared to a kingdom, a realm of rulership. Self-direction means you decide to become the ruler of your consciousness, you take over and ascend to the throne; now you're in charge, you "call the shots" and you're responsible for what is believed and accepted as truth. Self-direction also means to choose your own goals, objectives and purposes for your life. This implies becoming a so-called non-conformist, if necessary. It is a fact of human experience that we receive a great boost in our self-esteem whenever we have accomplished something that is truly and uniquely our own, even if nobody else recognizes it as important. The story is told of the American painter John Singer Sargent (1856–1925) that he would not sell one of his finest works because, in times of low inspiration he would look at it and say: "You did that, John!"

Becoming responsible does not mean refusing to ask for advice, not consulting anyone. We all need help, friendship, encouragement, intimacy but we also need to be ourselves. No one can live for us. Our next chapter explores what it means to slip into the driver's seat of your life and choose your own goals. Once we do this our feeling of self-worth will, inevitably, be enhanced. And we'll have the added boost of feeling that we are always growing and progressing toward becoming the person we can be, and perhaps, are meant to be.

3. **IMAGINATION** — We already know of the dramatic influence our imagination has on the creative force of our subconscious mind. By taking the opportunity to visualize, being your own confident self in whatever situation you wish, you set in motion the very "stuff" that makes it so.

The French author Emile Coué was fond of asking his audiences to imagine themselves walking a plank on the street between two houses. That was easy. "Now," he asked," imagine the same plank suspended three stories high between the windows of the same houses. Would you walk the plank now?" Everyone of course, with the possible exception of skilled circus performers, answered they probably would not.

"And why not?" Coué would ask. The answer was that now our

IMAGINATION dictated that it was too dangerous to do so. "So," he would say,"we can readily see what a vital role our imagination plays in the process of personal achievement."

Maltz goes even further and says that we cannot act otherwise than our imagination or self-image permits. Barksdale adds that if we try to do so anyway, it is at our peril, because the resulting distress causes agonizing headaches, high blood pressure, ulcers, arthritis and heart attacks. However, most of us can find enough motivation for our life roles simply by imagining ourselves in roles of healthy self-expression, enjoying the feeling of self-confidence surging through us, as we relate harmoniously to those about us.

4. **AFFIRMATION** — Here are proven techniques for strengthening your new higher course. Affirm, write down, repeat silently or audibly, the statements you are now defining about yourself that express the confident you which you desire to be. This is, of course, a personal matter and people's needs differ, but you may wish to write and say to yourself something like this:

- I am entitled to my own views and convictions, therefore I express them freely when it is wise to do so.
- I refuse to be too hard on myself. I am no longer a perfectionist. I let go of all my tendencies to be pleasing everyone whom I meet at the cost of my own integrity.
- If someone tries to put me down or insult me or tear me apart, I do not and will not accept such attempts, for I am myself and I am in charge.

According to legend the Buddha, some 2,500 years ago, visited a village where he was greeted by a man who heaped insult upon insult on him. When the assailant stopped for a moment to breathe, the Buddha asked him: "If I give you a valuable gift and you do not accept it, to whom does the gift belong?" "To the giver of course," replied the man. "Well," said the Buddha, "I do not accept your insults, they do not belong to me!"

Get into the habit of creating your own affirmations which exactly express your own convictions. They will work if you work them!

5. **ACTION** — It's vitally important for every one of us to do our own spiritual-mental-emotional work; it also does wonders for our self-esteem to, in Emerson's words, "do the thing and you shall have the power." Some contemporary philosophers, especially the existentialists have suggested that ACTING OUT whom you seek to be is of paramount value. French thinker Jean-Paul Sartre said: "Do you want to know who you are? Don't ask, **act**. Action will delineate and define you."

This sentiment appears to be born out by successful athletes. There's a young lady I know, who is a speedskater on the Olympic Winter Team of the Netherlands. She told me that her nervousness disappears the moment the starting gun sounds and she "explodes" (her own words) into action. Christine Aaftink has proven that action is a vital key to the self-confidence of a winner.

Jean Belliveau, admired by hockey fans as one of the all-time greats of the game, was asked if he didn't feel butterflies in his stomach before stepping on the ice in a championship encounter. "I do," he replied, "But they fly away the moment I actually step on the ice." Again, action made the self-esteem come to life, expressed it, and made it real.

Speaking in public, is for many people, the ultimate experience of dread. Yet, every skilled speaker knows that, despite the apprehension you feel before an engagement (which is normal and healthy), once you're on the platform and you deliver the first words into the microphone, you're O.K., thoughts and voice start to flow and your self-esteem has once more, seen you through.

So, let's decide to **do** the thing we fear to do, and, as the wisdom of the ages asserts, fear will disappear. Or we might say, utilizing an ancient truism: fear knocked at the door, self-esteem answered, there was nobody there . . .

Make it your business to be yourself, and only yourself, and you've taken the first step in mastering the art of motivation. You've turned the first key to success. Next we'll explore what the new Self we've cultivated is going to do, what goals, objectives and purposes are the right ones to be pursued. . . and how we may acquire that wonderful motivation that makes us feel authentically ourselves and alive!

Bibliography & Recommended Further Reading

Emerson, Ralph Waldo: Essays and Representative Men,Self-Reliance
    London: Collins, Library of Classics, 1962
Barksdale, Lilburn S. "Barks": Essays on Self-Esteem
    Idyllwild, CA: The Barksdale Foundation, 1977
Barksdale, Lilburn S. "Barks": Building Self-Esteem
    Idyllwild, CA: The Barksdale Foundation, 1979
Maslow, Abraham H.: Motivation and Personality
    N.Y.: Harper & Row, 1970
Maltz, Maxwell: Psycho-Cybernetics, A New Way to Get More Living
    Out of Life
    Englewood Cliffs, New Jersey: Prentice-Hall, Inc., 1960
Maltz, Maxwell: The Magic Power of Self-Image Psychology
    Englewood Cliffs, New Jersey: Prentice-Hall, Inc., 1964
Maltz, Maxwell: Power Psycho-Cybernetics for Youth
    N.Y.: Bantam, 1979
Maltz, Maxwell: Creative Living for Today
    N.Y.: Simon & Schuster, 1967
Maltz, Maxwell: Thoughts to Live By
    Markham, Ontario: Simon & Schuster of Canada Ltd., 1975
Buddha: Sayings of Buddha
    Mt. Vernon, N.Y.: Peter Pauper Press, 1957
Humphreys, Christmas: The Wisdom of Buddhism
    London: Michael Joseph Limited, 1960
Newman, James W.: Release Your Brakes!
    Thorofare, New Jersey: Chas. B. Slack, Inc., 1977

CHAPTER 7

GOALS: WHAT MAKES PEOPLE TICK?

*"Concentration of effort and the habit of working with a definite
chief aim are two of the essential factors in success which
are always found together. One leads to the other"*

The Law of Success
Napoleon Hill (1882–1970)

Given healthy, mature self-esteem, we're now ready to consider the right goals and objectives for ourselves. Without healthy self-esteem, the setting of goals will be, if not futile, extremely stressful, because the persons attempting to set goals do not believe, or only dimly believe, in their ability to succeed. That's why self-esteem is the number one factor in our discussion of achieving personal success.

With healthy, mature self-esteem, we simply cannot help but want to do something useful and productive with our lives, but we may not always know exactly what it is. Most of us, in our personal pursuit of fulfilment in life will have observed some fairly obvious facts about goals and goal-setting in our society; here are some apparent, major considerations:

Without goals no sense of achievement is possible — One of the most joyous feelings a person can have is that of accomplishing a task or objective one has set for oneself. A person who just drifts along through life may have moments of thrill or happiness but never experience the pride of "I did that!"

One of the foremost experts researching personal achievement in 20th Century North America was Napoleon Hill. He once analyzed the careers of 16,000 persons and noted that among those who considered their enterprises as failures, 95% did not have what Hill called "a definite chief aim." If the sail is not set, the wind will push you where you don't want to go.

All humanitarians and benefactors of civilization pursued definite goals — The ones we consider truly great had a vision of what they were meant to be and do and did not refuse to follow and express that vision. Just think, WHAT IF Jesus, Buddha and Albert Schweitzer had refused to share, what if Moses and St. Paul had refused to travel, what if Plato and Spinoza had refused to inquire, what if Florence Nightingale and Mother Theresa refused to express compassion, what if Galileo and Simone de Beauvoir refused to question, what if Thomas Edison and Henry Ford refused to experiment?

What if Christopher Columbus and James Cook refused to sail, what if Mozart and Beethoven refused to compose, what if Rembrandt and Pablo Picasso refused to paint, what if Horatio Alger and Napoleon Hill refused to teach success, what if the Wright Brothers refused to fly, what if William Shakespeare and Samuel Beckett refused to write plays?

What if Park Quimby and Carl Jung refused to heal, what if Elvis Presley and John Lennon refused to sing, what if Walt Disney and Lucille Ball refused to make people laugh? The world would be infinitely poorer and so would your world and home. The list, if you make your own, filled with the great names that have enriched your life, will be a testament to the truth that the world needs your dreams, your genius, and your goals.

Me? Yes, you, because you also are a member of that wonderful human fraternity whose potential it is to build a beautiful new world, a community of justice, peace and plenty for all.

We do have choices despite our environment — Many talented people feel limited by the influence of their background, family, education, age and other factors over which they have had no control. It is important to remember and recognize that we do have choices, that we do, in fact, set goals for ourselves daily without realizing that they are goals.

I met a lady the other day who owns a shop, but she's not happy with her business, so she's listed it for sale. "When I sell it," she said, "I'm going to get drunk." She may not be aware of it, but that is a personal goal!

With what we know about the creative power of our unconscious mind we realize that a goal is in the process of being reached, as is any firm belief we have accepted, although it may not be written down or defined as a goal. We choose continually, our lives are to a degree self-directed even if the action is unconscious.

Misfortune does not have to stand in the way of new goals — We may not be very happy with our accomplishments to date. We may feel life has been unfair, that people have betrayed our trust and that much of what you hoped for has turned out to be disappointing. We can learn from the lessons of "the school of hard knocks;" success researchers tell us over and over that we can learn far more from our failures than our successes. Whatever the past may have brought, today is a new day and in its hours you have the ability to make new, worthwhile choices. Pessimism and optimism are attitudes and we may choose which one we'll entertain.

Sometimes misfortune occurs because old goals, once achieved, have not been replaced with new objectives. Buzz Aldrin, the American astronaut who was one of the few select persons ever to walk on the moon, tells of the tremendous problems he encountered with living on earth once the great adventure was over; because he had never set any goals for himself beyond that outer space enterprise. An achieved goal is no longer a motivator. If you find your own level of motivation rather low, take a look at the area of your goals you have already reached. Trophies are wonderful and they have their important place but perhaps their most important function is that they can encourage us to do more, to come up higher, to seek a new objective.

Goal seeking and reaching can be learned — It is not really a difficult undertaking to do something definite about one's personal goals. It takes specific, sustained effort, but it pays off so well in terms of purpose of and feeling good about your life that not to do so would leave a tragic void in any intelligent person's life. What's the key to it all? You guessed it: give it your undivided attention.

Isaac Newton was asked how he discovered the law of gravitation. His reply was, "By thinking about it all the time." When we decide to THINK about the right goals for ourselves as individuals there are certain key elements that will help us make the choices of which we can be proud:

STUDY HUMAN MOTIVATION — If you have the opportunity to do so, study the subject thoroughly. Abraham Maslow has already been mentioned; there is so much vital insight in his work that it is highly advisable to familiarize yourself with it. During a considerable number of discussions with Frank Goble, the author of "The Third Force," a textbook which summarizes Maslow's teachings, he convinced me of the importance of this information, not only for choosing personal goals but also because as a result of this research, a key was discovered for reducing vandalism and crime. It is called character (or value) education. Applied in numerous American school systems it has achieved remarkable results and its impact and development is only in its infancy.

What is it that makes people tick? The history of human motivation goes back as far as recorded history. One statement, with which we can still identify, comes from Plato's Dialogues, where his mentor Socrates observes that human behavior, when consciously chosen, is commonly motivated by these factors:

Actions based on **Reward/Punishment**. We do something because we are promised a reward; we do it because we fear the punishment. This action does not consider others, it is pre-moral.

Actions based on **Exchange of Favors or Advantages**. "I'll scratch your back, if you'll scratch mine." It too is pre-moral action, "I'll help you providing you help me."

Actions designed to gain **Approval of a Group**. Here loyalty to group opinion determines what we do, including the "right and wrong" of it. To be "good" means to comply, to be conventional, to be accepted by one's peers, and to do what everyone does.

Actions based on **Authority/Law**. The state, employer or religion determines one's actions. Tradition is observed, convention maintained but the action could still be unethical, downright wrong and harmful. Plato said if we live on this level only, we do no better than bees and ants and apparently in his day most people did just that. What about our times?

Actions based on **Social Contract/Mutual Obligation**. This is the "principled" level of living; like a nation's bill of rights, the motivation and spirit of our actions keeps in mind the good of all people, the equal opportunity of all. In other words, we care.

Actions based on **Principles of Universality**. This is inspired action, carried out (selflessly) as a result of inner intuition. The highest value here is life itself, the equality and dignity of it. This action is associated with sages such as Jesus, who spoke of it in terms of "your reward will be great" and "you are children of the most high."

To choose to think and act from the highest level of motivation will result in experiencing great fulfilment, "peak experiences" and a sense of transformation into spiritual, unlimited being. This latter view is similar to the findings of modern motivational research. Our subject here touches on the topic of ethics and morality, the "right and wrong" of choices and actions.

Twentieth Century opinions of human motivation may be classified (very briefly here) into these three groups or "forces":

Freudianism: Associated with Sigmund Freud and the Psycho-Analytical School, the emphasis here is on the influence of the first five years of our lives or early childhood. We are motivated by what our parents and other adults taught and did, we (sort of) follow our role models. This is true enough, but does not take into consideration the fact that we can choose NOT to follow what we've been taught, and many of us don't.

Behaviorism: (Ivan Pavlov, John Watson, B.F. Skinner). The emphasis here is on the influence of the environment. We act in order to respond effectively to our environment; the Darwinian instinct to survive being the main motivator. This too is true enough. Consider the (true) story of twin brothers, growing up in an alcoholic family; one becomes a washed-up, gutter-type drunk, the other a teetotaller and successful businessman. When questioned as to the reason for their condition both responded with: "With parents like mine — how else could I have turned out?"

"Third Force" or Humanistic: (Abraham Maslow). The approach here is to study not the pathological but the healthy, self-actualized human being in order to discover what motivates the "champ" or the best of the lot. Answer: Human beings are motivated by basic and higher needs; we all strive to fulfil those needs, even if we are not aware of them. Maslow spoke of a "hierarchy" of these needs, that is, we seek fulfilment of the basic ones first and, when these are satisfied the "higher" needs knock at the door of our consciousness.

Very briefly, we start with (1) then go up to (2) and so on:
1. Physiological needs: air, water, food, shelter, sleep, sex.
2. Safety and Security needs
3. Love and Belongingness needs
4. Self Esteem and Esteem by Others
5. Growth needs; such as experiencing truth, goodness, beauty, playfulness, self-sufficiency, meaningfulness, aliveness and completion.

When we choose our goals it is wise to take into consideration the teaching of the wisdom of the ages as well as modern research. We too are the "humans" these findings talk about. We too have these needs. We too seek, if only unconsciously, to be fulfilled.

ASK: WHAT DO I REALLY WANT IN AND FROM LIFE? Have you ever asked yourself: What is my dream, what is my heart's desire, what is that "wonderful thing" I've always longed for? Many will say: I don't know, I want so many "things" or I've thought of a lot of activities, careers and functions in which I might be interested. One of the ways, is to go "within," to take time to reflect, to meditate and contemplate. To get in touch with our inner "fire of desire," those deep-down feelings that reveal the true nature of our potential. Our unconscious has the ability to reveal to us what it is we seek to know.

So, consult your own inner Wisdom, and do some real, uninterrupted THINKING. What skill, talent and expertise are uniquely yours that could help others? Finding and "setting" dynamic objectives for yourself could well become the most important motivator in your life. Usually, the secret seems to be to find what Napoleon Hill called your "definite chief aim." Comedian George Burns, a "legend in his own time" advises: "Do what you love to do." Sales motivators have urged people for decades to "find a need and fill it." Combine all of these to arrive at your unique, chosen goal.

APPLY THIS 7-WAY GOAL TEST. In my experience it is quite helpful, if we are not in the habit of choosing goals, or if we are doubtful, or tend to be timid or perhaps a bit too enthusiastic, to apply this little test to our goals. Your goals, to turn you on "must do" some of the following:

Be Realistic - that is believable, not out of reach

Be a Challenge - not something you do "with your eyes closed"

Get You Excited - or "turn-U-on" as we said in the 60's

Help You Grow - satisfy the "humanistic" needs

Not Hurt Others - not be designed to manipulate, harm or intentionally hurt another person or group

Be Measurable - that is, we must be able to put reasonable time and cost limits on it. "I'll do this by this date."

Feel Good - when you reflect on your objective and visualize its fulfilment, it should give us a warm, good "gut feeling."

CONSIDER TEN AREAS OF GOAL SEEKING — Beyond your "definite chief aim" there needs to be room for review of our entire lifestyle. Now's the time to take a firm look at what our life is all about and decide to do something about those areas where we feel a void exists. We may wish to look at the following areas, not listed in order of importance, — as this is different for different persons.

Physical Health. Where do we need to improve?

Material "things." What would truly enrich my life: the books of a favorite inspiring author, art?

Experiences. Do we want to travel, see a special place?

Career development. What are my professional desires?

Culture. Do I wish to explore music, theatre, poetry?

Spiritual. Do we desire to master contemplation, or the interpretation and understanding of obscure scriptures?

Relationships. The "significant other;" do I have needs in the areas of intimacy, sexual expression, close friendships, parenting, understanding relatives?

Self Growth. Do I want to break an undesirable habit?

Financially. What are our needs for security, future plans?

Socially. What cause in our society, community would we like to identify with? Are we interested in political life?

Your own awareness, upon reviewing these may take you well beyond the areas listed here. Goal seeking is a private enterprise and what your own heart tells you will undoubtedly take you well beyond any guidelines designed for general use. This is a good time to pause, decide for yourself which of these, or other goals, you wish to make your greatest concern. By the simple act of giving clarity to your goals you have begun the change to a better life.

UNLEASH YOUR DREAM — By unleashing we mean taking off the restrictions and limitations in our consciousness. If you have a dog, you may have taken it to an area where you take off the leash so your pet can have a free run — something all healthy dogs enjoy immensely! What ACTION can we take to unleash our dreams? What's there to do now to really set our objectives in motion? It's time for commitment, which means immediate action when due.

Bibliography & Recommended Further Reading

Hill, Napoleon: The Law of Success
    Chicago: Success Unlimited Inc., 1969
Plato: The Works of Plato (incl. the Dialogues)
    N.Y.: Modern Library, Random House, 1928
Goble, Frank: The Third Force - The Psychology of Abraham Maslow
    N.Y.: Grossman Publ., 1970
Goble, Frank: Beyond Failure; How to Cure a Neurotic Society
    Ottawa, Illinois: Green Hill Publishers, Inc., 1977
Goble, Frank & Brooks, B. David: The Case For Character Education
    Ottawa, Illinois: Green Hill Publ. Inc., 1983
Addington, Jack Ensign: All About Goals and How to Achieve Them
    Marina del Rey, CA: DeVorss & Co., 1977
Hughes, Charles L.: Goal Setting. Key to Individual and Organizational
    Effectiveness
    N.Y.: American Management Assn., 1965
Miller, Gordon Porter: Life Choices, How to Make the Critical Decisions
    N.Y.: Bantam, 1981
McKain Jr., Robert J.: Realize Your Potential
    N.Y.: American Management Assn., 1975
Bindra, Dalbir & Stewart, Jane, editors: Motivation
    Harmondsworth, England: Penguin Education, 1971
Maslow, Abraham H.: Toward A Psychology of Being
    N.Y.: VanNostrand Reinhold Co., 1968
Hoffman, Edward: The Right to be Human, A Biography of Abraham
    Maslow
    N.Y., St. Martin's Press, 1988
Skinner, B.F.: About Behaviorism
    N.Y.: Vintage Books, 1974
Skinner, B.F.: Science and Human Behavior
    N.Y.:Free Press, Macmillan Publ. Co., 1953

CHAPTER 8

FROM HERE TO PROSPERITY

"Do not hesitate to think that prosperity is for you. Do not feel unworthy. . . Think prosperity, talk prosperity . . . as your very own right . . . affirm supply, support and success."

Prosperity
Charles Fillmore (1854-1948)

Some wise person, who was no doubt familiar with the secrets of human individual achievement in a free society, said: "The first thing we need to do to make our dreams come true is to WAKE UP!" In other words, in order to move our goals into a forward motion, rather than to just stand or sit still, we need to discover and apply the means that will get us on our way to accomplish what we decided we would do. The two major ingredients of the art of motivation discussed thus far, Self-esteem and Goals contained as their concluding element the factor of "action" — unleash your dream, give it everything you've got, live a goal-directed life. Suppose we've made this suggestion our firm commitment — how do we now go about actually achieving that progress we seek?

What we are talking about here is prosperity. As is the case with so many key words that have become a part of our everyday vocabulary, the meaning of prosperity is not always the same for all readers. Many persons would equate it primarily, or even exclusively, with financial success. This certainly is part of what we mean by prosperity, because if the financial means for moving our goals forward is required but not available, we are not prosperous. But the idea behind prosperity is larger than money or its equivalent. The word is derived in our English language from the ancient latin word "prosperare" which means to do well, to thrive, to be successful, to be fortunate.

How can we, as individuals, improve our own prosperity? Let's remember what we discovered in THE ART OF THINKING - YOUR KEY TO WELLNESS section of this book. To change our lives, we must change our thinking, our beliefs, because our consciousness is the workshop where our creative achievement originates. Remembering that we are looking at our subject from a strictly individual point of view, let us not forget the tremendous benefit our knowledge of achieving more personal prosperity can have for our society. An abundance of prosperous, caring individuals can do much to alleviate general poverty with its concomitant suffering from loss of health and dignity, crime and war.

Poverty, says author Catherine Ponder, in her book "The Dynamic Laws of Prosperity" is a common vice. It is at the root of so much despair, fear, dependency, violence and squalor that, all us us need to do whatever we can to eradicate it from our planet.

As our consciousness is the creative origin of what we seek to achieve, what we need to do is build a consciousness of prosperity, to start believing in something better than what we have experienced. How then do we build a personal prosperity consciousness that will move us forward? Think of truly prosperous people you know, people whose lives are "doing well," you will most likely find among the deciding factors of their success the following key elements.

CONDITIONING:
REVERSE NEGATIVE BELIEFS ABOUT PROSPERITY.

Few persons would admit an awareness of beliefs in poverty, lack and failure. Yet these beliefs are being expressed continually in our culture and the outer and inner response to them leave people in the same mess they wish to escape. Below are a few examples of commonly expressed "poverty" beliefs we may hear almost daily:

— "Prosperity is not good," not spiritual. We are meant to be poor and needy. This life is sinful, a valley of tears and trouble.

— "Money is the root of all evil," the often misquoted Bible verse that is supposed to suggest we should not have or enjoy money. The verse actually reads: "The love of money is the root of all evil," in other words, greed is evil (1 Timothy 6:10). Someone has suggested the verse should have read: "The lack of money is the root of all evil!"

— "Money doesn't matter, we should be indifferent toward it. It's probably connected with corruption, so stay away from money. Rich people must be 'crooks.'"

— "Don't use the best things (dishes, crystal, furniture, clothes) you have, save them." Another belief in the postponement of enjoyment of prosperity.

— "Don't buy anything or spend anything if you can help it." Beliefs often going back to the "dirty 30's" depression years and earlier, as well as the two world wars. The fear of lack made people hoard. When the conditions change, the thinking often doesn't change with them. So people still hunt for that coupon-clipped bargain.

— "Times are tough, we're in a recession (depression) and things are getting worse. It's tough to find a job, to succeed." The media is usually the message here, or perhaps the culprit. Day after day, news broadcasters pour a stream of negative expectation out on the public. One announcement about a federal budget in Canada carried the subtitle: "Share the pain!"

— Jealousy, envious criticism of those who are perceived as being prosperous or having "more than" the jealous person. Wealthy people, royal families, corporate tycoons are often despised and hated by the very people who benefit from their enterprises and masses of "the public."

— "Success and prosperity are a matter of luck." Here too, the media have given (encouraged by government) tremendous publicity to multi-million dollar lotteries and other means of gambling, creating the belief that if you want to "be somebody" you'll just have to hope you'll be lucky one day. Otherwise, you "poor sucker". . .

— "Try to get something for nothing." This attitude was well portrayed by comedian-artist Red Skelton, whose character Freddy the Freeloader reminded us of people we know or knew. Is there a "free lunch?"

— Resentment toward paying taxes, fees, licences and permits. People go "livid" when income tax time comes.

— "My prosperity comes from taking." The poorest people are those who are stingy and won't share. They believe, if you give, you lose. They live as if they wish to play baseball, but are wearing two receiving mitts.

All of these poverty beliefs and many more you'll be able to think of, can be reversed and changed. If you detect a poverty belief in your own consciousness, arrest and reverse it now.

— Prosperity IS good, it is the natural expression of life to want to become more of itself. The spiritual giants described in the Bible and other scriptures always had their needs met and plenty left over unless they chose otherwise. Read the stories of Abraham, Jacob, Joseph and Solomon. To them, life was filled with abundance.

— Money and financial matters are not evil or dirty. We are simply discussing assets or means toward an end. It is the use we make of currency and its equivalent that determines the morality.

— Enjoyment and use of "things," spending wisely and helping worthwhile causes all promote more manufacturing, transportation, sales, employment and benefits to people who need them. There's no economics without demand and supply.

— Thinking is creative. Think depression and we create and attract depression. Think prosperity and opportunity and more of these will be generated. It is stupid to fill your mind with beliefs of hopelessness and pessimism.

— There is no need to be jealous, it will only harm the one who entertains such emotions. To reverse envious tendencies start thinking in terms of opportunity, plenty and infinity, realizing as Charles Fillmore observed, that prosperity is your very own right; you are entitled to your share of the abundance of this Universe.

— Taxes, fees, etc. need to be paid for a democratic society to function. If we're unhappy about it, the constructive thing to do is to become politically active. To upset your mind deliberately leads to illness and you become difficult to live with.

— Prosperity and success may be a matter of luck for only a few persons (many who have won lotteries have experienced that their lives become more stressful, not easier) but when we realistically desire to become prosperous and fulfil the goals we have chosen we'll find that it is not a matter of luck but of careful planning and hard work. So, when we've reversed and eliminated our poverty thinking we're ready to proceed to the next step.

EXPECTATION: CREATE YOUR OWN PROSPERITY PLAN

This is, of course, a personal matter, and the general ideal behind it is this: Let's sit down (seriously) and ask ourselves: How will I go about achieving my goals? What do I need to do, have or be to move forward? "Work" to some people is a "four-letter" word. To to those who understand that work is a blessing, there is tremendous joy in the process of achieving, happiness is in the journey, an opportunity to "DO" something is welcome.

Do I need more education, training, skills? How can I begin NOW (not when we seemingly have time, or when conditions are just right) to improve myself? Do I need to consult someone who knows about the business I'm going into? What do the experts in this field advise? What kind of organization do I need? Do I understand the recording and support systems needed to run my enterprise effectively? Do I need to acquire skills in bookkeeping, accounting, taxation, negotiation, administration, management? How will I market my services? What facilities will I require, what will my budget be, what do I need to purchase, with whom do I need to associate myself, do I have the resources necessary to succeed, do I have a practical PLAN for it all?

We become goal-directed persons when we begin to manage our lives along these lines. Then, at the start of the day we will ask: what am I doing TODAY to move closer to my objectives? We will eliminate those activities that do NOT contribute to our goals. Sound difficult? Not really. Self-management enhances our self-worth and the great feeling that goes with it. You start feeling alive, full of enthusiasm, worthwhile, — the person you are meant to be. It feels wonderful!

At the end of the day we may wish to observe the 3 R's of goal-directed individuals: **Relax** — so you won't fall asleep in distress; **Review** — did I get done what I wanted to do? Don't be too hard on yourself if you didn't. Life has a way of surprising us, so not all our plans are always being carried out the way and the day we wish. You did the best you could and tomorrow is another day. **Reflect** — it is important to master the art of contemplation described later in the book. In this way we never become part of the so-called rat race. We are not rats. Create ways to rise above rat-like living. Don't compromise on these ground rules.

CIRCULATION: BECOME A GENEROUS GIVER

How will your enterprise prosper, given that your plan is sound and in place? Every entrepreneur will tell you: you've got to give it everything you've got. We're not suggesting becoming a seven-day week workaholic, but rather, to live up to one's commitment. The ancient law of life, taught by the great sages throughout recorded history is: as you give, so you receive, as you sow, so shall you reap.

This applies in all areas of human activity as well as non-human organic existence. Your farmer friends will tell you that in order to obtain an abundant harvest, seeding must be both timely and adequate. Use no seeds and there cannot be a harvest. Your body functions by means of the same principle: breathe in, yes, but to continue to live, we also need to breathe out, to give back. Study the circulation of the blood, the processes of digestion and elimination and you'll find the same principle. "No circulation" results in stagnation and death. Your computer utilizes the same law: first the input, then the response by the program, finally the output or result. Put nothing in, and you get nothing out.

Take a look at human relationships. Refrain from giving your attention, your love and your effort and the relationship crumbles. Give these and it flourishes, providing of course the interaction is mutual.

Financially, this ancient law of prosperity is known as the habit of "tithing" or giving one tenth of one's gross income to the source of one's spiritual nourishment. The tithers I know seem to be not only happy, joyous persons but they also have that great feeling of knowing themselves as generous people.Their needs seem to be continually met, sometimes in quite unexpected ways. The same principle then applies here: as you give, so you receive and it's exciting to live this way because the surprises Life provides in response to one's generosity are often thrilling. Life is flow, circulation; we cannot play the game of life wearing two receiving mitts, it won't work. Have you ever met a happy, joyous miser? Giving is not losing, it is sowing and all of life is the soil.

What's holding people back from becoming prosperous through generosity? Fear, of course. Were you told to hang on to every penny you earned because "when you get old, you'll get sick and you'll need every bit of savings to support your condition?" How can we break the chains of this poverty thinking? One way is our next step.

AFFIRMATION:
FILL YOUR MIND WITH PROSPEROUS IDEAS

We have mentioned the often negative effect of the various media. Just turn around your TV dial and what do you see? An appalling amount of violence, shooting, stabbings, deaths, a diet of mental and emotional garbage. Are there exceptions? Of course, but far too much of our so-called entertainment can only motivate people to feel bad and act in concert with what they take in. When they watch the news, it gets even worse, because now we're told this is the real world. No one in their right mind would suggest that we need not be aware of what's happening in the world. The news, however, is usually completely inconsistent with the real world since it reports primarily what's "wrong" and not what's "right," healthy, successful, mature and happy.

I believe one of the major changes required in our society, if we wish to move to a better 21st Century, is a complete overhaul and clean-up of the media. When the creative principle governing the human organism, known as the interaction of the conscious and subconscious mind, is understood by enough numbers of people, we shall witness a dramatic change in the TV "diet" as well as the contents of the other media.

Meanwhile, what can we, as individuals do? We can prepare and implement our own prosperity diet consisting of prosperity and success audio cassette and video tapes, and of course, books. Consult the bibliography provided here with this chapter. Acquire some of these and other, similar titles. Decide to read one chapter in such a book every night consistently; fall asleep with these prosperity ideas on your mind and see if your prosperity experience doesn't change for the better! Watch those new ideas "pop into your head," be amazed at the people who will contact you or whom you just happen to "bump into," who can contribute to the fulfilment of your dreams. And watch how much better you feel! Talk with successful, prosperous people. Avoid the whiners, complainers, critics, cynics and pessimists. They never contributed anything worthwhile to our culture. Mix with "up" people, even if it means making definite changes in your current circle of friends, relatives and acquaintances.

Listen to inspirational and motivational cassettes while driving to and from work or other assignments. Time spent in traffic, one of the inevitables of our society, need not be seen as an annoyance and waste: make it an experience to which you look forward. Surround yourself with prosperous ideas, fill your genius mind with prosperous suggestions, to grow and flourish there.

AMBITION: PERSIST, DO NOT GIVE UP

Winston Churchill used to say: "Never, never give up," but of course many people do, when they do not see instant success after deciding to do something better with their lives. Giving up on a worthwhile dream is tragic and the people we know who seemed to be skilled, likable, good people who have now "lost it" are pathetic. They tried, perhaps for awhile, then dropped out. They return to the drab, grey environment they were used to, dependent, a "nobody" in a mass of people where no one is really motivated, where everyone's goal is just to be "secure," to earn a meagre but predictable income. The goal of life seems to be to make it to 4:30 or 5 o'clock, especially to Friday afternoon's "happy hour." This uninspiring scenario is only too common, and reminiscent of silver screen's W.C. Fields who said (tongue-in-cheek): "If at first you don't succeed, try again. If you still don't, the heck with it!"

Should we stubbornly stay with a projected goal, even when we don't have a reasonable chance of success? Of course not. Perhaps we need a different goal, perhaps our tenacity is an unwise left-over from the "tough neighbourhood" attitude of childhood. One never gave in, never admitted that one was wrong and never changed. This kind of obstinacy is foolish and when we reflect on our situation we'll know from within when it's time to "call it a day."

But far too many people give up the moment they encounter delay, opposition, disappointment and the requirement of extra effort. When we feel like giving up, we need to dig a bit deeper, we need to build a new fire under our desire. We need the ability to carry on despite disappointments and problems. We need to rise above our fears. We also need the ability to turn seeming failure into opportunity. All this requires more than merely being a "pencil pusher" in the office of life, it requires more than mediocrity, it requires leadership, it requires EXCELLENCE.

But this is such a big subject that we are devoting an entire chapter to it (Chapter 10). Sometimes, our tendency to quit comes from the distress of having too much to do and not enough time in which to do it. This too is a vital challenge and we are dedicating our next chapter to it (Chapter 9).

One more, concluding thought: let's be sure that our motivation is RIGHT, that we are indeed pursuing the right goals for us. Earl Nightingale, well known expert communicator on the subject of personal achievement, puts it this way: "It is an UNUSUAL person whose desire is larger than his or her distaste for the work involved!" But, for those unusual persons, the next chapter will assist them in taking their next step toward the fulfilment they desire and deserve. . .

Bibliography & Recommended Further Reading

Hill, Napoleon: Think and Grow Rich
    No. Hollywood, CA: Wilshire Book Co., 1966
Hill, Napoleon: The Master Key to Riches
    Greenwich, CT: Fawcett Publ., 1969
Hill, Napoleon: Grow Rich! With Peace of Mind
    Greenwich, CT: Fawcett Publ., 1967
Fillmore, Charles: Prosperity
    Kansas City, Missouri: Unity School, 1936
Addington, Jack & Cornelia: All About Prosperity and How You Can
    Prosper
    Marina Del Rey, CA: DeVorss & Co., 1984
Ponder, Catherine: The Dynamic Laws of Prosperity
    Marina Del Rey, CA: DeVorss & Co., revised 1985
Smiley, Emma M.: Bread of Life
    Wakefield, Mass.: Montrose Press, 1956
Grayson, Stuart: The Ten Demandments of Prosperity
    N.Y.: Dodd, Mead & Co., 1986
Ingraham, E.V.: Wells of Abundance
    Los Angeles, CA: DeVorss & Co., 1938
Ross, Ruth: Prospering Woman. A Complete Guide to Achieving the
    Full Abundant Life
    N.Y.: Bantam Books, 1985
Hoshor, John: Your Genie: Will Bring Everything You Want
    N.Y.: Creative Process Press, 1961
Andersen, U.S.: Three Magic Words
    No. Hollywood, CA: Wilshire Book Co., 1972
Schwartz, David J.: The Magic of Thinking Big
    No. Hollywood, CA: Wilshire Book Co., 1971

CHAPTER 9

IT'S ABOUT TIME

"One moment may be eternity. . . The fact that those who are happy do not keep a watchful eye upon the clock, indicates an emergence from mathematical time, a forgetfulness of clocks and calendars."

Slavery and Freedom
Nikolai Berdyaev (1874–1948)

People who decide to take over the driver's seat of their lives, and who become goal-directed soon find that "there are only so many hours in a day" — they would like to **DO** so much more than they have time for. . . They also experience distress when their persistent effort to get things done on time fails. This is a major problem for many entrepreneurs and achievers and it makes sense therefore, to look a little closer at the subject of time.

TIME is a fascinating (as well as necessary) topic — it plays a tremendously important role in our lives as everything we do and are is affected by time, even when we are unaware of it. There is a philosophy of time. One of its greatest contemporary exponents was the existentialist philosopher Nikolai Berdyaev, quoted above. He points out that there are a variety of meanings attached to the concept of time. Here are the three main distinctions:

Cosmic Time — Symbolized by the circle, it is connected with the motion of the earth around the sun. It is the time of your watch and clock which traditionally, though not the electronic version, displays a circular movement, going around over and over again, seconds become minutes, which in turn become hours, days and nights, weeks and months, years and decades, into infinity. It is the mathematical time of the diary and the calendar, the time of nature.

Historical Time — Symbolized by a straight line stretching out into the past but also forward into the future. It has to do with meaning. Events are not measured in terms of duration but in terms of significance. There is return and repetition but also the waiting for the disclosure of something new, even about events past. Historical time has to do with what you, as a human being, have experienced as you were aware of time and what you believe the time ahead of you holds in store. Collectively, it has to do with meaning of history, of the why's, how's and wherefore's of human activity throughout eons of time on this planet.

Existential Time — Symbolized by a point, it has to do with what we experience in this moment without specific reference to or awareness of past and future or clock time. It is in existential time that we experience a five-minute wait for a loved one as many hours and "one moment may be eternity." Realizing what philosophy has ruminated about time is not non-essential. It is important, when considering how to spend and therefore manage our time, to become aware of what is meaningful and purposeful activity and what is not. All these concepts are related in our considerations.

It is also wisdom to know something more about the nature of time than what we gather daily from our timepieces and calendars. It's exciting to consider the world of time as explained and explored in terms of our cosmos by such brilliant minds as Albert Einstein, Stephen Hawking and Carl Sagan. The expansion of our "ordinary" thinking is a vital and fundamental part of becoming an authentic person.

Continuing our quest: what can we do when we don't seem to have enough time to accomplish the things we want and need to do? The answers are important for two main reasons: first, so we will have the sense of accomplishment and success consistent with our goals; second, because we will avoid certain health hazards connected with the person who is always in a rush. Known as "Type A Behavior" by observers of human behavior and personality development, it is found in the person who is excessively competitive, aggressive, impatient and hurried.

Medical experts have been telling us for some decades that such individuals are likely to suffer heart and artery problems. Their lives are not peaceful and happy, but quite the opposite: they are about to "blow their top" (even if they don't do it), impatiently on the move, trying to do several things at the same time. Their letters and memos abound with words like "rush" and "immediate" and "urgent," while they have little or no time for listening to others, or relating in an informed way to what's going on around them.

How do we change to "Type B Behaviour," the image of the person who is relaxed and enjoying the trip while at the same time performing not merely as well as Type A, but even better?

The answer lies in the personal management and discipline of our time and there are several areas of activity that can help us achieve it. Novelist Michael Ende creates an imaginary society in his story called "Momo" where people are able to deposit left over time in a bank as we do money. You can then save time and withdraw it when you need it. It seems impossible science-fiction theorizing to suggest that we can have more time when all of us are given the same twenty-four hours a day in which to work, eat, play and sleep, yet with the implementation of efficient time management the results will seem just as magical.

KEY IDEAS OF TIME MANAGEMENT

ELIMINATE inefficient use of time, time-leaks; arrest the "thieves of time." It has been called by different names but the idea is the same: to know what to do next we must first know what we are doing now. Make a list of the ways in which you are aware, in your own daily experience, you are "losing" valuable minutes, perhaps hours. Think again of what we discussed about goal-directed living; to achieve our goals we need to actually <u>pursue them</u> and not something else. Your list of time-leaks may include items such as these:

— My desk is cluttered with files and papers — I can't find what I'm looking for WHEN I need to.
— I do things that really don't matter much, they are unimportant to my overall objectives.
— I keep and save and store "stuff" I don't and never will need again.
— I jump into doing a job before thinking it through and planning it properly.
— I forget appointments and promises.
— I like to do things that give me pleasure first and put off everything else.
— I do things that are not part of the job at hand.

— I do things that could just as well be done by other people.
— I do not communicate with my boss and associates before going ahead with a job.
— I mix personal concerns with business.
— I allow the telephone and visitors to interrupt me while I am working on something important.
— I spend a lot of time complaining instead of changing unwelcome conditions.
— I try to "remember" messages verbally communicated to me rather than writing them down.
— I tend to say "yes" to every request for my time and attention.
— I spend too much time talking on the telephone.

Whatever your list may look like, now that you have yours, you are in a position to do something about wasted or unproductive time - you now know what requires your action. You might want to add another experiment: keeping a personal time LOG. That is: record your activities in 10 to 15 minute blocks of time for a week or so. It will become even clearer to you then where your time is spent in activities other than goal-directed objectives. Now we are ready to stop time leaks by taking the next personal action step.

PLAN your day, week, month, year as well as your "station." Organizing your life may sound dreary and boring but it can and does pay off in many wonderful ways. The initial distaste for tackling it will be far outweighed by the benefits. Think of planning in the following ways:
Plan Long Term — Count the cost when looking at a project. When we want to grow a garden we know it will take time. How much? What do we have to do to have this time available? Do other objectives have to be shelved? What does this mean to the harmony of my life? What to my relationships?
Plan Short Term — Plan your day: keep track of each appointment, follow-up calls, etc. Keep a "day-timer" type diary and know what you want to accomplish that day. Develop a "things-to-do" list.
Schedule your work in terms of priorities, that is, do things in order of importance, "first things first" and this priority should be reflected

on your list of things-to-do. Whenever and wherever possible, break down your schedule into time slots or a time table so your day is planned not only showing your appointments with others but also with yourself.

Organize your work into projects, or jobs, each with its own file or at least card (or equivalent if your work is computerized). Your project is monitored by your control sheet or card which has a time-date-action plan. Review each morning, or agreed period, for progress. Keep notes on all calls, memos, correspondence etc.

Manage your information, sources and functions. Do you know where to find telephone and fax numbers, addresses, postal codes, prices, data that are necessary to be "at your fingertips" when you need them?

Organize your work area; know where everything belongs and keep resources in their place. Get rid of clutter on your desk or station.

Take a close look at those "habits" of working that may not be useful any more. If not sure, apply this 4-way "profit and loss" test: (1) Why do we do this? (2) Do we profit or benefit by doing it? (3) What would we lose if we didn't? (4) Would we profit more if we didn't do it or if we did it differently?

Do things in multiples. How often have you obtained an item from some distance away, only to have to do it again the same afternoon or the next day? Instead, we can bake several casseroles at a time, we can invite three persons instead of 1, buy items in quantity, write the same memo once and send it to several people, plan several errands on one trip.

Get rid of files that are not essential to your current work-in-progress or future projects. If necessary develop an "archives department" that's not in your way.

Utilize your waiting time. See time spent in waiting rooms, commuting, driving in traffic as an opportunity for learning and growing. Carry books that you have wanted to read, with you in your car. Acquire inspirational, motivational, personal development audio cassettes you can listen to while driving from point A to point B. You'll start LIKING the time you previously considered wasted.

Confirm in writing your important communications and make notes to
    yourself continually as you participate in telephone calls, interviews,
    conferences and meetings.
Learn to conduct efficient meetings and discussions.

CONCENTRATE on what you are doing and implement effective
controls on interruptions. The best slogan here is the hotel room sign
that reads "DO NOT DISTURB." Of course, we do not always wish to
"be this way" - managers know how important it is not to appear aloof
or authoritative. We wish to be in communication with the people
around us and an "open door" policy facilitates that desire. Yet, it is not
inconsistent with a warm, friendly attitude and genuine interest in others
to allow yourself the opportunity to get your work done. Most people will
respect privacy when it is necessary for you to "plough ahead" and finish
your project.

One of the greatest benefits in human communications came with
the invention of the telephone. But, as with all technology, the blessing
can turn into a curse if not managed wisely. We've all waited at wickets
and counters only to be interrupted by a telephone call which, in too
many organizations seems to receive priority over the client with whom
the employee is speaking. Result: hurt feelings and a waste of time. To
control your telephone so it does not become a monster but the
marvelous assistant it can be, try these ideas:

Think, plan, write down your ideas before punching or dialing that
    number.
Select a special (most-likely-"in") time for your calls.
Use a telephone answering service so you will still receive those
    messages even though you are not at your telephone or you are
    concentrating on an essential project.
Stay with the purpose of your call. Of course we wish to be social,
    friendly but — remember those time leaks — so much time, prime
    quality time, is spent in conversations that add nothing to the
    objective of the call.
Leave clear messages with the person answering the call or the
    tape, if the person you wish to reach is not available.

Keep notes on your calls, made and received and follow-up in writing, as soon as possible, when called for.

Decide on the best time for you to answer your phone and to respond to messages.

Keep basic information materials nearby and handy, to answer questions by phone quickly and accurately.

With all this "controlling," do be flexible and do not lose your sense of humor and above all, don't be too hard on yourself: it is said that only Robinson Crusoe could have everything done by Friday!

DELEGATE work, tasks, duties, errands, chores . . . to others who can do, or can be taught to do, the job just as well.

It takes a healthy degree of self-esteem to delegate tasks to others. People who are insecure do not want to delegate for fear of losing a position or function. Perfectionists believe they are the only ones that could do the job properly. But some of the real dangers of delegating are, naturally, that the work will NOT get done as well or as quickly as you had planned. Some ideas to keep in mind here:

— When delegating put controls in place so the work is subject to auditing.

— Make sure the person who is asked to do the work is both qualified and has the time to do it.

— Provide adequate information about the job to be done and about the way in which you expect it to be carried out.

— Be open to questions and problem solving which the person doing the job cannot handle.

— Make the delegated task seem like a challenge and fun rather than a drudgery and a bore. Of course this can only be done if it is sincerely meant but a positive attitude is helpful with all kinds of work that could be seen as a chore.

— Become comfortable with the feeling of risking. Life has an element of risk in it and it is healthy.

— Many persons to whom a new task was delegated have turned out to be both creative and efficient. What may have started as "I simply must give this job to someone else" may wind up as a creative and intelligent solution to a stubborn challenge, where the new associate in the project is just the right person to handle the situation, perhaps for some time to come.

CONTEMPLATE — When we start and conclude our day with a contemplative, meditative review of what we want to do and what we have done and have yet to do, we break the awful chains of distress due to the hurry-worry habit.Too many people we know do not allow themselves time to pause and THINK before plunging into the day.

Arrange your time schedule so you <u>do</u> have that bit of quality time to review quietly. You will begin your day in a peaceful mood instead of in a rush and you will end your day serene, with the best chance for healthy sleep, instead of popping pills and inviting nightmares. Stop, slow down, take time to be yourself, to feel what you need to feel, to care about others and our environment, to get in touch with your spiritual self and the spirit of the universe.

You'll be surprised how often new ideas, new ways of doing things, time-saving ways will come to you as you allow the intuitive part of your unconscious to function freely. To manage our time effectively is but one way toward the goal of living our lives at the level of excellence.

Bibliography and Recommended Further Reading

Berdyaev, Nicolai: Slavery and Freedom (Transl: R.M. French)
      N.Y.: Chas. Scribner's Sons, 1944
Ende, Michael: Momo (Transl: J.M. Brownjohn)
      N.Y.: Doubleday, 1985
Barnett, Lincoln: The Universe and Dr. Einstein
      N.Y.: Bantam, 1974
Hawking, Stephen W.: A Brief History of Time — From the Big Bang
      to Black Holes
      N.Y.: Bantam, 1988
Sagan, Carl: Cosmos
      N.Y.: Random House, 1980
Reynolds, Helen and Tramel, Mary E.: Executive Time Management,
      Getting 12 Hours' Work Out of an 8-Hour Day
      Englewood Cliffs, New Jersey: Prentice-Hall Inc., 1979
Harris, Thomas A. and Harris, Amy B.: Staying OK
      N.Y.: Harper & Row, 1985
Waitley, Denis and Witt, Reni L.: The Joy of Working
      N.Y.: Dodd, Mead & Co, 1985
Von Franz, Marie-Louise: Time, Rhythm and Repose
      Golborne, Lancashire: Thames & Hudson, 1978
Priestley, J.B.: Man and Time
      N.Y.: Dell Publ., 1968
Bliss, Edwin C.: Getting Things Done — The A B C's of Time
      Management
      N.Y.: Bantam, 1980
Robert, Henry M.: Robert's Rules of Order
      Westwood, New Jersey: Fleming H. Revell Co., 1969
Parkinson, C. Northcote: Parkinson's Law
      N.Y.: Ballantine, 1964
Peter, Laurence J. and Hull, Raymond: The Peter Principle
      N.Y.: Bantam, 1976

CHAPTER 10

AIMING FOR EXCELLENCE

*"The most important of all factors in your life is the mental diet
on which you live. It is the food which you furnish to your mind that
determines the whole character of your life."*

Power Through Constructive Thinking
Emmet Fox (1886–1951)

There are so many signs now in our global village that point to a much gentler and fairer society. Even our environment could cause us to be encouraged to strive for far higher aims than the carrots of materialism and the basic, legitimate desire to "make a living."

The megatrends we may observe, as we move swiftly toward the 21st Century, have in a significant part, to do with success in a much grander, richer way than the equivalent of monetary values. We see enterprises everywhere whose aim it is to provide a better quality of life, to improve the humanity of humans. We are becoming a part of the universal movement to create a new age, where we think in terms of goals that lead not just to making a living but building a good life.

With the break-up of the communist empire it now seems likely that a new global economy is in the making wherein it will be exciting for the individual entrepreneur to participate. While material needs are increasingly being met for more and more millions, other, even more rewarding riches will come into focus. Abraham Maslow envisions on a personal level, inner riches of beauty, truth, music, literature, art, philosophy and community. Those of us who are becoming more aware, regardless of our age, of our enormous potential for choosing personal objectives with opportunities for prosperity and self-management, will experience moments of ecstasy when we reflect on what life offers us, right here and right now. . .

What will it take to fully participate in the development of the new world order, which, in the process, will also fulfil us as individuals? As we begin to practice the factors we have already learned, a certain new FEELING comes over us. It is best described, as the desire to leave the average and the mediocre behind, to rise above the recordings of statistics and the average, to aim for excellence!

We are no longer waiting until all the conditions surrounding us are just right before we begin. Why? Because we have decided the good life begins now, it begins with the decision to express the highest and best of which we are capable. Nothing less than excellence, is our aim.

Our next question then arises: what are the ingredients of excellence at the personal level? What do people who truly become excellent actually do? This is an exciting question and my own experience has convinced me that there are five major qualities which contribute to personal excellence. They each have their own component causes, all of which help build that marvelous "something special" we detect in those whom we could call the true "mystics" of life, in the original sense of that word, the ones who know the secret.

PERSEVERANCE — Our word comes from the original latin "per" which means "intensify" and "severus" which means "severe." In our discussion on Prosperity (Chapter 8) we concluded that persistence is an important quality of character because so many have failed in their enterprises as they gave up too soon. We all meet people who have grandiose ideals, they'll tell you what they are going to do, but they never do it. Many give up even before they start. Many soon after. Why?

There are many reasons, depending on the particular circumstances, but the main ones seem to recur, over and over again:

— When things get tough, the tough get going, but the rest quit. They cannot stand the "heat in the kitchen," they thought it would be much easier.

— The goals chosen are not appropriate to that particular person. The motives are not right, the "feel" isn't there.

— Inadequate business plan, so the enterprise cannot win.

— Lack of enthusiasm, because of criticism from others.

— Inadequate skills, including not learning from previous failures.

What does it take to acquire that perseverance we all need to break through the tough barriers that we all experience? Let's consider two major factors:

<u>A Sound Business Plan</u> If your plan is indeed sound, you will have such faith in it that you just won't quit. We should avail ourselves of some of the good books which can explain to us the many items we must know to be a success. We should have intimate knowledge concerning the product or service we wish to supply. Who are your potential clients, your competition? What will your costs and price structure be? Who will be your partners and employees? What volume of business will be necessary to be successful? How much financing will be required, can you find and borrow sufficient capital?

All these have to be in place, documented and realistic. Without them, no one can succeed and perseverance would equal stubborn stupidity. Trying to go into business without these basic facts will ruin what could potentially be a fine opportunity. Get the informed help you need to establish your business plan, plan one in which you can deeply believe, and you will be well on your way to success.

<u>Enthusiasm</u> All studies on the secrets of the truly excellent personalities show that they were totally devoted to their objective. The famous 19th Century French painter Pierre Auguste Renoir is said to have painted every day of his adult life. In his late years when arthritis in his fingers made it impossible to hold his brush, he asked for an assistant to tie the brush to his hand, so he could continue to create. This is but one of thousands of examples of a person of excellence, filled with enthusiasm until the very end of earthly existence, who did not have to acquire or find persistence, because he already had it, in the reservoir of the unconscious.

We all have such a reservoir but it cannot be reached when the motivator that produces the enthusiasm is not there. Money, greed, envy of others won't provide it. Your motivation has to be more noble than mere personal gain. It has to be nothing less than your heart's desire, as the great spiritual motivator Emmet Fox pointed out.

Enthusiasm or zeal is really a spiritual quality, but when you've discovered it inside you, it isn't too difficult to cultivate expressing it. The secret then is simply this: act the way you'd like to be and soon you'll be the way you act. Start your day enthusiastically by taking time to meditate and to reflect on your goals and the opportunities life offers you right now.

The wisdom of the ages has always given this kind of instruction. Said the ancient philosopher Plotinus around 250 AD: "The wise man recognizes the idea of the GOOD within him. This he develops by withdrawal into the holy place of his own soul."

CREATIVE THINKING Excellence means being capable of producing new ideas, solutions and answers where ordinary thinking knows not what to do. To most people this ability is a total mystery and it is usually believed that one must be endowed with some quite special talent for creativity, as some unusual persons such as Wolfgang Amadeus Mozart had a rare talent for composing beautiful music.

But creative thinking can be learned, as it is mostly the un-learning of previously conditioned modes of thinking. Everyone has access to new combinations or conclusions of thought.

As part of our culture we all have available a vast range of information, facts on reference, available to us: names, dates, places, events, sequences, sentences, interpretations, commentaries.

Beyond this encyclopedic fact there is the more subtle computing that takes place in your unconscious (review chapter 2) which comes as the result of having inherited the great thoughts of our ancestry — intellectual, cultural, philosophical, spiritual. Within us live the thoughts of Plato and Spinoza, of Moses, Jesus and the Buddha, of Albert Einstein and Albert Schweitzer — providing we have requested our inner need for their wisdom. When the best that our worldwide, historical culture has to offer is actually ingested by our mind, it will "feed back" to our consciousness the exact right thought or interpretation when we need it. Intuition, also developed through contemplation, makes liberal use of the outer reference system as well as the inner one. The richness of what we know and appreciate unconsciously comes together later in unexpected, unrehearsed ways, just when you are looking for that solution.

Too many people get distressed when pressed for an answer. The secret is to "let go," you have done what you can do, now relax. That's perhaps at first quite hard to do, but it is the only way. It has been observed by researchers on creative thinking that the desired results appear to pop up into our minds' consciousness in "the bed, the bus and the bath" — precisely in those places and at those times when the conscious mind is paying attention to another, mundane or habitual task.

Here are a few helpful questions to ask ourselves to encourage more creative modes of thinking: Do I listen to and welcome or avoid new ideas? Do I write down and test new ideas? Am I utilizing my memory to full potential? What am I feeding my mind that will be helpful later? Am I in a rut or am I curious? Do I ask questions, dig, research, read creative books, see creative videos? Do I associate with creative open-minded people? Am I taking time to develop my intuition? Do I apply imagination to my goals and plans? Am I willing to take risks involved in working with innovation? Am I aware of the contents and meaning of my dreams, visions and promptings from within?

EMOTIONAL MATURITY A life of "hard work" and taxing circumstances does not always lead to balanced emotions. Many of us grew up with "role models" who were moody, angry, upset, much of the time. One of the main challenges for the person who strives to live an authentic life of excellence is the management or control of negative, destructive emotions. We live an intellectual, rational life, the one seen and noticed by those around us. We also live an emotional life, sometimes noticed by others, when we have an "outburst" of feelings — we laugh, we cry, get angry or upset, are suffering from moods — and the person who probably suffers most when our feelings are negative is ourself. So, what can we do to control our feelings?

We have all heard of the advice that we should not show our feelings at all, be tough, macho, and "don't let anyone know how you feel." This course of action (naturally) leads to repression, and as we have seen when considering self-healing, leads furthermore to disease and other problems. So there is the advice that we should EXPRESS what we feel — if you are angry, show it, blow your top, let them have it, etc. We all know that this course of action also leads to trouble, as others refuse to put up with our violent anger. Soon after the outburst we regret what we did, feel ashamed, remorseful and apologetic.

There are some suggestions that may be of help when we are trying to "cope" and we are attempting to keep our emotions healthy yet managed:

—   Change your reaction. Realize it is not events and persons that upset you but your reaction to them. A lady says: Oh, I'm so upset, how could my mother have treated me so badly, it is unbelievable, I am so upset, I can't sleep, I have to take pills, my husband can't stand me anymore, my blood pressure is up . . . and so on and on it goes. What is really the problem here (and the part she can control or modify) is her own expectation of her mother's behavior. It was obviously too high or too different from what the factual behavior is. What needs to be done is: change, perhaps lower the expectation, or have none at all. We can all change our reactions to various events and people's actions.

—   Take responsibility for your own feelings; don't blame them on others.

—   Let it be. If you cannot change it, drop it. There is a recurring phrase in the King James Version of the Bible that goes like this: "It came to pass. . ." Perhaps we need to remember more often that everything and everyone comes to pass, to move on.

—   Don't live in the past. Often, the event that upsets us is long since gone, but we are still stewing. Set your watch to the right time, the now.

HANDLING WORRY SUCCESSFULLY   Closely related to the management of feelings is the management of thought habits, and the one that is the most useless and quite destructive is the worry habit. Dale Carnegie wrote an excellent work on this subject, "How To Stop Worrying and Start Living," highly recommended. I have come to believe that it is admirable but too idealistic to expect that anyone can actually stop worrying. However, we can so adjust and change our thinking patterns and habits that the amount of worrying we do is greatly reduced. This anyone who wants to, can do. Some helpful ideas:

—   **Limit your responsibility**: Some of us worry about every situation we hear about in the media and from people around us when it isn't remotely our business. This frame of mind was symbolized by Atlas in ancient mythology: he carried the entire globe on his own shoulders! Let's remember our station: in "outer space," in the Milky Way alone, there are 400 billion stars, each moving with complex, orderly grace, yet we did not have anything consciously to do with this cosmic fact. If we could travel eight billion (9 zeros) light years from planet Earth, we would still be in the Cosmos. . . Consider the Infinite Intelligence that indwells and surrounds you and quit worrying so much!

— **Limit your thinking to the actual problem.** It has been estimated by world famous communicators such as Earl Nightingale, who devoted a lifetime to probe these matters, that only 8% of the problems we worry about actually deserve our attention since there is a danger or risk present.

— **Accept responsibility for issues and situations that actually <u>are</u> yours.**

— **Avoid escaping into dependencies** such as drugs, alcohol, excesses. They make things all much worse.

— **Use the law of substitution.** When you realize you are worrying again about something you don't want to think about, change the thought to something else. Emmet Fox put it this way: "Thought control is the key of Destiny — the only way to get rid of a certain thought is to substitute another one for it." You can think of your home this very moment but you can change that image this instant by thinking of a friend's home or the home in which you grew up. You control your own thought processes.

— **Use a problem solving formula.** Too often we just worry "up in our heads" without ever getting a handle on the thing that bothers us so much. Instead, follow a simple formula such as this one:

Write down (the best you know how) the exact nature of the problem — what is it you are worried about?

Write down all the possible factors that may have given rise to this situation. What and who caused it?

If you have a lot of blank spaces or unknowns about this situation, now gather that additional information necessary and write it down also.

Think of all the possible solutions that may come to you and write them down separately again, no matter how unlikely or ridiculous they may seem to you.

Consult any resource or reliable, informed person who may know a great deal more than you do about the subject area of your problem, and write down the advice you obtain.

Let it be for awhile. Before going to sleep at night ask your subconscious mind to give you the answer or insight into the situation, and mentally, emotionally, expect that such an answer will be conveyed to you quickly, but at the right time.

Make your decision and act on it without delay.

CULTIVATING COOPERATION FROM OTHERS Only a limited number of people can hope to achieve their goals and a high level of personal excellence without the active help, involvement and cooperation of other people. Too frequently there has been the impression that motivating is insincere, a selfish attempt to cajole or trick others to do what we want them to do to serve our own ends. This kind of pressurized motivation seems to be gradually on the way out in Western society. When we set ourselves goals for the new times of equal opportunity and freedom for all, we work not only from the point of view of one person's interest, but from the objective that all must benefit from the enterprise.

When others need to become involved, we must show friendliness between all levels of workers, with satisfactions and joy in accomplishment for all. Communications, even if expressed in the most modern ways, still convey feelings. Our basic attitude toward people is crucial: it is <u>either</u>: love, respect, open-minded, asset and potential oriented <u>or</u>: superiority, judgment and condemnation.

When we sincerely and heartily <u>respect</u> another human being, soliciting their cooperation is not a difficult task. Remember to include in your business relationships:

—   Challenging goals in which they have a part. This creates a feeling of importance, value of the individual.

—   Recognition, approval and appreciation. It is a joy to work when we and they receive them liberally.

—   Opportunity, freedom and initiative. The greatest feeling your associates can have is the chance to grow, to develop, to become.

—   Security. Fear is the basic negative emotion people often seek to overcome. Therefore, create an atmosphere in your enterprise where people are being informed about what is happening, so they can feel secure and happy within their situation.

—   Responsibility and accountability. Let the rewards be directly related to the performance, and the quality of the work will constantly increase. Give people the responsibility; most of them are looking for it.

—   Justice, fairness and trust. All strikes and demonstrations that involve labor unrest have to do with conditions being perceived as unjust. Wisdom teaches us to place a firm foundation of trust and honest-to-goodness fair play under our enterprise. We then create an environment of helpfulness and mutual understanding and, as we know, in such an atmosphere, excellence thrives and prospers!

The subject of relating to other people is part of the lifestyle of authenticity we seek. These brief ideas touched upon here are only an introduction to the fascinating, intriguing area of human relations which forms the next "world" we are about to enter . . . and the next "art" we are about to master. . . the art of caring!

Bibliography & Recommended Further Reading

Goble, Frank: Excellence in Leadership
    N.Y.: American Management Ass'n, 1972

Peters, Thomas J. & Waterman, Robert H. Jr.: In Search of Excellence
    N.Y.: Harper & Row, 1982

Hickman, Craig R. & Silva, Michael A.: Creating Excellence
    N.Y.: New American Library, 1984

Ray, Michael & Myer, Rochelle: Creativity in Business
    N.Y.: Doubleday & Co., 1986

McGregor, Douglas: The Human Side of Enterprise
    N.Y.: McGraw-Hill, 1960

Naisbitt, John & Aburdene, Patricia: Megatrends 2000
    N.Y.: Wm. Morrow & Co., 1990

Feinberg, Mortimer R.: Effective Psychology for Managers
    Englewood Cliffs, New Jersey: Prentice-Hall Inc., 1965

Posner, Mitchell J.: Executive Essentials
    N.Y.: Avon, 1982

Bolles, Richard Nelson: The Three Boxes of Life, and How to Get Out
    of Them — An Introduction to Life/Work Planning
    Berkeley, CA: Ten Speed Press, 1978

Hill, Napoleon & Stone, W. Clement: Success Through a Positive Mental
    Attitude
    Englewood Cliffs, New Jersey: Prentice-Hall Inc., 1971

Hill, Napoleon & Keown, E. Harold: Succeed and Grow Rich Through
    Persuasion
    N.Y.: Hawthorn Books, 1970

Bullock, Alan (Ed.): 20th Century Genius
    N.Y.: Exeter Books, 1981

DeVille, Jard: The Psychology of Leadership
    N.Y.: Mentor, New American Library, 1984

PART THREE

THE ART OF CARING
YOUR KEY TO RELATIONSHIPS

"In truth, society has been all about me from the day of my birth; it is in the bosom of that society, and in my own close relationship with it, that all my personal decisions must be formed."

The Prime of Life
Simone de Beauvoir (1908-1986)

CHAPTER 11

RELATIONSHIPS IN A NEW KEY

*"There can be no other truth to take off from than
this: I think; therefore I exist. There we have the
absolute truth of consciousness becoming aware of
itself— In order to describe the probable, you must
have a firm hold on the true."*

Existentialism and Human Emotions
Jean-Paul Sartre (1905-1980)

Life without other people and other forms of life would be
unthinkable. The supreme fact of human existence is that there are "the
others," that we are not alone. As Simone de Beauvoir so aptly put it, we
find ourselves in the bosom of a society. As individuals, born into this
dimension of life, our survival depends on our relationship with those
members of society closest to us. It is because of our parents and
caregivers that we reach a point of self-consciousness that allows choice,
growth, understanding, maturity and the pursuit of our personal goals.

Our need for harmonious relationships is one of the greatest
requirements of a happy and satisfying life. The more years of life
experience we accumulate, the more we realize our need for establishing
relationships that work, that facilitate the results we want for ourselves,
as well as the highest good of "the others."

The two major revolutions in our global society or world
community of the second half of our 20th Century are the establishment
of social justice and the development of self-realization. To have the kind
of society we really want, we not only desire the empowerment of each
individual to achieve personal potential, but we desire to bring this about
for all human beings. This means the understanding of (and practical
application of) what a relationship is and how it can express this high
ideal.

While we're being idealistic — and doesn't everything we create
begin with a dream — perhaps we can think of the art of relating in
somewhat the same way as we think of the art of music. There is a right

way of playing or singing a song, but sometimes we do it off-key. To attain the fullness of beauty inherent in a score, we must find the right pitch, the correct key. Sometimes you play a song on a keyboard and it just doesn't sound right, or it doesn't have the depth of harmony or feeling you know it could have. So you try another key and you find the great sound you desire and intuitively knew was available.

Can we look at relationships in the same way? No matter what kind of relationship, being a client, customer, employee, patient, consumer, manager to being a parent, child, relative, spouse, lover, can we not assume that here too there are right and wrong "keys?" If things are going badly, we are acting in a key inappropriate for this situation. Find the right key, and the relationship moves smoothly, famously. Getting quickly to the right "key" for each new relationship is a worthwhile quest, but where do we start?

Shall we begin by tackling the awesome challenges of international politics, the relations between the global hemispheres? For most of us that's a bit much. Shall we discuss the relationships between nations, cultures, religions, corporations, states, provinces, language groups, special interest groups, economic classes, cities and townships, urban and rural populations? Or shall we stay within our communities, our neighborhood perhaps, or the organization with which we work, or our street, our family? No matter where we may direct our attention, we meet PEOPLE, women and men and children, human beings. It would seem to make sense that we first try to get to know something of the nature (and the limitations) of the persons relating. What truths can we discover about our concept of ourselves, as individuals or humanity in general?

It is interesting that our word relationship is rooted in the latin "relatum" which conveys the idea of bringing back, giving back, carrying back and connecting again. To what true concept, what authentic blueprint can we connect our understanding of whom we really are? The quest we are on has been and continues to be the subject of study and practice of major cultural disciplines, religion, psychology and philosophy. It is a quest engaged in by the best minds of recorded human history. It is the challenge of much of literature, poetry and lyricism. It is the occupation of much of what art and fashion are all about. It is at the heart of our celebration of the highlights of human connectiveness, it is the key question in courts of justice. But above all it is what motivates those of us who, in Leo Buscaglia's words, "are eager to encounter themselves before their death."

Indeed, one of the tragedies of life is that too many never understand themselves, let alone others. The results have been described in numerous ways in novels for centuries, in our time rarely more clearly than by Simone de Beauvoir in "The Woman Destroyed" where she lists what happens to a person who doesn't know herself. She is "the incarnation of everything we dislike." In her leading role she is pretentious, will do anything to succeed, doesn't "possess a single idea of her own," is devoid of sensitivity and simply goes along with whatever is the fashion of the moment.

The voice of awakening Simone de Beauvoir represents, known as Existentialism, is one which has had the courage to break with traditional thinking which failed to withstand the devastating experience of two World Wars. Our culture needed and still needs, a revolution in self-understanding and acceptance. So, we're not alone in our quest — let's think about what some of the most profound thinkers of our time have said concerning human nature.

Jean-Paul Sartre, de Beauvoir's lifelong companion, French philosopher, playwright, novelist and social thinker, was active in the French Resistance during World War II and prior to that was a prisoner-of-war. He suggested we begin to appreciate our freedom to choose and to take responsibility for our choices. He wrote in one play about "hell" as being "other people," about how so many people pursue life as a useless passion. But he also showed that the way out starts with the recognition of our ability to think, self-consciousness.

Sigmund Freud pointed to the instincts and drives, including sex and power that are already there; we simply wake up to discover them. In the tradition of Charles Darwin, he felt this was the result of eons of evolution. There is a need for the management of these drives because to cooperate with others doesn't seem natural to us. Humanity's aggressiveness, violence and destructiveness are apparent everywhere. Add to this the influence of what we experience in life. This, according to the Behaviorist school (B.F. Skinner, Ivan Pavlov) is a most important factor in determining human behavior, especially during the first five years or so of our childhood.

But there's more that goes into making up our "self" and our personality (which may not be the same thing). Carl Jung has drawn our attention to the fact that much of what we are is unconscious, as we saw in Chapter 2. We are connected by a collective unconscious which influences us; there is synchronicity in the events of our lives which highly involves other people and our relationships to them. There is also a spiritual element, taught by the mystics of all religions, where we may perceive ourselves as the incarnation, child or expression of a Universal, Cosmic Spirit which indwells us and represents the dynamic innermost self. Perhaps the "blueprint" for what the human self is meant to manifest is found there. Some suggest we may discover it through meditation and contemplation and sometimes through significant dreams.

Beyond Freud, Abraham Maslow emphasized that our instincts and drives, while themselves already "there" nevertheless represent in rough, natural form, the potential which seeks to express itself through us. In Maslow's interpretation, we behave with the objective of fulfilling certain needs that are both good and natural. So the best members of society become our "role models," not the worst, as we so often see portrayed in motion pictures, fiction, television, video and other media.

Phineas Parkhurst Quimby was a 19th Century visionary whose ideas are still not widely known nor appreciated in our time, yet they fit our discussion well. We are belief expressed — we are a bundle of beliefs walking around, acting upon and experiencing the contents of our consciousness. We are responsible for our beliefs and the good news is that beliefs can be changed; there is an inner Wisdom available that can guide us to a better understanding, and hence a better life.

All of the above is a brief summary of some of major contemporary viewpoints on human nature. Volumes have been written about our subject and the interesting thing is that there is truth in all of these observations. At first they may seem contradictory and if we wish to be academic in a traditional sense, only seeing the merit of one major viewpoint, we will have division and controversy forever. But rising a little higher in our attitude, we can find a common truth in them all.

More importantly, we can begin to BENEFIT from all these theories and use them to enhance our relationships.

We have shared this lengthy introduction to practical application for better relationships because, as a wise commentator has said, there's nothing so practical as a good theory. Our theory here is not dogmatic or narrow but what is called "eclectic" with elements drawn from various sources. We need to widen our horizon if we want to see more. If we don't want to remain inside the valley, we have to rise higher. The old ways of cultural isolationism haven't worked, so let's look at relationships from higher ground, or to change the metaphor, as sung in a new key.

Here are five ideas, which, when kept in mind as we relate to and communicate with others, in whatever situation, may enhance, enrich and ennoble those relationships. Think about these ideas for awhile, contemplate them, reason about them. Consider what would happen if they were applied in actual situations you vividly remember and consider also the alternative, what the absence of these ideas would mean in our human relationships.

WE ALWAYS RELATE TO OUR IDEA OF ANOTHER PERSON

This is not just a philosophical observation, but a truth, that lies at the source of much conflict between people. We think we know what the other person is all about, but in reality we don't. You don't know any more than another person really knows about you. Yet we think, evaluate, perhaps even judge, speak and act as if we know her or him. Do we know how another really feels, what their conditioning through childhood, adolescence and adulthood has been, what motivates them, the level of their self-esteem?

Not even between two lovers, who have for several years been engaged in a most intimate relationship, is there necessarily an adequate understanding of the content of the other person's consciousness. Spouses often discover, when faced with the betrayal of their trust, that they did not really know their partners. Counsellors, who interview the two members of a marriage which is in trouble, more often than not find that one partner has little idea of how the other partner feels. This is not only due to the much publicized lack of communication, but also the boundaries of our individual consciousness.

Every person we know, have ever known and will ever know, lives as an image, a concept, an idea in our own consciousness; when we address that person in thought, word or deed we do so solely on the basis of what we THINK that person is like. And that, as we have so often later learned, may not be the truth. The sages of our civilization have always known this. Jesus suggested that we judge not "according to appearances" and on another occasion that we not judge at all.

William Shakespeare wrote: "Make not your thoughts your prisons." There is a rule of military strategy, when faced with unknown territory that could be very dangerous, proceed with extreme caution. Is it really that difficult to relate to another human being? Suppose you asked that question while seeking honest advice from someone whom you felt had their relationships "really together." The answer would probably be: "No, but it helps to remember how much you really DO NOT know about your friend, let alone about yourself."

THE PAST IS OUR OPINION WHICH CAN BE CHANGED

Have you had the experience of getting hurt in a certain situation and not wanting to get into that same situation again? People who get injured in a car accident refuse to get into a vehicle again even though driver and conditions may be different. Whenever we get close to, in our perception, a scenario in which we got hurt, we back off. The 19th Century American humorist Mark Twain told of his cat who jumped on a hot stove once, but never again would jump on one, not even a cold one.

People get hurt in a divorce or break-up of a relationship, then say no to every opportunity of a new relationship. Yet, the past is only our own opinion, our personal perception. We can hang a label on it that reads:"Never again!" or, "To be continued in the same way." But we can also write other slogans: "Never mind!" "Learn from the past and walk on, wiser." If your memories are a barrier to what could be a new opportunity for you, change your opinion of that memory. You cannot erase a memory but you can cancel the negative impact it has on your life and your decisions today.

SOUND RELATIONSHIPS ARE BASED ON ATTENTION

Have you ever stood at a counter in a department store, asking for information and the salesperson picks up the phone, or is interrupted by another employee and so ignores you? How does that affect you? Unless you are highly motivated to purchase the product you are enquiring about, you are inclined to move on. Yet, so often we take a relationship or a friendship for granted and that relationship deteriorates. David Viscott, after years of experience with thousands of people in the field of advice on relationships, says "relationships seldom die because they suddenly have no life left in them. They wither slowly . . ." Let us remember that a relationship is not a goal which, once achieved, no longer continues to motivate our energy. We need to nourish it with our attention, verbalized and in terms of listening.

BEHIND EVERY PROBLEM LIES THE TRUTH

The truth of a situation is usually hidden and we are getting upset dealing with the appearances, the effects, not the causes. Example: Here is a teenage daughter who seeks help from a counsellor because she says, her problem is her mother. Well, what about her mother? Does she abuse her daughter, neglect her, lie to her, treat her unfairly, etc.? No, none of these things. The problem is: Mom is too pretty, too attractive, too sexy. So, when she's out, on the beach, at school functions, in shopping centers with her mother, "the boys" whistle, look at and want to date her mom, not her. It's downright embarrassing! Please, can't you tell her to dress down, to look more "her age," to be less "seductive?"

The real problem here is not the mother who has chosen to express herself in a way consistent with her self-esteem, but the daughter who has a self-esteem problem. She needs help in discovering, accepting and expressing her own unique, attractive and beautiful personhood. The truth is not always apparent but it is always there and we need to dig for it.

Plato assumed that behind every created phenomenon is the process that put energy and ingredients together to build it. Behind the process is the right plan and behind the right plan is the idea. Back of the idea is the mind that perceives the idea. We can reason back in our own mind about the idea we have of what every relationship OUGHT

TO BE LIKE. Re-think that idea if the experience you are having does not correspond to the idea. What ingredient in the process is different from the pre-conceived idea? Is that ingredient under your control and direction or is it someone else's domain? Do we then have to revise our idea because it was, in part, based on an illusion, a myth, perhaps a desire, but NOT THE TRUTH? Would we build a house knowing that the blueprint is flawed? In your current life are you working industriously, but from a plan with basic flaws?

Perhaps now is the moment to go back to your basic plan, make the necessary corrections before wasting more time and energy? When you arrive at the truth you'll know what to do.

GO EASY ON CRITICISM - Most of us relate to other people in similar style to our parents or early "role models." The habits of perception, judgment, attitude, speech and behavior are formed, not as a result of conscious choice, but learned example. Of course we do have choice, nevertheless, as a rule, we don't change our attitudes with people until getting into deep trouble. One of this century's master teachers on human relations and success in sales was Dale Carnegie. Working with people in New York City in the economically difficult between-the-wars years, he discovered a major reason why so many people failed on the job, even though the opportunity seemed promising. The problem was badly misdirected energy: the person was continually working hard, not at the job, but at criticizing, condemning and complaining.

Our times are not different in this respect. The reaction to recessions and depressions is still, for many, a learned response: bitch, bitch, bitch. But no situation ever improves that way unless the criticism is constructive, to the point and includes suggestions for solutions. No one likes to be criticized, but most mature persons welcome suggestions for improvement. Why do we criticize so much? Out of ignorance and habit, not realizing how it destroys the good and finer feelings people may have had for us.

Poor self-esteem and jealousy are often at the root of a critic's lifestyle: Oh, if only I could have what others have — but I can't, so I'll diminish them. By tearing down another, I'll build myself up; by comparison, I don't look so bad. People have reasons for their critical stance, but not one of them is justified if the objective is better relationships. The alternative? Try love. To this we shall direct our attention in our next chapter.

BIBLIOGRAPHY & RECOMMENDED FURTHER READING

de Beauvoir, Simone: "The Prime of Life" (autobiography)
    N.Y.: Lancer, 1962
Francis, Claude and Gontier, Fernande: Simone de Beauvoir,
    A Life . . . a Love Story
    N.Y.: St. Martin's Press, 1987
de Beauvoir, Simone: Letters to Sartre
    London: Radius, Random Century, 1991
de Beauvoir, Simone: "The Woman Destroyed"
    London: Wm. Collins Sons, 1985
Sartre, Jean-Paul: Existentialism and Human Emotions
    N.Y.: Philosophical Library, 1957
Sartre, Jean-Paul: No Exit and Three Other Plays
    N.Y.: Alfred A. Knopf, Inc., 1948
Cohen-Solal, Annie: Sartre, a Life
    N.Y.: Pantheon, 1987
Gay, Peter: Freud for Historians
    N.Y.: Oxford University Press, 1985
Buscaglia, Leo F.: Personhood, The Art of Being Fully Human
    N.Y.: Fawcett Columbine, 1978
Fromm, Erich: The Art of Loving
    N.Y.: Harper & Brothers Publ., 1956
Viscott, David: How to Live With Another Person
    N.Y.: Pocket Books, 1976
Addington, Jack and Cornelia: Drawing the Larger Circle, How to Love
    and Be Loved (Marina Del Rey, Calif: DeVorss & Co., 1985)

CHAPTER 12
REDISCOVERING LOVE

*"And think not you can direct the course of love,
for love, if it finds you worthy, directs your course."*

The Prophet
Kahlil Gibran (1883–1931)

What does the word "love" mean to you? The several ways in which the terms "love" and "loving" are used in our culture make it necessary to define exactly what we mean when suggest "try love" to improve our relationships. This need for clarification is evident when we consider the virtual absence of courses of instruction on the subject of love in our educational systems. Where is the college or university that offers the degree of Bachelor of Love, or Master of Love, or Doctor of Love? It is indeed a rare teacher who, as Leo Buscaglia did, develops a course in loving, what it means and how to apply it in daily living. So, the vast majority of us grow up vaguely sensing, based on what we hear around us and the promptings within us, that love is most important and desirable; yet we're not sure how to go about satisfying what Abraham Maslow suggested is a dire need in all of us, to love and be loved.

Where does it all start? The truth of Maslow's assertion is only too clear to us all: without love none of us would have survived our early days, months and years in this dimension. Most people have some impression of happy memories from their time as toddlers recalling the feeling of security and warmth of which they were the recipients. For some fortunate ones, the love they received was unconditional. That is, it didn't matter how they behaved, or what happened within or outside the family, they knew they were loved just the same, and this continued as they grew older.

For many, this was not the case: receiving love, attention, rewards, peace and security, depended on how well they conformed to the behavior model that was expected of them. Love became conditional on their degree of obedience to the source of power in charge. Religion in its various institutionalized forms usually approved of this scenario because of the belief that the husband of the family is "the king of the castle" leaving wife and children dependent and easily victimized. Simone de Beauvoir, an outstanding scholar and social researcher of our times, pointed out the historical background of the superior male, lesser female status could never lead to a happy and satisfied, let alone loving situation. It was, in effect, and still is, a moral and social outrage.

De Beauvoir's book "The Second Sex" opened the eyes of many, both women and men, and became the initiating force of the contemporary feminist movement. This social revolution, sometimes quiet, sometimes volatile, resulted in many changes in our society, with increased equality of opportunity for both men and women. But what has this development done for love? We see radicals and fanatics on both sides: fundamentalists wanting to return to the "good old days" that were never good, even for the master/father, for how can one be truly in love and happy with a doormat/wife? We also see ultra-outspoken feminists who do not have one good word to say about men, who despise and hate and with whom no man could hope to have a satisfying personal relationship. So love often becomes a lost cause in the midst of a controversial confrontation. Are we, after all, engaged in a battle, a struggle, a war. . ?

In recent decades motion pictures, novels, television, videos and advertising, have often portrayed an illusion of "love" — with the male protagonist as not much more than an animal macho-stud and the female character an incarnation of the "dumb blonde." She is helpless and dependent, unhappy unless the right stud "falls in love" with her, marries here and magically they "live happily ever after." Such images have had an unfortunate effect on our impressionable younger generation as all counsellors are well aware. Of course there are exceptions to our description of the media; there are fine, sensitive novels and scripts. But the overall effect of the worst representations of love in the media, plus what remains of patriarchal ethical mores, means that available resources for the learning of a genuine art of loving are difficult to find.

There appears to be little interest in developing a sound educational program on the subject of loving. Sex education and biological information made available to students in order to prevent communicable disease from spreading are healthy and welcome but this is hardly teaching how to love. Can it be done? What should our approach and reasoning be? Let's turn back to our findings about "relationships in a new key" in our last chapter.

We discovered that consciousness is the governing factor of all our experiences, past present and future. This means, in relationships, you and I are relating to our idea or belief we have of another person and we are limited by **our** awareness and opinion of that person. Our responses and actions based on those beliefs may therefore not be the best.

Our own capacities, potentials and qualities are also our beliefs or our self-concept and this too is limited by our awareness and brought accordingly into the relationship. Therefore we can never really know the other person's consciousness. If we could, the other person, and we too, would be truly free, for everything would be revealed. Since behavior follows belief, it is of the utmost importance that our beliefs be accurate and complete, yet they never are and cannot be. Like ourselves, the other person does not wish to share her or his authenticity, usually because of the fear of rejection. "If you really knew me, you wouldn't like me," hence, I fear to communicate what's inside me, what I feel, what I experienced, what I perceive I'm really like. With the individuals on both sides blocking off an honest exchange of their thoughts we have an existential impossibility and this is precisely why love is needed.

May I share here a personal experience? I was the accountant office manager for a manufacturing company, when I took my first "self improvement" course. The program combined the teaching of communication skills, including public speaking, with the development of human relations techniques. One of our assignments was to select the person we least could get along with, probably at work, and apply a few simple human relations guidelines in order to improve that relationship. The "other" person was not to know about the experiment. Among the suggested techniques were: not to criticize, condemn or complain, to give instead honest, sincere appreciation and to become interested in the other person. In our company there was an employee who had many years of faithful service to her name, was highly skilled, worked hard, was prompt and efficient but she was almost always in a bad mood, often sour and hard to get along with. I wasn't alone in this opinion. Her co-workers would rather see Leona go than come. If you said "good morning" to her, she might respond with a grunt or if you were lucky, with a "what's so good about it?"

I decided I would apply what I was learning to my relationship with her. Since I knew little about her personal life, I decided to speak privately with our company manager whose secretary-assistant she was. He confidentially informed me that while she was still a child she had lost her father; her brothers and sisters had left home to marry, leaving her living with her elderly mother who was sickly and cranky. She had had several men in her life who had proposed a closer relationship, but her mother went to incredible lengths to discredit these male friends as not being "good enough" for her. She was also raised in a strict religious faith where "honoring thy father and thy mother" was deeply impressed on her mind. Consequently she felt trapped and miserable, undoubtedly envious of her co-workers who were "married with children" or in a functioning relationship.

This knowledge produced a change in my attitude toward her. Instead of thinking (and no doubt sending out "vibes" of) "oh, why don't you go fly a kite" and similar negative scenarios, I decided — actually it wasn't so much a decision as a feeling — to "send" her thoughts of love, compassion and friendship. I smiled at her, and utilized every opportunity I had to show my appreciation for the work she did. I made her job easier in "any which way" I could. At first this procedure was so out of character for me that I surprised myself, but I kept at it and the result of my newly chosen habit was that she became friendlier toward me. When I left that company a few years later Leona and I had become great friends; when we parted, we both had tears in our eyes.

This was one of my first experiences in understanding how love, in the words of a beautiful song, can build a bridge, and transform a relationship for the better. It had nothing to do with forced diplomacy or hypocrisy or sex. The work, if we can call it work, was done in my consciousness. It had to do with CARING and this is why I believe we can, in all simplicity say, that the art of loving is first and foremost the art of caring. But the big question of course remains: How do we bring about this change of consciousness that results in our becoming loving, that is, caring persons, despite all the environmental and cultural conditioning to the contrary?

As we seek to bring our understanding of love into full realization with those about us, in the home, the workplace, at recreation, etc. let us first make clear that love exists in several broad categories:

FRIENDSHIP, the love and caring that flows between, and is felt by, two persons who find themselves in a reciprocal relationship. We speak also of brotherly, sisterly, fraternal love. The ancient Greek term is PHILIA (as in Philadelphia, city of brotherly love.) Our words affiliation and philosophy (love of wisdom) are derived from this source. It implies loyalty, trust, goodwill, humanism, compassion and a willingness to help and assist. Philia may include animals: "a dog is a woman's best friend."

PARENTAL LOVE, the love and caring that flows between, and is felt by, a mother and a father and her, his or their child(ren). This love may be extended to include the love felt by all relatives, grandparents, aunts and uncles, including adopted children, plus those friends so close they feel **bonded** to this intimate circle. Children responding with reciprocal love within such families will find it natural to extend that love to even wider circles, the neighborhood, village, city, area and the family of a nation, or a culture. Many social commentators today believe that the strengthening of the **family** unit will also result in a more caring society.

EROTIC LOVE, the love and caring that flows between and is felt by, two persons who find themselves sexually attracted to each other. Our word SEX is derived from the Greek Sexus, which means all forms of seeking and attaining sexual experience. Our word erotic also derives from the Greek, namely the term EROS, which meant passion and appetite, not necessarily sexual, but could apply to a passion for food, or any pursuit of pleasure. In its most selfish form it is called "lust" and can lead to the demeaning practices of rape and sodomy. Eros is often onesided and interested in self-satisfaction to the highest degree. However, the dawning of the knowledge that the experience is less satisfying unless the partner is also gratified, can be the beginning of reaching the higher planes of love.

SELF-LOVE, or the love and caring we feel for ourselves as individuals. It really means self-esteem or self-worth. Without that respect for our own being we are down on ourselves and usually feel guilty for not having lived up to some pre-conceived ideal. Healthy self-esteem is based on the realization that we are spiritual beings, the expression of the wisdom and intelligence of the cosmos. Or, if you like, be proud and glad you are a self-conscious, free human being with unique and wonderful potential for excellence and loving. By Self-love we do not mean selfish. A selfish person wants everything for him- or herself, feels no pleasure in giving, only in taking and judges others from the point of view of their usefulness to him or her. Selfish people usually suffer from poor self-esteem and a poverty consciousness. The mature "lover" has no need to hurt anyone since loving and sharing satisfy and fulfil that person. Self-love includes those passions that express dynamic individual growth and development of constructive potential: "I love what I do."

SPIRITUAL LOVE, the love and caring that flows between and is felt by, the individual and the Universal or Cosmic Spirit within that individual. Spiritual love is also felt and realized by two or more persons who share the same or similar spiritual awareness. It may be felt when contemplating the beauty of nature but also the spirit, grace and attractiveness of a human being, animal or plant. Philosophy calls it aesthetics. The realization of truth, the recognition of some high purpose or the revelation of what was a profound secret, all have elements of this divine, spiritual love. To the true mystics of all religions and cultures it means the mystic union of the individual and the universal, or cosmic consciousness. "I and the Father are one" said Jesus. To those who have felt this union, it is the highest degree of love of which we can become aware.

Perhaps this is a good "point-in-time" to realize we are not alone in our quest and the sages of "the Wisdom of the Ages" are indeed our elders in enlightening us. All the great ones who have helped civilization take a step forward have said and understood the same truth: that we must become so natural around the feeling of love and caring, that it becomes our nature. The great mystics have always believed that at the central core of our being we find love as our true nature. This is quite different from the fundamentalist notion of man as a sinner, incapable of any good deed; if that were really true the Cosmic Spirit or Infinite Intelligence is flawed in the act of its own creation and would be a monster giving birth to monsters. We fare no better if we follow the Freudian path where the belief in man, as by nature being an aggressive brute who needs to be constantly managed and controlled, hardly produces a better role model.

Jesus' teachings are filled with the instruction to love the Universal Spirit, "God is Spirit," your neighbor and yourself. In the Gospel of John, chapter 13, Jesus makes it clear that we cannot claim to be his followers unless we are love. In answer to the question as to how one might attain "eternal life," Jesus replied, by loving and by expressing compassion — see the Gospel of Luke, Chapter 10. Out of his awareness of God as Spirit, and ourselves as "children of the most High," whom he taught to perceive God as their "Father" or parent, he showed that our own nature is spiritual in essence. Hence, we are meant to express love, truth, beauty and wisdom, not as some sort of added after-thought, but as our natural inheritance. St. John added to this understanding the concept that "God is Love" and "he who dwells in love, dwells in God." St. Paul authored one of the supreme statements on love in what is known as the 13th chapter of his first letter to the Corinthians: "Love is patient and kind . . . Love never gives up, its faith, hope and patience never fail." To him, love is the only quality that endures. There is also the idea that love matures within us, as the mystical union becomes more real to us.

From the Eastern world we find similar thoughts on love from the teachings of Gautama the Buddha. As teacher, he taught his disciples to let their minds pervade the wide world with everyone and everything in it, with thoughts of love. While seeking to lift those about him to the fullness of all that they could hope to be, he taught meditation and contemplation (which transforms consciousness). When asked by his followers on what they should meditate his answer was: love.

Buddha's first meditation is that of love, or the longing for the weal and welfare of all beings, including one's perceived enemies. Other meditations emphasize compassion, joy in the well-being of others and serenity which rises above conflict. In our own century one of the most wonderful literary expressions of this natural human spirit of love and its wisdom is found in Kahlil Gibran's masterpiece, "The Prophet." While we will focus on the art of contemplation later, let us remember that the transformation of human consciousness to its natural state or mode, is greatly facilitated by contemplation of the object of its desire. Meditate on, give your attention to, the love the sages teach, and you will become the lover you are meant to be, and you will (finally) feel GOOD. . .

When the mystic returns to earth, so to speak, new questions arise on how to apply this awareness to commonly experienced human situations. This we shall explore in the next three chapters. But for now, let us consider one subtle point that arises in many individuals' minds who are adventuring onto the pathway of love. It appears at first, as a contradiction or paradox: If we love another person with true love, does the oneness that occurs at all levels of our being imply less individuality, less independence, less freedom, more sameness, more compromise? Does this not bring us into conflict with our wish to be individuals, uniquely ourselves?

We sometimes hear single persons who have developed an individualistic, independent, often professional lifestyle, say: "Oh, I don't think anyone would want to live with me, I'm too independent, I'm too used to having it all my way!" A legitimate comment. Yet, when we see what happens when we become intimately involved with another person as spiritual lovers, we find the apparent contradiction dissolves. When we view the lives of the truly great humanitarian lovers, we see that they too were or are highly individualistic, original and unique, yet these qualities enhanced their capacity to help and relate to others. The mature lover brings so much that is warm and wonderful to a relationship that the one who "falls in love" with him or her is incredibly enriched and ennobled. Thus, both partners' uniqueness and potential are realized to far greater heights than would have been possible separately.

One of this century's great psychologists, Erich Fromm taught that there are four essential elements of the mature love we seek: Care,

Responsibility, Respect and Knowledge. In his fine, scholarly book "The Art of Loving" he explains these aspects in logical detail. Anyone who follows his line of reasoning rediscovers love, a love we may "fall into" but which we also develop, through study and practice. How? By having more respect for others, more caring for their needs, being responsible for our duties in our circle of influence, ever developing a deeper knowledge of who we, and they, are as part of Creation.

Bibliography & Recommended Further Reading

Gibran, Kahlil: The Prophet
N.Y.: Alfred A. Knopf, 1963
Buscaglia, Leo: Love
N.Y.:Fawcett Crest CBS, 1972
Buscaglia, Leo: Loving Each Other, the Challenge of Human Relationships
Thorofare, New Jersey:Slack Inc., 1984
de Beauvoir, Simone: The Second Sex
N.Y.:Vintage, Random House, 1952
Sorokin, Pitirim A.: The Ways and Power of Love
Boston: Beacon Press, 1954
Sorokin, Pitirim A.: The Crisis of our Age
N.Y.:E.P. Dutton, 1941).
Kaufman, Barry Neil: To Love is to be Happy With
N.Y.:Coward, McCann & Geoghegan, 1977
Buddha, the: Sayings of Buddha
N.Y.:Peter Pauper Press, 1957
Ikeda, Daisaku: The Living Buddha, an Interpretive Biography
N.Y. Weatherhill, 1976
Humphreys, Christmas, ed: The Wisdom of Buddhism
London:Michael Joseph, 1960
Gard, Richard A.: Buddhism
N.Y.:Geo. Braziller, 1962
Phillips, J.B., transl.: The New Testament in Modern English
London: Wm. Collins Sons, 1958
Bucke, Richard Maurice: Cosmic Consciousness. A Study in the Evolution of the Human Mind.
N.Y.:E.P. Dutton & Co., 1962

CHAPTER 13

OVERCOMING LONELINESS WITH FRIENDSHIP

"What is the greatest need of human beings?
What is it they seek from me always? Intimacy. Being able to reveal
themselves."

The Diary of Anais Nin, Vol. Six
Annais Nin (1903-1977)

Our individual living experience usually starts and continues for some dozen and a half years within a relationship called family. The fortunate ones among us have a genuine experience of what it feels like to be loved within that family and so we also learn to become lovers ourselves. When we leave our original family, or that relationship ceases to exist, we lose that warm affection and attachment. Even if we are living in close physical proximity to other persons, we become aware of a LACK, a loss of affection in our lives. Certainly one of the most insistent needs of human beings today is to overcome this loneliness and experience once more "warm affection," friendship, intimacy and love.

Why do we become lonely? My work has taught me that there are certain basic causes for human loneliness in our society. Before taking a closer look at these let us remember that we are not speaking of aloneness when referring to loneliness. Queen Wilhelmina of the Netherlands, who was a reigning monarch for fifty years, experienced a lonely childhood in a protective environment. Feeling people distancing themselves from her for so many years, she entitled her autobiography "Alone but not lonely" (transl. mine) to indicate it is possible to be and live alone, yet not be lonely. Conversely, you may live and work in the midst of a crowd of people and yet feel lonely. To feel lonely is to feel that nobody really cares about you, to feel forlorn, a terrifying sense of being un-connected, separate.

Mahatma Gandhi once remarked: "To a man with an empty stomach, food is god." We might say that to a person whose life is empty of affection, friendship is god. The pursuit or worship of this god is quite evident in bars and pubs all over the world, come "happy hour" when so often we find people thrown together by the same unexpressed need for closeness and intimacy. But what are the causes for loneliness, how do we get to feel this awful way? Let's consider some common origins of personal loneliness:

Poor Self-Image. People believe themselves to be boring, uninteresting. "Who'd want my company?" they ask. Sensing they are not worth much, they could be considered, in the French existentialist sense "de trop," that is, not necessary to anyone or society. They are uncomfortable with themselves, often feel no need to look attractive. They lack spiritual depth and do not understand their own psyche. This state is usually the result of negative conditioning. The same family "nest" that can provide us with an enormously wonderful sense of belonging, can also be the cause of self-rejection. Tell a child often enough that he or she is a miserable sinner, or stupid or ugly or "no-good" and the poor self-image is formed within that vulnerable subconscious.

Shyness. Shy people also have a concept of themselves that makes them uncomfortable in the presence of others whom they consider their judges. The roots of that feeling are also usually found where judgment is the order of the day. Shy persons may respond to the attention of others, whom they actually may wish to attract, in terms of blushing, sweating, a pounding heart and other attacks of panic. The fear of judgment and rejection is so strong they are unable to get close to another person.

Emotional Hurt. As previously observed, many people, once hurt (as in a painful divorce), protect themselves unconsciously from a repeat performance by refusing to get close to anyone else. Riders who fall off horses must get on a horse again without delay to prevent fear from causing them to fail. In actual fact, an emotionally hurt person who keeps potential friends at a distance, rejects her- or himself on the basis of having first been rejected by someone else such as their "ex." Often self pity and depression and a subjective simmering arrogance plague the emotionally hurt and loneliness is the result.

Self-Centeredness. It has been said (as a truism) that a human being can get used to anything if it lasts long enough. When people don't experience a personal closeness and live alone for a long time we sometimes hear them make statements such as: "I'm O.K. by myself. I couldn't imagine myself sharing my home, my bathroom, my toothpaste, with another person. I can come and go as I please without having to ask of or answer to anyone. With my lifestyle I don't think I could STAND the presence of another person." Such individuals believe that to share with someone else would take away from "me," that they would be less, or losers, in the bargain. People who feel this way may not be socially selfish. They may be excellent volunteers and contributors to humanitarian and cultural causes in their community. But their stance of self-centeredness causes them to become lonely.

The Stranger Identity. There are folks who move away from their original home and hearth and never in any other place feel at home again. They don't seem to be able to "click," don't seem to want to identify with their new environment and so remain strangers in their new city or country, feeling they are "always on the outside looking in," hence lonesome. We observe this culturally and collectively in the formation of ethnically based communities and churches on the North American and Australian continents. Immigrants sometimes refuse to learn the language and lifestyle of their adopted country, thereby making life for themselves and their families more difficult. Many thousands remain strangers in a strange land for most of their lifetime, because of stranger identity.

The Dependency Belief. In a culture where for too long we were made to believe that no happiness and acceptance is possible unless you become one half of a couple, too many people have been conditioned to believe that it is necessary to conform to the couple culture: Another person must make me happy, I cannot be complete without him/her. They are thus forever looking, not for genuine love, friendship or intimacy but the **form** of relationship, perhaps the replacement of Mom and Dad. Such individuals make others responsible for their happiness and when these others (including the community in which they reside) do not live up to their expectations, bitterness and disappointment lead to an ever deepening loneliness.

Family Changes. When children grow up and leave "the nest" mom finds herself unprepared for the resulting emptiness. If motherhood does not always live up to expectations here's one reason why. We are generally not ready for these changes, we have no other relationships to take the place of the old ones where we felt needed. Thinking that we are not needed any more is an invitation to the loneliness mode. Loss of spouse or companion due to divorce, separation or death can lead to a similar scenario.

Family Abuse. There are those who feel terribly lonely within a family situation because they are being physically, mentally and/or emotionally abused. Many modern women have left relationships because of abuse and neglect. Feeling so abandoned, disappointed and angry, they seem to be in a perpetual state of war, especially with men. As a result of personal abuse, believing that nobody cares about you, is too often the explanation for much of the pathetic loneliness and resulting suffering we see in our society.

What are practical and sensible answers to modern loneliness? Could we magically change all adverse social conditions, destructive human behavior and negative conditioning, the answers would be easy. I have met many a frustrated, overworked, depleted social worker who has been unable to cope with the burden of misery seen on their daily round. Yet, there are also points of light, hope and transformation and to find these we must return to the basic consideration about human relations we referred to in the previous two chapters.

Life is consciousness (Emmet Fox's statement of truth). We experience it as consciousness, no matter what may or may not have happened to us. We are here now, we feel and what happens (next) is largely a matter of consciousness. The eight causes of loneliness we have reviewed here are like colored glasses giving tints to our minds of the world about us. The shade or color of what we believe we see will seem justified in the minds of people who have been hurt. Nevertheless, when dark colors of our beliefs make us feel forlorn, desperately lonely and miserable, the time has come for tough self-love, namely accepting the realization that BELIEFS, like differently tinted lenses, CAN BE CHANGED. When they are, the feelings they produce, as Marcus Aurelius once taught, will change as well.

Let us explore how we may go about doing this in actual practice. I have seen people make these changes in attitude with marvelous, sometimes seemingly miraculous, results. The goal here is simply this: we wish to replace **loneliness** with **friendship**. One of the clues to this solution is to become more interesting, appealing, attractive and alive, so the right person(s), those who share our lifestyle and philosophy will be attracted to us. The primary requirement for this change is contained within our first major step:

LEARN TO LIKE SOLITUDE. "What?" some may ask at this point, "do you want me to LIKE being alone?" The answer is YES, but not being lonely. We are essentially alone as self-conscious beings. We are not born half-a-couple, not even if we are physical twins. Each person is unique and that exclusivity, as an expression of the wisdom and intelligence and energy of the Cosmos, presupposes that the mastery of individual life and living must take place within consciousness. When we learn to so contemplate and meditate that we reach a spiritual, mystical level, we shall feel, not lonely, but uniquely ONE WITH all life, human, cosmic and in every other expression. When that enlightenment comes, our aloneness and solitude turn into sources of transformation and creativity. Moreover, we will tap into the inner resource called intuition, which may guide us to our next right decision.

Try the experiment of expecting to be guided, to have the right idea conveyed to you from the spiritual level of your unconscious. Before falling asleep gently say to yourself:

"Infinite Intelligence within me knows the answer to my present situation. May it now reveal to me the answers and solutions of which I need to become aware. I fully expect this to happen and am grateful that being one with this Cosmic Wisdom, I am now guided in the right way."

Your words, to become most effective in your consciousness, should preferably be your own. Even as the symbols of your dreams can only be adequately understood through your own consciousness and the meanings that exist there, so too, meditation, contemplation and affirmation will be of the greatest meaning using your personal language and symbols. From time to time make changes in the symbols so that they are in terms of current needs and you will avoid repetitive, mindless rituals.

Simplified, all this means: learn to contemplate, to be at ease with your own thoughts, direct them in positive, constructive, spiritual ways. Be open to hunches from within. When you feel comfortable with yourself, others will feel more comfortable with you and you with them.

One tool, found helpful by many seeking to grow in these areas, is to keep a journal or diary of our deeper thoughts, dreams, and experiences. Take a little time to study some of the works of the great diarists of our century and note how they enriched their lives, as well as the few people with whom they shared, WHILE THEY WERE LIVING LIFE. We are thinking here of such literary giants as Virginia Woolf, Franz Kafka, Albert Camus, Jean-Paul Sartre, Simone de Beauvoir and Anais Nin. Keeping a personal journal can be easily learned and may prove for you to be a vital step toward liking and enjoying solitude.

LEARN TO BE INTERESTING. The answer to the belief that you are boring and nobody would be interested in meeting you, is to become interesting, exciting and enthusiastic. The starting point here is to move away from cultural and personal isolation. Start becoming more aware of what is actually going on in your community, your country, other nations, global happenings. What are the truly significant events among the rapid changes on the planet in these momentous times? **Be informed** so you can converse and interact with confidence. Pursue interests you have in common with other folks and support worthwhile causes. Develop the skills and abilities that are within you but which you have never exercised: perhaps you've always wanted to paint, or sculpt, or dance, or sing, or ski or master an instrument. Go for it, whatever it may be. Expand your intellectual horizons, and your people horizons will also.

LEARN TO COMMUNICATE. Once our curiosity about the world, the family of (wo)man, of history and the meaning of today's happenings is awakened, and we added the development of our personal unique potential, we cannot help but become interested in our neighbors, local and international. But to become really involved with people we need to feel free and comfortable in our communication with them. Do we feel uncomfortable speaking to people? Do we dread phoning, striking up a conversation, making a sales call, writing a letter, delivering a talk?

If so, it's time to learn to communicate. Read books about speaking and writing, find out about the lives and practices of "super" communicators, take courses in public speaking and writing skills. Learn what to say after you say "hello," how to express your views, opinions and feelings in such a way that people warm up to you, so you know you are making friends, not enemies.

LEARN TO CARE. Often, lonely people think they are the only ones who feel this way. But of course, they are not and most likely other folks feel just as "uncared for" and they are present all about us. People who are professional or volunteer caregivers are not masochists even though their work requires much effort. They find that, despite the inevitable challenges, they usually GROW as a result of caring. They enjoy widening their circle of friendship and feel the love coming back to them.

A lady I know was obliged to spend a few days in hospital. She is 87 years young. Many folks "her age" are in institutions lonely and forgotten; not this lady. She had so many visitors in her hospital room that it was almost necessary to issue numbered tickets for those in line to see her. Her secret? She has been, a volunteer worker in that hospital for the past 26 years! She is a caring person.

Compare the response you feel when someone says to you "I don't care" or "I could care less," with when a person says: "I care, you can talk to me." By caring we do not take over another person's life and we do not take away their responsibility or choices. What we do is become their friend, and we give them an opportunity to become our friends. Caring includes listening, just as communicating includes listening. Too often we find, in conversations with another person, that he or she doesn't hear what we are saying, they are merely waiting for us to stop, so they can have the floor. Genuine, authentic interaction between two persons implies making every possible effort to UNDERSTAND what the other person means.

The joy of becoming a friend of someone who was a stranger is partly felt because we are beginning to understand another person better and better. Once we learn to appreciate and become friends with a few people about us, our loneliness vanishes.

LEARN TO EVALUATE. How do we know that another person is "right" for us? When you are considering a closer relationship with someone, who has become your friend but about whom you don't really know very much, how do you know what is "the right thing to do?" Should you continue to build that acquaintance, take a "wait and see" attitude or "cool it?" Frequently we see lonely people so afraid of loneliness that they rush into an intimate relationship, or marriage, without due consideration of the wisdom of such a step. In our next chapter we will take a more detailed look at what happens when two people do decide to live in an intimate and committed relationship. For now, let's consider the tell-tale signs that may not predict the future course of a relationship but nevertheless give us good insight as to our likely prospects.

Questions we ask ourselves at this juncture run something like this: What do my feelings tell me about this person? When I contemplate and visualize a more intimate scenario, how does this make me feel? Do we have mutual goals and expectations for our lives together? Do we BOTH benefit from these objectives? Does this person care about me, adore me, like me, listen to me, respect me, accept me, forgive me, love me? And how do I genuinely feel toward her/him?

Do each of us have not only the right but also the encouragement TO GROW AS INDIVIDUALS while in this relationship? Do we respect each other's privacy and chosen solitude? Do I feel secure with this person? Can I really trust him/her? Is he/she responsible? Are we comfortable about our financial arrangements? Can I be myself when I'm with this person or do I have to act, wear a mask, play a part, keep my defenses up? Are we at home with each other intellectually, physically, sexually, emotionally, spiritually? If I enter into this new relationship will I become what I believe I am meant to become and is this also true for her/him? What about her/his family, children, relatives, buddies, friends — how do they affect this relationship?

Yes, we can overcome loneliness with friendship! The level of interaction at which this takes place depends on individual taste, choice and wisdom. The "bottom line" is: there are so many people all around you who need you, that there is really no need to be lonely. Having agonized and suffered enough, all that is required is to make the decision that we shall be lonely no more, and act on that decision.

Bibliography & Recommended Further Reading

Nin, Anaïs: The Diary of Anaïs Nin. Volume Six
        N.Y & London: Harcourt Brace Jovanovich, 1977
Seabury, David: How To Live With Yourself
        L.A.: Science of Mind Publications, 1972
Phillips, Gerald M.: Help For Shy People
        Englewood Cliffs, New Jersey: Prentice Hall Inc., 1981
Sartre, Jean-Paul: The War Diaries
        N.Y.: Pantheon, 1984
Camus, Albert: Notebooks - 2 Volumes
        N.Y.:Alfred A. Knopf, 1969
Woolf, Virginia: The Diary - Volumes I, II, III, IV & V
        N.Y.: Penguin, 1983
Lehmann, John: Virginia Woolf
        London: Thames & Hudson, 1987
Simons, George F: Keeping Your Personal Journal
        N.Y.:Paulist Press, 1978
Progoff, Ira: At A Journal Workshop
        N.Y.: Dialogue House Library, 1975
Skinner, B.F.: Notebooks
        Englewood Cliffs, New Jersey: Prentice-Hall, Inc., 1980
de Beauvoir, Simone: Memoirs of a Dutiful Daughter
        Markham, Ontario: Penguin, 1975
de Beauvoir, Simone: The Prime of Life
        N.Y.: Lancer Books, 1966
Kafka, Franz: The Diaries - 2 Volumes
        N.Y.: Schocken, 1974

CHAPTER 14

LIVING TOGETHER - PLAY BY PLAY

"Try honestly to see things from the other person's point of view"

How To Win Friends and Influence People
Dale Carnegie (1888–1955)

Most of us, starting when we are little children and increasingly through our young adult years, dream of someday entering the fulfilling life of being happy parents. "Motherhood and apple pie" was a truism on the North American Continent for many generations and the idea is still widespread today. Nevertheless, today we find ever-growing numbers of people whose dream of a happy "couple" is turning into a nightmare. Yet, to those who succeed, the rewards in terms of fulfillment and happiness seem to be more than compensation for the efforts spent to achieve it.

In this chapter we will explore (a) the values we seek to express and treasure in good relationships, (b) the major causes of conflict in relationships, (c) the usual reactions to conflict; and (d) the options two people (and other family members) have for working themselves out of conflict into harmony.

These observations are mainly based on my own experience in working with people over many years. While the picture may not be the same everywhere, values, behavioral patterns, causes and effects emerge with repeated regularity. My experiences in seminars and workshops, at conventions and speaking engagements in the major metropolitan areas of the United States of America and Canada, as well as my acquaintance with Europe, have taught me that our ideals, our experiences, our reactions and our solutions are remarkably the same the world over.

What are the **values** most people treasure in a relationship that is committed, and we include here, family relationships? What do we want to experience, feel, have, cherish together that we do not accomplish alone? What do we "expect" from each other in the living-together-scenario? It seems to me that we can distinguish a number of value areas which have survived depression, wars, and the cultural revolutions of the beat- hippie- and me-first generations. These still appear to be what being "at home" with one another is all about:

Caring. What makes us human if it isn't that we express our love, our caring for one another? What a wonderful feeling to be able to come home, and no matter what may have happened to you that day or night, you know there is someone there who CARES how you feel! To me, civilization's continuance can only be assured when caring families continue to thrive. Our educational systems were never intended to replace the family as the cradle of civilized living.

It is within the family we are first cared for and meet our role models for living. It is here we learn what love, freedom, truth, beauty, justice, courage are all about. Lacking quality experiences during childhood in a good home, how much we have learn later on. How much pain and has been suffered when human beings are allowed to grow up without respect, tolerance, integrity and attention! Parents who care - this is where it all starts.

Responsibility. Income tax forms tell us parents are raising "dependents" but the successful family generates in each participant the sense of personal responsibility for her or his own actions and choices, that also creates a sense of being needed and of being important in the scheme of things. Each plays a part that can only be enacted by that individual.

Fairness. We first discover order, management of things and procedures, rules and guidelines for living in a family setting. Without that basis, we would be hard put to strive for justice in society at large. The skill of managing a "fair" family requires mastering the art of "forgiving and forgetting." It is within the family that we learn to cope with stresses and the demands of others while at the same time eliminating the possibility of exploiting those who are weak and ignorant and learning. The term we now use is "tough love" and it works wonders. Honesty is the key.

Self-discovery. We have seen earlier in this book that, young or old, rookie or mature, we always seem to live up to the self-image we have of ourselves. The effective family encourages the development of a healthy self-image for each of its members, including mom and dad. Where else would we "pick up" our self-image? Much modification in later years is unnecessary when our self-worth is rooted in what we felt before we could even walk.

Creativity. The great satisfaction mature and intelligent parents in feel later years is NOT to have molded their children into clones of themselves, as they might have preferred. Our deepest gratitude to our parents comes, when we have the impression that what they desired most for us, was to become that unique person we ourselves felt we could, and should, become. Home is at its best when mom and dad, as well as "kids," feel the encouragement of "all the others" to be themselves, to be creative, to grow into what we have chosen as our objective and delight.

Challenge Having observed a great many families where the opportunities for development of the individual were far greater for the children than they once were for the parents, we can detect the understandable attitude of these parents, who say "I don't want my child to go through what I had to endure!" Protection from known dangers, harm and suffering, is then extended to include healthy challenges and barriers. We see immigrant parents provide everything for their children, to the point that frequently the son and daughter prefer to "leave the nest" at an early age because they seek, want and need the challenge to achieve for themselves. The goal is excellence, not ease. Happiness comes from being able to say with pride and mean it: "I did this!"

Appreciation. Have you known families where "all they ever did" was criticize each other? How can those raised with the standard of unattainable perfectionism ever form their own loving relationship with a new partner, without having to overcome that learned habit to nit-pick everything others do? The answer is appreciation, learn to praise, to express gratitude, to say "thanks." The psychological genius William James wrote in the early days of behavioral sciences: "The deepest principle of human nature is the desire to be appreciated."

Trust. The media tell us daily that it's hard to trust anyone or any institution. What a relief it is to be able to go home, be with other members of the family, finding an environment where you can just be yourself (without defenses and masks). Old-fashioned trust was once the foundation of the human community. How we need to teach and practice it!

Fun. The greatest moments I remember about the family I grew up in are filled with laughter, funny stories and marvelous humor, the roots of which went back for many generations of family bonding. How terrific we feel when home is not a place of duty, obedience, competition and seriousness but an often lighthearted fun place where we can be just as happy as we feel. Here at the family hearth we can still be happy even when facing crises and disappointments. List a sense of humor under assets here.

Relaxation. If stress, tension and worry are among the main culprits of modern living, the main solution has to be an environment where the opposite is the order of the day. People want their home and their relationships to be the outpicturing of serenity and relaxation, of which the old ideas of the hearth, homecoming and Christmas are fitting symbols. All these are what we want but unfortunately, what we get is too often quite different. The question is: Why not? Why do so few succeed in building a truly happy, albeit not perfect, relationship and family?

The causes of conflict in intimate, committed human relations are many but in my observation in working with many such situations, there are a number of identifiable causes. Most of these can be prevented or avoided because the symptoms are there before "the knot is tied" or the commitment to live together is acted upon.

Inauthenticity A character in a comic strip, depicting continuous conflict between spouses, lamented: "I thought loneliness was the worst thing in the world, until I got married!" Why do so many feel this way? Why all this reversal of behavior "after the honeymoon?"   What happened to that courteous courtship attitude, now changed to "I don't pay any attention to you, I could care less about you?" What happened to all the kissing, hugging and lovemaking? How can a person change so drastically in such a short time?

The answer is, they don't: they were always the sloppy, competitive, uncaring, macho, abusive, violent, impolite, uncivilized, badly smelling, addicted persons they now appear to be. The courtship attitude was not authentic, it was a phoney, put-on act to achieve a goal, namely to "hook" that partner, to marry into that family, to obtain that status or security, to show our peers or parents what we can do. So when the enchanted prince turns into an ugly old or young frog, and when Snow White looks more like a dishrag, there has been no sudden transformation, but rather a revelation of what was there all the time.

"Too High" Expectations Many a disappointed groom or bride was well aware of the serious and undesirable flaws in the personality and behavior of their spouse but they believed they could and would make her or him over. "Oh, he'll stop drinking after we marry" is only one variation of a theme we hear too often. But he or she cannot be changed by another person, not even by the best intentioned and sincere lover; they can only change themselves. The expectations were false.

Another Lover One of the results of lack of communication and trust, and of the disappointment of inauthenticity is the attraction to someone else who appears to possess what is lacking in our own partner. The excitement of the affair, the secrecy, the attention, the newness of new love all lead to causing the relationship to deteriorate. Closely related to this development is the next one.

Boredom When there are no exciting common goals both can pursue, life becomes a bore, a drag and a burden. Everything becomes commonplace and drudgery. The other person's behavior becomes almost totally predictable in given situations. We want to escape, because home is now a trap, a boring hell.

Lack of Common Interests   When one partner wants to grow, develop her or his potential and experience new things, places and feelings but the other one has settled down to mediocrity and sameness, the relationship gets stretched like an elastic band to its limits.

Distress   or negative stress due to money worries, debts and poverty. It's hard to keep a home happy when we're constantly bickering over finances, when there's lack, want, abuse, addiction, exploitation and poor management of assets and liabilities. Distress also sets in when there's not enough time for each other, when work and things become more important than our lover, and when there's intentional competition between spouses.

Lack of Understanding of how the other person thinks and feels. Unaware of the challenges, problems, the workload and worries of our partner we are no longer providing the understanding shoulder to sigh or cry on. The caring has stopped here.

Lack of Respect   Too many boys have grown up without or with little respect for their mother and sisters and too many girls heard and felt "not much good" about "the old man."   When people enter a committed relationship without a healthy respect for their other-gender-partner we are again looking at a cause of an uncaring situation.

Sexual Conflict   Being unaware of or uncaring about the sexual needs and desires of our partner is another cause of drifting apart. Sometimes gay or lesbian relationships are of more importance than the commitment originally entered into by one or both parties. Interests change, intimacy may have been too difficult to achieve or express in a strained environment of conflict. Sometimes lack of information about one's own sexuality prevents the development of a mutually satisfying relationship. Then there are the old Victorian attitudes toward sex as being sinful and the repression of healthy desires, feelings and fantasies because of the condemnation of an ignorant and prudish partner, and perhaps relatives and friends as well.

Television, video and/or other technological "monsters" that have become the core and center of all the attention in the home and we pay little or no more attention to what other members of our human family say or feel. This, is in turn related to the next problem.

Lack of Communication is easily the foremost cause of relationship breakdown and almost always a significant contributing factor. Most folks simply do not tell their family members what they are thinking, what they feel, what they want, what they are going to do, when and with whom and why.

Lack of Commitment Too many people are not serious about their relationship. They are lazy, selfish, and uncaring; never having witnessed anything better, they often believe that what they are doing is perfectly normal.

Crisis A serious illness, accident, disaster or calamity can prove to be too much for one or both partners in a relationship. Usually unexpected, the person who gives up does not have the inner resources to carry on, or the wisdom to know how to handle or resolve the crisis.

Children Contemporary families frequently include children whose natural parent(s) are not present. Divorce and re-marriage or new relationships often result in children being moved and transferred back and forth between parents, grandparents, various ex-es etc. New relationships sometimes just cannot stand the strain of learning to relate peacefully with a host of new intergenerational or ethnic, cultural lines of communication.

How do people usually react to these conflicts? Perhaps you have been involved in or been a bystander of these seven fairly common responses that usually neither improve nor resolve the conflict situation: (No Exit: beware!)

Enduring One reaction with a long history in our culture is to try and "live with it." Some people would like to "split" but are afraid of loneliness, poverty, disapproval of church and relatives, "I must bear my cross, cheerfully. . ."

Withdrawal With some, you really don't know what they are thinking for they are not saying. However, some changes in behavior begin to show: there is more drinking, more eating, more silence, more sulking and more repressed simmering. There's also increasing ill health because one cannot be practiced without the other.

Ignoring People hope that, like inclement weather, the bad scene will pass, it'll go away, so just ignore it and wait. But relationships are not healed this way.

Attacking "You're not going to push ME around, I have just as much ammunition, if not more than you do." So the mental, emotional claws and guns come out, the fighting starts, flares down only to start up again. Home is now a battlefield, war is the normal state. We discover and push all the buttons that lead the other person to become angry and upset. But all this fury doesn't resolve anything, the blows simply cause more injuries and all the finer feelings are destroyed.

The tale is told about Sir Winston Churchill meeting a stern judgmental and disapproving lady at a party who said to him: "Winston, you are drunk! Shame, shame on you!" Whereupon the old warrior retorted: "Yes, milady, I'm drunk but you are ugly. And tomorrow morning, I shall be sober, but you will still be ugly!". . . Now, what's resolved?

Forgiving These are the good souls who will keep on forgiving and trying to forget but who won't SAY anything, won't look for help, won't communicate, won't DO something about the (often abusive) situation. Result: things only get worse.

State of Shock Some folks react in disbelief, always saying to themselves: This couldn't be real, this isn't true, I must be dreaming, or misinterpreting, surely this must be my mistaken concept of the situation. They deny the severity or reality of the conflict in disbelief and shock, and resolve nothing. Often too, they keep running, finding more work to do, to fill time.

Consolation Persons in trouble at home often will turn, not to their partner, nor to a qualified counsellor, but to a friend or relative, to pour out their heart, to tell all or some of it, often to exaggerate, gossip and belittle, to betray trusts and to solicit sympathy and pity. In most cases, if you too have tried to help people resolve conflicts with their significant other, you'll discover this process is of little or no help.

What does help? There are five effective "self-help" steps to resolve the conflicts we have been discussing but this approach does require a definite preface, or perhaps we should say: pre-requisite. Not all relationships in trouble have a chance of recovery and transformation. How do you know which one does and which one does not? In my experience, we need to precede any mutual or joint attempt to heal a relationship with an honest personal EVALUATION. This requires some time "apart," perhaps away from the scene of the trouble. Take time to learn to MEDITATE, then use this subtle connection to your higher consciousness to contemplate and heal yourself and your relationships. This is the way to get in touch with your true and deepest feelings, as well as your unconscious level of intuition.

Ask yourself: how do I really feel about him/her: do I still love him/her? Why did I "fall in love" (if I did) with him/her in the first place? Did I "fall for" an illusion — is the "thing" I was, and still am looking for simply not there, or is it but dormant, hidden, unexpressed?

This kind of evaluation, which you do by and for yourself, will include an honest inventory of all your mutual assets, the qualities and the "things" that are good and desirable as well as the liabilities. Weigh how serious the negatives in the relationship are, how much you still care, how strong and how authentic your desire is to continue to live with this person, what your motivations are and what your intuition is conveying to you.

Our next chapter tries to help us deal with the situation if we find we do not wish to or just cannot continue our relationship, for whatever reasons. If however, your answer and the conclusion of your personal evaluation definitely is that you wish to improve, save and heal your relationship AND THIS IS ALSO THE SINCERE DESIRE OF YOUR PARTNER, these five essentially self-help steps have proven (again, in my experience with many such situations) effective, sometimes even seemingly miraculous.

FIVE STEPS TO RESOLVE "COUPLE CONFLICT":

1.   **LET YOUR FEELINGS OUT** - Get together, the two of you, in a private setting, and start TALKING about everything you **feel** about your relationship, what may or may not have been happening, all your expectations, disappointments, positive and negative evaluations. Don't blame, don't get angry, avoid emotional outbursts, but also don't pretend, don't try to be nicey-nicey, don't cover up. Be honest, communicate clearly and accept what is being said. We are now honestly communicating and, perhaps for the first time in years, becoming aware of how the other person really FEELS. Dale Carnegie's and other fine counsellors' valuable advice to see things from the other person's point of view cannot be heeded unless we know what that other person's point of view actually is.

2.   **LIST YOUR NEEDS** Write down, each separately, what you want from this relationship. List all your desires, wishes, expectations, goals and even dreams. Make it clear cut, so there's no doubt about what each of you mean. This may take a little time, say even a week. Both agree to the time limit, then meet again with the purpose of taking the next step.

3.   **WORK OUT A NEW COMMITMENT** You now have two lists of individual goals that need to be blended into one mutual list of relationship objectives and guidelines. Go over and discuss each item carefully. Define your solutions and agreements together and be sure to write them down at that time. "Rules" of workload, chores, behavior, financial arrangements, entertainment, hours spent together etc. are now being agreed upon. Perhaps for the first time in years of living together, you have consciously become aware of what you both can happily live with through compromise. Be definite, but also flexible.

4.   **PRACTICE AWARENESS** You now have the opportunity to become more sensitive to your mate's needs. Add more appreciation, praise, compliments, forgiveness, interest and caring. Stop talking the faults of the past, phone if you are going to be late, look more attractive than before, make her/him feel important (because she/he is) and don't shout (unless there's an emergency). As we get to know our partner better, we also become more aware of what his/her hidden personal needs, dreams and desires are. This is your opportunity to start anew, but this time you are both AWARE of what you are really all about, hence it is within your reach to make it work.

5.   **WEEKLY "STAFF" MEETING** A key factor in the success of a productive business enterprise is the regular communications session. Here problems, concerns, ideas and goals are openly discussed among management and staff. The same principle, based on the formation or creation of a "master mind" in Napoleon Hill's Laws of Success theory, can be applied in family and couple relationships. Meet at a pre-planned time slot during the week when it is convenient and without interruptions. Then simply "do" your planning of all the projects usual and special to the functioning of the family unit; communicate any concerns, any unresolved issues, feelings and fears. Express joys and thank you's, discuss what needs to be ironed out or decided. Include long-range planning of events to be looked-forward-to.

       Don't overlook the motivational value these regular get-togethers can provide. It's more than clearing the air, straightening out a mess or even just managing the household. It can be the highlight of the week, because it may well provide the incentive that "turns us on" to create a relationship that makes us feel really good. Keep the atmosphere affirmative, avoid turning your meeting into a complaining session.

Privately, remain affirmative too. Re-enforce your hopes, dreams and commitments by defining affirmations that reflect your intentions: "This is a wonderful relationship and it is getting better and better every day and in every way. I am becoming more loving, more patient, more understanding and more caring every day and so is my partner (my child[ren])."

Affirmations need to express **your** deepest desires and convictions in your own words and can become even more powerful when agreed upon and used every day by all participants in the relationship.

Also privately contemplate such absolutes as love, compassion, beauty, harmony and truth; let these philosophical values gently and often pervade your consciousness. Let these sentiments soften your soul and emotions; join the sages of the wisdom of the ages in rising above conflict into a realm of the ideals of eternal verities, for they are the transcendental origins of all that is admirable in us, and in civilization.

But, as observed earlier, not all relationships can be healed nor do they endure. To consider what may happen then we now turn our attention to the next chapter.

Bibliography & Recommended Further Reading

Carnegie, Dale: How To Win Friends and Influence People
      N.Y.: Simon & Schuster, 1952
Carnegie, Dale: The Quick and Easy Way to Effective Speaking.
      Revision by Dorothy Carnegie
      N.Y.: Pocket Books, 1962
Carnegie, Dale: Lincoln, the Unknown
      Garden City, N.Y.:Dale Carnegie & Ass., 1959
May, Rollo: The Art of Counseling
      N.Y.:Abingdon Press, 1939
Viscott, David: Winning
      N.Y.: Pocket Books, 1987
Viscott, David: Feel Free
      N.Y.: Pocket Books, 1987
Viscott, David: Risking
      N.Y.: Pocket Books, 1979
Viscott, David: The Language of Feelings
      N.Y.: Arbor House, 1976
Viscott, David: I Love You, Let's Work it Out
      N.Y.: Simon & Schuster, 1987
Baker, Robert & Elliston, Frederick, ed.: Philosophy & Sex
      Buffalo, N.Y.: Prometheus, 1975
Paulson, J. Sig.: To Humanity with Love (Poetry)
      N.Y.:Hawthorn, 1975
Patterson, Yolanda Astarita: Simone de Beauvoir and the
      Demystification of Motherhood
      Ann Arbor, Mich: UMI Research Press, 1989
Madsen, Axel: Hearts and Minds - The Common Journey of Simone de
      Beauvoir & Jean-Paul Sartre
      N.Y.: Wm. Morrow & Co., 1977

CHAPTER 15

LIFE AFTER DIVORCE

"Nobody realizes that some people expend tremendous energy merely to be normal"

Notebooks IV
Albert Camus (1913–1960)

Since everything in life is potentially final, all relationships eventually come to an end. Death and the grief that accompanies constitute one of the great challenges of living. Some relationships however succeed for a lifetime; we usually admire this phenomenon and to some of us, it is one of the most desirable and sought after "states" of living. When an intimate and at first committed relationship ends because it just doesn't work and becomes unbearable, "breaking up" or divorce, in case of marriage, becomes necessary. For some this is unthinkable because of their religious beliefs, or because they lack the courage and vision to proceed on their own. As we noted, some people simply endure a hellish situation, resulting in unnecessary suffering for many. Death, either of oneself or of one's spouse, then becomes a welcome relief. Someone has said that nobody can be sick for much more than ninety years. So everything, in this case, gratefully does end.

Our concern here is with those who find themselves "going through" separation and divorce as this writer did. How do we meet this challenge — one for which no one is quite fully prepared. . .

As you may have discovered, if you have experienced divorce or separation of a committed relationship, or if you have tried to help someone faced with this challenge, there are many difficulties. Apart from the CHANGES in financial, social and parental relations, the most difficult area is what goes on INSIDE. Life is consciousness and what we are now facing is a barrage of mixed feelings, the likes of which we have never known before. Our emotional life is filled with rapidly alternating uppers and downers. If "storms of life" was ever an appropriate metaphor this is it: the grief because of loss of love and security, the joy of sudden freedom, the agony of anger and guilt, the ecstasy of newness and the bleakness of loneliness, depression and self-pity.

Then there are the arrows of panic, resentment and hostility but also the wonder that life somehow beckons on with the promise of an unknown future and hope. Finally, there's the distress of broken ideals and dreams and the shaking of our courage, self-respect and self confidence, to say nothing of having to cope with the reaction of other people, the judgments, condemnation, loss of friendship, shunning and all the rest of it.

What is the constructive, realistic reaction to divorce that will result in a really new "life after divorce?" My own experience added to that of the many others with whom I've been associated and worked with for several decades suggests five major helpful considerations to which we all have access . . . It is not necessary to be like Françoise, the protagonist in Simone de Beauvoir's novel "She came to stay," who "did not know what to do with her body or her thoughts." What can we know and what can we do?

EXPERIENCE YOUR FEELINGS - Rather than looking at yourself as being weird or strange (I've heard many people ask: Am I cracking up?) realize that it is NORMAL to have all these reactions and feelings. When we study and understand what our unconscious is all about (recommended resource: Carl Jung) we realize that ALL emotions are a natural, normal part of us and that is it a tremendously valuable experience for us that we give permission to ourselves to feel what we feel.

Why should this be so hard for people, especially men? Look back to where your value system originates. Were you told it is **not** manly or masculine to cry? Did we learn to repress rather than express our feelings, be they joyous love or melancholy grief? Like sex, emotions have in our culture had a "bad press," we have lived as if they weren't there and the more we repressed and acted "cool," the harder living became. No wonder that the great writer, Albert Camus noted that for some people to appear as normal, they have to expend tremendous energy. How much easier and sensible to be yourself, to be in touch with your feelings, to experience them totally. Release the pain by crying it out, as often as you feel like it. Without bothering or harming others, do whatever helps you to release it all. Recognize, that letting this state of mixed feelings come to the surface, is teaching you much about your unconscious consciousness. Surely this will motivate you to want to get better acquainted with the totality of your mind through the practice of contemplation and meditation. (see next section in this book)

For starters, simply take a half hour or so, on a regular daily basis, be quiet and do not let anything or anyone disturb you. Now, just watch the stream of consciousness that seems to well up from within, like a parade at some holiday celebration. Experience it all, relax and enjoy it and don't think of yourself anymore as abnormal or strange.

Then go a little further and become still; from a deeper, spiritual level of your being, without any effort on your part, a feeling of peace and calm strength and courage imparts itself to you. You may not understand its origin, it doesn't matter. There is a deeper, spiritual self in all of us and if we give it half a chance, it will make itself felt. This feeling is somewhat different in quality from feeling the emotions of anger, resentment, remorse, guilt, joy, curiosity, happiness and even wonder. The spiritual feeling does not have the temporary upper and downer, swinging back and forth temperament. It is existential, it does not seem to fluctuate or be subject to duration as we meet it in our "inner space." Rather it just IS and we know it.

This doesn't as yet solve anything, but it does give us the impression, and then perhaps the conviction that solutions are available and that they will be revealed to us. The Buddha spoke of "the uncreate," the realm of the unexpressed yet present potential that we have access to in meditation. To experience all your many feelings consciously, without judgement, then to know this spiritual empowerment is the beginning of the personal transformation you need, deserve and desire. These personal sessions of awareness with yourself may well become the most precious times of your daily existence. There's nothing ritualistic, magic or esoteric about this. You are simply and naturally, getting to know yourself better and better. This approach leads logically to the next step.

INTERPRET THE PAST - The "mixed feelings" we were experiencing, like dreams, are there for a reason and the reason is that we have to **DO** something within ourselves to arrive at a state of harmony again, if ever we were there in the first place.

What may our feelings convey? Probably that we blame ourselves for some part or all of the causes that led to the divorce. We feel we could and should have done differently and better. So, we feel guilty, our self-worth is diminished. In addition, there's no doubt a range of feelings best described as anger and resentment. How could he or she have done such a thing, etc.?

Both emotions may be healed by the realization that both you (and your "ex") have always done THE BEST YOU COULD according to your prevailing awareness. Of course, we don't think so. We say: but I (she, he) knew better, yet I got drunk, lost my temper, reacted childishly, anyway. Think it through: if we really did know better, we would have acted differently, but the truth is, we always act in accordance with, neither better nor worse than, our state of consciousness permits. Now how does this help us? It helps because it eliminates the need to punish oneself as well as seek revenge on the "ex" and anyone else that may be involved in the dissolution of the marriage. This is one form of for-giving, the healing technique taught in all civilized philosophies, religions and cultures. We give one balanced and realistic feeling for another that was false, illusory. Getting rid of the destructive emotions of guilt, blame, anger, resentment and the like is a tremendous relief but there's more.

There are other useless, harmful emotions that appear to be more noble, such as, what Emmet Fox described as being "a tragedy queen" (or king) when we feel so sorry for ourselves as to be continually seeking the sympathy of friends and relatives, symbolized by a long face, unkempt appearance and handwringing. All of which solves nothing. The sooner we know that we can and will create a new life for ourselves, the better it is for all concerned, including ourselves.

The past can never be changed but it can be re-interpreted so you can live with it and then put it behind you. Don't force yourself to forget because it cannot be done. Memory is one of the greatest assets of consciousness you have, don't tell it to stop functioning. You wouldn't want to be in the shoes of those to whom this has actually happened. It is one of the greatest human tragedies, so don't facilitate it happening to you. You do of course remember, but you take the sting out of the remembrance by applying the measure of compassionate forgiveness that Jesus practiced when he prayed for his cruel adversaries: "Father, forgive them FOR THEY KNOW NOT WHAT THEY DO." Everyone lives at her or his own level of awareness and that's the way it is. Period. But there's more.

Whatever it is that we have gone through, and it can be terribly inhuman, I know, we can always ask ourselves: what am I to learn from this, how do I grow, how can I become different, what is the meaning of all this? Value the challenge of asking yourself honestly these and similar questions. Keep a journal of your feelings, evaluations, comments, inner discoveries and revelations. The closer you are to knowing yourself and what happened to and through you, the better and brighter your chances for a new and more desirable future. But that is unlikely to happen until we realize this next step:

PRACTICE CENTERING - Remember your thoughts weave the pattern both of your feelings and your destiny. And as long as our belief persists and prevails that another person (your ex, a lawyer, a relative) can make us unhappy and prevent us from becoming the person we want to be, so long shall we suffer accordingly. It is one of the greatest discoveries in the art of living when we realize that we can choose to CENTER our thinking within ourselves, so that the decision what reaction to experience next becomes ours. Then we no longer live at the mercy of those who do not wish us well and who have known all along what buttons to push to set us off. Each new day is a new opportunity for you to improve and enhance the quality of your life: discover the controls, for they are within you.

Center within yourself, live from your own deep, quiet center. No one can disturb you unless you let him or her do it to you.

SEEK NEW LOVE - It is not always easy for divorced or separated persons, both male and female, to feel that they deserve and can attract another significant other into their lives. The main barrier is the old protection mechanism, where we will not go ahead into a potentially dangerous situation as perceived by the person who was and feels hurt. We stay away from closer contacts because we don't want to get hurt again. With this often comes the feeling that we are not very lovable because we have been rejected, or so we think. But, life's experience all around us shows that the loss of love of someone does not have to mean the loss of love always, unless we accept this.

Once centered we now know that our happiness does not depend on another person; however, that does not mean that another person's presence could not and would not add to our fulfillment in life's experience. Remembering that the past is not, and never needs be a precedent for future events and possibilities; let's meditate, seek guidance from our intuitive level and, given the affirmative response, let's see how one might proceed to find new love embodied and expressed in a (to us) new significant other.

A lady I know who did this went about it successfully, in this way (and I know of several others who have proceeded in similar fashion with wonderful results). We may call this, in Jungian terms, synchronicity or simply the result of conditioning one's subconscious, so its own law could attract what it is designed to do. She first got rid of all the old hurt feelings and resentments and poor self esteem that had resulted from her divorce. She then realized herself progressively more certain as the expression of an Infinite Intelligence and meditated upon this daily. She obtained the intuitive conviction that there was the right male person "out there" for her and that she was the right feminine person he was seeking. This dual belief was firmly accepted by her before doing any further inner work.

She then proceeded to write down a description of the type of person she wished to attract into her life. She read several good books on relationships, psychology, personalities and the mind. The picture began to form in her consciousness of what the person she wished to attract was like; her heart told her and she defined it carefully and patiently. She then affirmed quietly twice a day that this person was now "on his way" to her and she included the statement that she was all that he was wishing for in his heart. It included such qualities as mutual trust, integrity, caring, love, compassion, understanding, communication, tenderness, intelligence, kindness, spiritual awareness and responsibility. This woman met and subsequently married the man who exactly fit her imaged objective. What's more, she is exactly what he had, with profound and sincere desire, been looking for.

Consult your inner wisdom, define your heart's desire, affirm your expectation — all these and also the next and concluding step:

BECOME A PEOPLE PERSON - You and I probably know quite a few people, who can tell you what they want — the fantasy Princess or the Prince Charming — but these same people unfortunately give little or no attention to the question as to why these ideal persons should be attracted to them!

It really isn't difficult to work on becoming more of the interesting person we already are deep inside. We're not suggesting putting on an act that would, as we have seen in Chapter 14, only lead to eventual discovery and disaster. We need not act when we become authentic and begin to live the wonderful, caring, spiritual person we already really are. Those who recognize this about themselves know they aren't perfect, they make mistakes, they have a lot of growing to do, but, like royalty, they already belong in the Universe, so we can now close the door on pretence and become truly ourselves.

Our objective is to find a loving, interesting person, and, in Emersonian terms, we therefore, need to express the very "things" we seek to attract: to have a friend, be a friend. To find interesting people, be interesting. Develop your communication skills, be informed, become a good listener, become interested in others, encourage people, be positive, radiate love and goodwill. Respect yourself and others too, recognize basic human rights, reach out compassionately, speak constructively, and practice the art of caring toward every human being, every animal and our planet.

A new, significant and desirable relationship is a precious and wonderful "thing," quite beyond adequate descriptions because it is ecstasy; it goes far beyond healing and the restitution of self-esteem. It is a fulfillment; it may not be for everyone but let's be careful not to reject what may yet be "out there" for us. One way of becoming more sure about what we can do, be and have, is to master the Art of Contemplation. To this we now turn our devoted attention.

Bibliography & Recommended Further Reading

Lottman, Herbert R.: Alberta Camus, a Biography
    N.Y.:Doubleday, 1979
Kafka, Franz: Letter To His Father
    N.Y.:Schocken, 1974
Dewey, John: Experience and Nature
    N.Y.:Dover, 1958
Johnson, Robert A.: HE, Understanding Masculine Psychology
    N.Y.: Harper & Row, 1974
Harris, Amy Bjork & Thomas A.:Staying O.K.
    N.Y.:Harper & Row, 1985
Waitley, Denis & Witt, Reni L.: The Joy of Working
    N.Y.:Dodd, Mead & Co., 1985
Jung, Carl G.: Modern Man In Search of a Soul
    N.Y.: Harcourt, Brace, 1933
de Beauvoir, Simone: She Came To Stay
    London:Fontana, 1985
Brée, Germaine: Camus
    N.Y.:Harcourt, Brace Jovanovich, 1964
Johnson, Robert A.: SHE, Understanding Feminine Psychology
    N.Y.: Harper & Row, 1976
Bolen, Jean Shinoda: Goddesses in Everywoman. A New Psychology of Women
    N.Y.: Harper & Row, 1984
Johnson, Robert A.: WE, Understanding the Psychology of Romantic Love
    N.Y.: Harper & Row, 1983
Bolen, Jean Shinoda: Gods in Everyman. A New Psychology of Men's Lives and Loves
    N.Y.: Harper & Row, 1989
Smiley, Emma M.: Not Guilty

L.A.:Scrivener, 1960

Riley, Glenda: DIVORCE, An American Tradition
     N.Y.:Oxford Univ. Press, 1991

Krantzler, Mel: Learning to Love Again
     N.Y.:Thos. Y. Crowell Co., 1979

Krantzler, Mel: Creative Divorce, A New Opportunity for Personal
     Growth
     N.Y.: M. Evans & Co., 1974

Hootman, Marcia and Perkins, Patt: How to Forgive Your Ex-Husband
     — and Get On With Your Life
     N.Y.: Doubleday & Co., 1983

Derlega, Valerian J. & Chaikin, Alan L.: Sharing Intimacy, What We
     Reveal To Others and Why
     Englewood Cliffs, New Jersey: Prentice-Hall, Inc., 1975

Romney, Ronna & Harrison, Beppie: Giving Time A Chance — The
     Secret of a Lasting Marriage
     N.Y.: M. Evans & Co., 1983

Wallerstein, Judith S. & Blakeslee, Sandra: Second Chances: Men,
     Women & Children A Decade After Divorce, Who Wins, Who
     Loses and Why.
     N.Y.: Tichner & Fields, 1989

PART FOUR

THE ART OF CONTEMPLATION
YOUR KEY TO PEACE

*"Each soul will feel and know that the entire universe
with all its good and with all its beauty is for
it and belongs to it forever"*

Cosmic Consciousness
Richard Maurice Bucke (1837–1902)

CHAPTER 16

THE GENTLE WAY TO SERENITY

"The mind acts only in so far as it understands . . ."

The Foundations of the Moral Life
Benedict de Spinoza (1632–1677)

Have you noticed — in your observations of your own life as well as the quality of life others enjoy, regardless of their personalities, introvert or extrovert, and regardless of their goals and objectives in life, everyone wants to FEEL GOOD. That is, we wish to feel at home in life, we wish to have a sense of belonging — with the persons we normally associate with, but also in the universe, in life as a whole. Perhaps our most urgent mode is our wish **not** to be upset and angry all the time.

Wouldn't it be wonderful if there was available to us a strategy, the application of an art that would result in a permanent feeling of SERENITY, so that no matter what was happening in your life, you would not be torn apart on the inside? Instead of getting "hot under the collar," we would remain calm and cool and comfortable under any garment? We've already seen how vital it is for our health and wellness as well as effectiveness, to have a firm check on distress. But for all of the aspects of our daily living to be enjoyed and lived to full efficiency demands a state of mind that is calm, balanced and serene. However we may wish to describe it, it is this serenity that is at the bottom of the quality of life and living we ultimately strive for. How shall we gain it?

We are going to suggest a definitive answer here; the way in which this answer may be realized, however, is to be traced very carefully. As "Baruch" Spinoza realized: for the mind to proceed it must first understand. So it needs to be said here that our approach to a subject that appears to be somewhat, if not entirely, irrational is rational. We believe what we are studying, while it may have appearances of being mysterious and even strange and weird, can and should be thoroughly understood. Ours is not the acceptance of the uncertain and the unknown, but the pursuit of the knowable and the evidence of what can be proven and tasted in the experience of every serious devotee.

To return to our question: how shall we achieve inner serenity while living in a world that constantly suggests we are going to be upset? The question is a big one and it invites, another question as so often is the case when we start "digging" for existential understanding. The second question is this one: where does the "upsetting" take place? The answer, of course, is in consciousness, in our awareness. There's no getting away from the basic truth that we get upset, not by an event, but by our response or reaction to that event. Therefore, the direct and obvious answer to our questions is: if one could master one's consciousness or awareness, one would achieve serenity.

Check it out: think of the last time YOU were upset, uptight, stressed out, wound up or otherwise feeling uncomfortable because something happened "out there" that "did you in." Now, whatever you may have done, whoever may have helped you, you presumably calmed down again. Where did this "calming down" process take place and whence came the ability or "power" to do so? Always the answer is: it came from somewhere within the unconscious realm of my consciousness. The resource is within you. The requirement therefore is to activate and develop that inner resource to such a degree of skill that it becomes effective continuously. Eventually it will not have to be consciously directed because it has become automatic.

This process and the practise of the skill of mastering our consciousness we call the art of contemplation. It may be called by many terms but the terminology needs to be thoroughly understood. These terms have been and are being widely used, especially in the media, without their meaning being explained, hence there is in the minds of a great many people in today's society much confusion about thes subject.

There are five major considerations we need to direct our attention to, before we can explain and apply the art of contemplation. These are integral to the "thing itself" and in our experience, necessary to be understood in order to attain success. We cannot "skip" the context if we are to grasp the true nature and significance of this precious art. There is also the fear of the unknown and with that the reluctance to proceed when it is suggested we do so on the basis of some outside authority. Nevertheless let us go ahead with intelligence and an open mind.

UNDERSTANDING OUR TERMINOLOGY

Words spoken or written can only become meaningful to us if we know the meaning that was intended by the author. If we do not know this, we will attach our own opinion to it, and as Quimby would say, we may wind up with an entirely different concept from what was intended. Here are clarifications of terms we will find useful when approaching the art of contemplation.

Meditation — This word is derived from the Latin "meditari" which means: to reflect upon, to study, ponder and think. The Oxford English Dictionary on Historical Principles states that meditation means: "sustained reflection or mental CONTEMPLATION; the continuous application of the mind to the CONTEMPLATION of some . . . truth." (caps mine) The main thrust of meditation, historically speaking, is clear: it is to *contemplate* a truth, to realize communion with a Greater Reality though still including our ordinary sensory existence. It is NOT to suppress or banish thought and emotion, it is NOT willing, or pretending, to bring about a vacuum in one's awareness. Neither is it "brainstorming," ritualistic behavior, nor directed logical thinking for the attainment of a certain goal. There are tremendous benefits to be derived from the practise of contemplative meditation, yet we do not deliberately set out to attain such benefits; they are by-products, not pre-planned.

Consciousness — From the Latin "conscius," which means, knowing in oneself or knowing something with others. It is the state of being conscious or "aware," the totality of thoughts and feelings which make up a person's conscious being. In describing our mental activity, the term consciousness implies the inclusion of both the immediate thoughts as well as **un**conscious or **sub**conscious aspects of a person's mind. Here, mind and consciousness mean the same thing, and it is always dynamic and creative.

Metaphysics — A term widely in use with different meanings. Originally its use was derived from the ancient Greek philosopher Aristotle's library which was divided between works on the physical world and everything else, "beyond physics," which came (over the many years' usage) to mean: preceding the physical form is the impulse, the idea, the thought, the mental blueprint. Plato, who was Aristotle's mentor, thought that each phenomenon in the material world (thing, person, organism) has a perfect idea back of it, or the "Truth" of that phenomenon. If we could become aware of this Truth, we would be able to understand whatever we give our attention to. In the process of deeper contemplation this is actually what is happening: "Truth" is conveyed or "revealed" to us from the spiritual realms of our unconscious mind.

Spirit - Spiritual — Origin: the Latin spiritus or breathing. This term seeks to convey the animating or vital principle of life. It may, in some contexts mean "God," or cosmic presence and power, infinite intelligence, universal creativity which gives rise to "worlds," dimensions, phenomena, organisms and persons. If perceived as self-conscious or "a being of consciousness," its ideas are (Plato's) Truth; incarnated in a human being, the spiritual self, or in Christian metaphysics, "the Christ."

Mysticism — Derived from the Latin mysticus, or initiate, literally "one who knows the secret." Which means the belief in the possibility of conscious, realized union with the Divine nature by means of contemplation. Implied also is the idea of reliance on a spiritual essence.

Intuition — from the Latin intueri, look upon, consider and contemplate by means of insight, as a means of acquiring knowledge of mysteries inaccessible by other means. A mystic is therefore not a weird, other-worldly, half-crazy person but a supremely natural, self-realized individual who "tunes in" to the spirit and nature of the cosmos itself, as a musical instrument may be finely attuned to the master musician or composer.

Psychic — Our English word is derived from the ancient Greek psyche, meaning "of the soul." In our usage we mean by psychic mental influence, extra-sensory perception, relating to phenomena which appear to lie outside the domain of physical law. That which we designate as psychic is not necessarily genuine, authentic, spiritual or "good." It may be illusory, counterfeit, deceptive and mental garbage. Current usage is therefore very different from the original meaning. The psychic requires unassailable verification to become acceptable as a constructive or useful tool.

THE NEED FOR CONTEMPLATION

Within the application of this essay we identify a three-fold human need for the Art of Contemplation:

To find personal serenity, inner peace in an often difficult and challenging world. This includes the reduction of stress (and therefore improvement of health) and enhancement of one's functioning.

To develop intuition or direct knowing, guidance from within enabling one to make right decisions, to think more clearly, to awaken and develop creative abilities, to cope better with change, to discover more purpose and meaning in one's life.

To experience union or oneness with divine or infinite intelligence, the spiritual ground and source of being. This experience is often referred to as Cosmic Consciousness or Mystical awareness. Ultimately we might say it simply means to feel "at home" in the Universe.

THE THREE LEVELS OF CONSCIOUSNESS

Richard Maurice Bucke, the eminent Canadian scholar in this field during the latter part of the 19th Century, developed a theory to understand what it means to reach for or aspire to a higher state of being than the one we've experienced up to now. In his marvellous book "Cosmic Consciousness" he points out that we are already aware of the two levels of consciousness which we encounter every day; he also adds a third, higher level:

Simple or Animal consciousness as in your dog and cat, a state of awareness we as humans share.

Self- or human consciousness, which is self evident

Cosmic or divine, spiritual, universal consciousness.

The mystics claim that it is possible to participate in and become aware of the Cosmic spiritual process, and that the difference between it and self-consciousness, is about as great as the usual difference between simple and self consciousness.

Whatever we may initially think of this theory, it is only by living victoriously through the events of our daily round that we cope with and "master" the multitude of daily "highs" and "lows." The degree of mastery, success and fulfilment we have depends on the level of consciousness we have attained and use. The higher governs the lower and as consciousness expands and improves so does our understanding and ability to live life as we want to live it. To be continually aspiring to an ever higher level of consciousness is an incredibly wonderful and practical adventure.

THE CREATIVE DYNAMICS OF THE MIND

What we are participating in — contemplation of higher truths — is a creative, dynamic process and not just a temporary escape from the raw realities of life and living. This three-fold process we may observe in ourselves continually, day and night, chosen and aware or not.

Within your mind ideas, suggestions, information and the interpretation of the reports of our senses, "exist" not just as "being there," but as influence. This influence is either destructive (if based on inaccuracy, ignorance, illusion, lies, negativity, misinterpretations, etc.) or constructive (if based on scientific evidence, spiritual intuition, rational intelligence, etc.). The reason the conscious activity is perceived as influence is because it affects an inner medium (see Chapter 2) we call: *the subconscious mind.*

This basic mind receives from the conscious its impressions, learns, accepts, understands, remembers, forms beliefs and sets in motion its own causes which may be destructive or constructive.

There will be continually changing behavior and feelings (moods) produced by the interaction of sensory reports with the subconscious. When destructive in conscious origin, the experience is distress, confusion, failure, trouble, addiction, feeling "down", etc. When constructive in conscious origin, the experience is health and happiness — well-being, success, freedom, peace, full of love, wisdom and functional excellence. (our terminology originating with Phineas Parkhurst Quimby, the 19th Century genius who discovered psychosomatic relationships)

Since this dynamic process is relentlessly proceeding within each of us it is easy to see why the art of contemplation is so tremendously beneficial; it is the direct and clear cause of all that we desire to experience in our private and public lives.

THE PURPOSE OF CONTEMPLATION

It is clear from the above description of our need for contemplation that we seek to achieve an inner serenity and activation of our intuitive faculty as well as increased spiritual awareness.

The ecstasy and sublimity of the mystical path are not easily conveyed in material language. My experience in personal practise of spiritual contemplation for over thirty years has taught me, gently but nevertheless convincingly, that the ancient metaphysical philosopher of Greece, the mystic Plotinus perceived the essence of this intensely private activity in a candidly clear way. Here is my interpretation of his thought:

Each individual participates in and partakes of the intangible nourishment of the fullness of the Cosmic Spirit, the wholeness of Infinity, but we realize it only to the degree of our own spiritual receptivity. "Each is there in All and All in each" (Plotinus, Enneads V-8). The purpose of the art of contemplation, as I perceive it, is to recognize our own highest, divine and spiritual identity. We are one with the cosmos and the cosmos is one within us.

Bibliography & Recommended Further Reading
Goldsmith, Joel S: The Art of Meditation
    N.Y.: Harper & Row, 1956
Goldsmith, Joel S: The Infinite Way
    San Gabriel, Calif: Willing, 1961
Goldsmith, Joel S: Living the Infinite Way
    N.Y.:Harper & Row, 1961
Goldsmith, Joel S: Consciousness Is What I Am
    N.Y.: Harper & Row, 1976
Goldsmith, Joel S: Practicing the Presence
    N.Y.: Harper & Row, 1958
Goldsmith, Joel S: Living Between Two Worlds
    N.Y.: Harper & Row, 1974
Goldsmith, Joel S: A Parenthesis in Eternity
    N.Y.: Harper & Row, 1963
Goldsmith, Joel S: The Mystical I
    N.Y.: Harper & Row, 1971
Sinkler, Lorraine: The Alchemy of Awareness
    N.Y.: Harper & Row, 1977
Addington, Jack and Cornelia: The Perfect Power Within You
    Santa Monica, Calif: DeVorss & Co., 1973
Steinem, Gloria: Revolution from Within
    Boston: Little, Brown, 1992
Hall, Manly P.: Daily Words of Wisdom
    L.A.: Philosophical Research Society, 1973
Holland, Jack H: Man's Victorious Spirit
    Monterey, Calif.: Hudson-Cohan Publ. Co., 1971
Holland, Jack H.: Your Freedom To Be
    Salinas, Calif.: Hudson-Cohan Publishing Co., 1977
Holmes, Ernest: The Science of Mind
    N.Y.: Dodd, Mead & Co., 1958

CHAPTER 17

HOW TO MEDITATE

"To expect immediate results from the practice of meditation would be the same as expecting to play Bach or Beethoven after the first music lesson"

The Art of Meditation
Joel S. Goldsmith (1892–1964)

Reaching higher levels of consciousness is not exactly everyone's everyday business. We are all conditioned to "perform" the usual human functions every day — we eat, drink, walk, answer the telephone, read, drive our cars, function as practitioners of certain skills and find nothing unusual in it all. We even have the problems of routine and boredom because there's insufficient challenge in life.

But when it comes to reaching out, or rather inward, to achieve an expansion in awareness, who is there to guide us? And what fears arise of this unknown territory? Is there a rational and intelligent strategy we may study, understand and apply that will take the art of contemplation and meditation out of the atmosphere of mystery and anxiety and into the realm of the accessible and practical? There certainly is and what we are about to discover could mean the beginning of the greatest adventure on which you will ever embark: the exploration of your own inner greatness!

Let us first recognize that observing various levels of consciousness in ourselves is perfectly natural. Every twenty-four hours all of us "fall asleep" and while unaware of our environment, we enter into a world where time and space as we know it in our ordinary consciousness, do not apply. Nevertheless we believe this dream world to be real and we function in it, with a different awareness of form and organism and of time and duration. All this is very strange, particularly in view of the intelligence expressed through it and its references to this life, here and now. (see Chapter 5).

We raise the subject of "dreaming" here again because it is a natural and normal activity of our consciousness to "exist" or "have being" at different levels. Therefore, when we suggest that it is possible and natural for us to "exist" at a spiritual, mystical level this may not be as novel an experience as we formerly thought, and should not frighten us in any way. In the contemplative state we feel somewhat different from the so-called "normal" state (what is normal?) but you'll find that, after you've practiced contemplative meditation for awhile, this state too becomes perfectly normal and natural. You may even prefer to be in "it" for it embodies deep and good feelings, and the further we proceed in our universe within, the more we will find ourselves at home. In this state we are perfectly relaxed, mildly aware of our physical environment, but not asleep and usually feeling absolutely wonderful, peaceful.

But how, in this hectic, stressful world of ours are we to achieve this? Experience of the many mystics throughout recorded history (see bibliography at end of this chapter) teaches us clearly that there are several stair steps to climb for effective practice of contemplative meditation. Although the number and height of the steps may prove different for various individuals here are five which have proven common to many meditators, they can be your guide to begin right now.

FIVE STEPS TO CONTEMPLATIVE MEDITATION

STEP I: PERSONAL COMMITMENT: As we have seen in our study of motivation and success, without your own definite no-nonsense personal commitment no enterprise has a chance of succeeding and "paying off." While the art of contemplation is a different, intangible and private pursuit, the same principle applies. How many people have you talked to who will tell you that at one time or another they've tried to meditate but gave up on it? Just how serious are these people? What happens when we say we'd like to be able to play the piano, synthesizer, violin or flute? No one would expect us to be able to do this successfully without taking some lessons and becoming familiar with the instrument and practice, practice, practice! Nor would anyone be surprised if after a few lessons, as Joel Goldsmith, one of our century's master teachers of contemplative meditation, points out, we still cannot play Bach or Beethoven!

Let's be realistic: without commitment, don't even try this art — you'll only be disappointed and more frustrated. We do not say this because it's a hard and difficult task, but because practice, correct understanding and consistency have proven to be indispensable ingredients of the mastery of this art.

When you are paying a bill, you may make out a check to the party to whom you owe the funds. It isn't until the check is signed that it becomes an instrument of value. Sometimes it's helpful, as with goal seeking, to write out a promissory note to yourself that clearly states the commitment you make to **yourself** to become a meditator. Some people have found, within themselves, that to commit themselves to a practice for an indefinite period or lifetime is just too much for them and it would weaken their resolve in other areas if they made a promise that feels like an impossible task or burden. This is not a burden or an additional duty in your life — it is a privilege and an incredible opportunity; so let's not move into is as an awful area of duty to be performed.
Rather, see it as an adventure you freely and happily embark upon.

Do give yourself a fair and practical chance to find out what it's really like. Commit yourself to one month of daily practice — let this be your "initial" period in which to give it your "best shot," an honest try. If after one month you feel it's not for you, you can discontinue the practice and not feel that you're either "too dumb" or that you've let yourself down. My guess is that your month long commitment will "automatically" become a wonderful daily habit you won't want to do without. What exactly is it we're going to commit ourselves to?

STEP II: CAREFUL PREPARATION: Just as you wouldn't consider stepping into your car to drive onto the highway if it wasn't in good driving condition, so we don't jump into the meditation practice without careful and thought-out preparation.

Choose Your Resource Material As you start your practice you need IDEAS, spiritual, positive, constructive, philosophical IDEAS to fill your consciousness with delight allowing you to expand your consciousness and heighten your awareness as the mystics and sages have always done. These great thoughts will give direction to your awareness and will lead you to achieving a sense of oneness with life, a cosmic consciousness. Reading and study is not the objective or content of contemplative meditation, but it is the starting point.

What do the mystics recommend? The scriptures of the great world religions have for centuries been a resource of spiritual ideas: the Bible, the sayings of Buddha, the Zen and other Buddhist writings, the Upanishads, the Gita and other vedic Hindu scriptures. Also recommended are the works of the great mystical and metaphysical philosophers, the spiritual poets, books by and about genuine mystics and texts by contemporary authors on meditation, contemplation and mysticism.

The key here is that the resources you select are inspirational and enlightening to **you**. Every person, as we all know, is different, and experiences a different level of consciousness from everyone else. And we are changing, hopefully growing all the time. That is why you may today pick up and open a book and find an inspirational treasure house there, while five years ago the same book might not have meant anything to you. The book and its author haven't changed but you have. Moreover, the same passage or saying, when we contemplate it, will likely reveal meanings we hadn't thought of before. It is as with dreams which may seem puzzling at first, but when seen in the light of symbolic insight and life events comparisons, may become abundantly clear.

So, begin, if you haven't already done so, to build your own personal library of philosophical, and spiritual masterpieces. Consult the bibliographies in this section of our book. Select what really and truly makes **you** feel inspired, "good," and enlightened. There is not any prescribed tradition or ritual here. This is your meditative practice, it should be based on what you are finely "tuned to," reflecting your own deepest sense of wisdom. These works are not controversial or problematic but "lifter-uppers," inspirational wisdom of the ages.

Choose Your Time and Place If you wish to meet with someone, say for lunch, you know that by saying "someday we must have lunch," nothing ever happens because "someday" is not definite and is merely a tool of procrastination. What we need to do is set a definite date — time and place, agreed to by both parties. It may sound somewhat of an oversimplification to mention this with regards to the practice of meditation but here too, the same "business" principle applies; this time the promise is once more to yourself.

What is the best time and duration for contemplation? It is a personal matter, as observed previously; for many active, creative people a brief affirmative meditation session of from five to ten minutes at the start of the day is likely suitable. For your daily period of deeper contemplation it is important that there are no vital time limitations that would cause you to keep looking at your watch to see if there's enough time left — this causes distress and defeats the purpose of our practice. So, for most, the end of the day will be the most suitable time. Decide to give yourself ample time, say half an hour at the start. It could be less, most likely it will become longer but the strict "setting" or outlining of time limits is, again because of the nature of the practice, not helpful. Be sure to select a private place for your meditation time. Do not permit interruptions, not even the telephone. This is **YOUR** TIME and so **you** are the priority — everything else, T.V., radio, video, stereo, other persons is off limits.

The master teacher Jesus suggested that this kind of practice was like a going "into the closet" of one's own consciousness where the inner realm would be found, where all inspiration and guidance originate, where the source of all life and thought may be found. So, decide on your definite place and time(s) for consistent daily practice.

Relax and Be Comfortable Many a prospective devotee of meditation has been "scared off" because some instructor suggested bodily positions that were painful and entirely unnatural. All this is mental/emotional garbage. The only requirement is to be comfortable, because you want your attention to be directed to the subject of meditation and not to your physical body or any object or condition in your environment. Since comfort is once more a personal matter, you need to get in touch with your own feelings and decide what's right for you. It could be sitting up straight, with your feet flat on the floor and hands in your lap. It could also be lying down, totally supported physically without any effort on your part.

If you find it difficult to be relaxed, despite the creation of a comfortable environment, "do" a little relaxation affirmation for yourself, by saying quietly to yourself: "I am relaxed, my body is relaxed, every part of my being, every muscle, every fibre is relaxed, I feel totally relaxed" or (your own) words to that effect. It may also be helpful to direct your attention to the various parts of your body and gently suggest that they are now relaxed, such as "my legs are relaxed, my shoulders are relaxed" etc.

If you go over your whole body in this way, gently and quietly, you will find yourself becoming more and more relaxed. Or, you may wish to address your suggestion only to those physical areas that seem stressed to you. You will find, with a little practice that in this way you will be able to eliminate distress, tension and pains. Your body has no choice but to respond to your subconscious mind which controls it and it in turn is subject to the firm, first person, present tense suggestions pronounced with quiet conviction by means of the conscious mind. Biofeedback technology has in recent decades confirmed what meditators and mystics have known for ages.

STEP III: SELECT YOUR THEME

Why not just "sit there" and see what "comes?" Well, what "comes" is likely a "stream of consciousness" consisting of images, situations and problems from your "memory bank" of the subconscious which you will find anything but peaceful and uplifting. You want to achieve a sense of serenity and if possible, a picture of the "archetype of perfection" (C. Jung's expression) within you. Therefore you select a thought, an idea, a paragraph, a saying from your inspirational literature which seems right to you at that moment; even the selection of that thought will be an almost or entirely "guided" event. Your unconscious knows your desire and also your needs of which your spiritual self is aware and delivers a theme appropriate for your contemplation at that moment. It is in just the same fashion that our inner intelligence selects, "writes," produces and delivers an appropriate dream at the right moment to resolve a problem.

So, if you have chosen, for example, the theme "Peace, be still" (Jesus' frequent greeting-affirmation) it will, or may, feel to you that somehow, the theme has "chosen you." This is not unusual and much to be welcomed: we are "on the beam" of the Infinite. Joel Goldsmith speaks of it as "grace."

STEP IV: THINK GENTLY ABOUT YOUR THEME

You may wish, if you have selected your theme as a result of reading a few paragraphs of inspirational writing, to review again the context of the theme that "clicked" with you at that moment. Then take the theme within you, perhaps repeating it gently a few times, asking as it were, what does this mean to me at this moment? What is the feeling that comes to me when I think about this idea, and what is its cosmic, universal meaning? Is this the meaning the inner wisdom conveys to me to calm or heal some area of my life's experience?

Take your time, better yet you won't actually be aware of time, in this process. Play with your theme in your mind, seeking for the significance of the idea. Do not allow your mind to dwell on particulars of circumstances, challenges, past experiences or problems of any kind. Don't hurry or push your thinking, simply contemplate, reflect and let the inner meaning of your theme occupy your entire relaxed attention. Likely, other thoughts, images and ideas, similar to the one that is your main theme, will come into your awareness. If they seem "in tune" and enhance the meaning you are contemplating you'll welcome this spiritual addition, and continue your enriched reflection.

You may wish to maintain a journal of your meditation experiences, including your main themes and the other meaningful ideas and feelings that come to you, much in the way you'd keep a dream journal. This too, allows for an interesting record not just of your "progress" in the practice on the contemplative path but also in terms of additional insight into what's happening in your unconscious. Perhaps the most fascinating aspect of your practice is the concluding "step," which is described as . . .

STEP V: LISTEN IN THE SILENCE

Contemplation and philosophical reflection as suggested in this book lead to a deep peace and also, to a need for creative silence where words, images, activity cease — yet you are awake and aware. At this point in your meditative experience, you may find that the universal wisdom-in-you has "something" to convey to you, uniquely your own private experience. Be open, be quiet, be receptive to this "intuitive guidance." No one can predict in what way your contemplative silence will communicate what you will need to know at that time, any more than you will be able to predict the contents of your next dream. It is unusual for many people to anticipate such an experience because we are so used to competitive, directional, controlled thinking processes. Welcome the change for it enhances the quality of your individual life beyond words to adequately describe.

But — even if "nothing happens" of any unusual nature — this too is all right. There's no prescription and no failure here. There will always be an increased awareness of feelings of peace, serenity and a sense of oneness with life as well as mastery over one's emotions and thinking. The "end" of your meditation will come as naturally as the end of a dream or a meal. You will know and you will cherish that wonderful relaxed feeling for some time. If sleep is your next "planned thing" (can we call it that?) you'll find this an excellent choice of sequence, for your sleep will now be more restful and beautiful, and your feelings of well-being as well as all aspects of your health and the meaning of your dreams will be enhanced. When dawn comes you'll be better prepared for a creative day than ever before and you'll love your new-found life.

Chapter 20 will expand on the intuitive development hinted at here. But before that we need to direct our attention to two related areas of our learning of the art of contemplation: how to overcome the difficulties we may experience when deciding to commit ourselves to this practice and alternate techniques of meditation. And so, our fascinating inner journey continues in our next chapter. Meanwhile, if you have made the decision to become a meditator in the manner suggested by the above five definitive steps, you have now joined that invisible, yet very real, relatively small number of human "souls" who though we dwell in the physical dimension of life on this planet, are aware of another, greater dimension where the limitations of life are less certain and the promise of real fulfillment and awareness of cosmic infinity are felt as an increasing possibility. Then, the unknown beckons with real delight and fear is finally replaced by an ocean of understanding wisdom. The former lonely self becomes one with all intangible life, energy, warmth and beauty, the belongingness of the Infinite.

Bibliography & Recommended Further Reading

Underhill, Evelyn: Practical Mysticism
    N.Y.: E.P. Dutton & Co., 1943
Underhill, Evelyn: Mysticism
    N.Y.: Meridian, 1960
Waite, Arthur Edward: Lamps of Western Mysticism
    N.Y.: Rudolf Steiner Publ., 1973
Stace, Walter T.: The Teachings of the Mystics
    N.Y.: Mentor, 1960
Godwin, George: The Great Mystics
    London: Watts & Co., 1949
Zaehner, R.C.: Mysticism, Sacred and Profane
    N.Y.: Galaxy, Oxford Univ. Press, 1961
Staal, Frits: Exploring Mysticism
    Markham, Ontario: Penguin, 1975
Happold, F.C.: Mysticism
    Baltimore, Maryland: Penguin, 1975
Jones, Rufus M.: The Flowering of Mysticism
    N.Y.: Macmillan Co., 1939
Gaynor, Frank: Dictionary of Mysticism
    N.Y.: Philosophical Library,l 1953
Huxley, Aldous: The Perennial Philosophy
    London: Fontana, 1958
Plotinus: Enneads Vols. I, II & III - Transl.: A.H. Armstrong
    Cambridge, Mass: Harvard Univ. Press, 1966
Grier, Albert C. & Lawson, Agnes M.: Truth and Life
    N.Y.: Little, Ives, 1922
Unity School: Daily Word, monthly publication
    Unity Village, Mo.: Unity School of Christianity, each month
Sinetar, Marsha: Ordinary People as Monks and Mystics. Lifestyles for
    Self-Discovery
    N.Y.: Paulist Press, 1986

CHAPTER 18

IN THE GARDEN OF TRANQUILLITY

"We should have done well, I think, to be satisfied with
the aspect of peace."

The Diary, Volume I
Virginia Woolf (1882-1941)

Just as a splendid garden of trees, shrubs and plants is nourished and supported by the soil in which the vegetation is firmly rooted, so the beautiful results of peace, guidance and oneness in our personal experience are impossible without the unwavering support of the invisible unconscious garden of the mind. It is in this garden of tranquility that the nourishment of the spirit and the conditioning through consistent practice have done their beneficial work. All contemplative meditators, no matter what their cultural background, are aware of this intangible nursery of tranquillity in which they "dwell." In this atmosphere of peace and serenity the devotee is able to cope better with all the vicissitudes of life without becoming disturbed.

So, having taken the basic and essential steps to contemplative meditation we are now prepared to proceed with the cultivation and design of our own garden of tranquillity. We shall look at several practical considerations. Considerations is the correct term because these suggestions need to be considered and applied carefully, not just read and left alone. Let us remember our personal commitment to give it our "best shot" in terms of a controlled period of time and now extend that commitment to ourselves to include the removal of barriers that have plagued those who have tried but gave up. Development of our consciousness is not difficult — but it does require consistency.

However, even given a sincere person's determination, if the expected results are not realized in a reasonable period of time, that person will not continue. The following considerations are designed to overcome the difficulties most people experience when taking up contemplation and are intended to prepare the way for future beneficial exercise of this practice.

LET YOUR SUBCONSCIOUS HELP

One of the functions of your subconscious mind is to automatically produce a certain state of being after that state has been repeatedly consciously induced. We call this a conditioned reflex and it is by means of this process that we learn our skills such as driving a car or typing. A repeated motion becomes subconsciously accepted and we perform it under the same circumstances "without thinking." This "law of mind" may be applied to help us become more effective meditators. The ancient Hindu practitioners knew this and in the Vedic scriptures, among the oldest of known literary efforts, the "mantra" (Sanskrit: "instrument of thought" or literally "man/think") is suggested as a prayer or incantation to produce a quiet state of mind. A word-sound consistent with a meaning will produce the state of consciousness intended.

The easiest way to understand and apply this principle is to take one word, for example "peace" and become consciously aware of it whenever you feel really peaceful. Every time you allow yourself to relax and feel peaceful, regardless of the means, quietly repeat to yourself the word "peace." It could, be any word that you designate as meaning peace to you, serenity, tranquillity, calm, etc. or a translation into another language known by your subconscious mind. You could even select a meaningless word and give it the meaning of peace, just for you. Now, let us assume that we are saying consciously "peace" (or the chosen word) whenever we really feel peaceful and we keep this up for a week or so.

Now, suppose that there is an occasion when you feel you're going to be upset — in dense traffic for instance. At the moment you feel the anger rise within you, deliberately say "peace" in the same way you have repeatedly done when you did feel peaceful. What happens? A peaceful feeling will come over you and replace the tendency toward anger. Autosuggestion of this nature has a powerful ability to help us balance our emotions. Keep a few choice "mantras" of meaningful words or phrases in your mental storehouse to be used when stressful conditions are at hand. It will not replace the main objective of contemplation, but it will be useful as a preface to it. There is no need to mystify this procedure or to make some sort of elaborate ritual out of it.

Keep it simple, use it "as required" as you would a recipe or prescription. Meaningful words such as peace, love, truth, beauty, light, joy and wisdom are excellent key words to utilize in this way.

EXPAND YOUR PRACTICE

Contemplative meditation practice should not be looked upon as "the only way" or "the right way" to meditate, but rather as a "highway" whereas there are many creative ways to go beyond the technique described in our basic steps. Here are some suggestions of methods and aids that have been tried and found helpful in numerous courses of instruction and in meditation literature.

a. **The Counteraction Method** Sometimes we find ourselves in a state of fear and worry that makes it impossible to keep focused on our chosen theme no matter what we do to try to relax and concentrate. Then it is time to do some rational thinking. Analyze what's happening to you, what **emotion** dominates that you don't want. Identify it and choose a theme that counteracts that undesirable emotion. Let's say its worry over what might happen to someone you care about. Now think of all the statements of wisdom you have access to that affirm the opposite, the sure confidence that there's nothing to worry about and that everything will work out just fine.

Supposing you have selected the statement "All things work together for good" or harmony. Take this saying for your theme, concentrate on it, let it sink in and proceed as per our basic instruction. This is an effective way of dissolving the worrisome mood and what's more, to instill a sense of optimism and confidence. Since thought is creative, this kind of meditation also helps, at unconscious levels to bring about the desired solution to the problem that triggered the worry attitude in the first place.

b. **The White Light Method** We are all caring persons and it isn't always easy to dismiss the images of perceived suffering when we've witnessed scenes of disease and deterioration such as encountered in a hospital. What do you do when you can't help but think of that "patient" there? A relative calls you and informs you of an accident that involves someone you deeply love. Can we still meditate? Yes, we can, but now it's wise to use your faculty of positive visualization and make the picture of that person the subject of your contemplation. Not as an individual "suffering" but by imagining her or him well and whole and surrounded by a bright healing light that is dissolving all the shadows of infirmity. Hold that picture of divine perfection until you can feel its warm, healing effect on you, then silently, gently give thanks to the Infinite Healing power and presence in you and your loved one for the healing now being affected. If you find it too difficult to fully accept a complete healing, imagine it as a process, something that is now set in motion and is being carried out with incredible intelligence and energy.

c. **The Koan Technique**   Thanks to the long and interesting tradition of the Zen Buddhist teachings (see bibliography) we have access to another beautiful and sometimes humorous technique of contemplation. It too is a form of imagination as the "Koan" is a short story or fable that plays as a brief video through the workshop of your mind. The imagery creates a certain feeling that sometimes leads to an enlightening insight in your world, sometimes it takes you beyond the rational world of predictable thinking.

An example is the story of the Zen master, who couldn't teach a particular student any wisdom, because the pupil wouldn't stop talking about his own opinions. At the tea ceremony the master poured tea into the student's cup, until it was full and still he kept pouring. Of course, the recipient protested loudly. When the master stopped pouring he explained: "Just as I cannot pour tea into a full cup, I cannot give you Zen (the way or wisdom) as long as your mind is full of your own ideas. Empty the mind first." Now, this little story seems almost too simple to deserve our attention. Yet, as you allow yourself to dwell upon it, to play it through your mind and then repeat the next day and perhaps again a few days later, you may be surprised what may "come" to you as a result. Try the koans, you may get to appreciate them as many mystics have before you.

d. **Audio as Meditation Background**   Some people prefer to contemplate in complete silence, while others prefer relaxing music in the background or sometimes even as their main object of contemplation. Experiment, use what appears to be helpful to you and make it yours.

e. **Art in Contemplation**   Viewing a great work of art such as a painting or sculpture and letting your feelings and emotions flow freely through your consciousness can be an enriching way of contemplating. Videos also can be helpful.

f. **Symbols in Contemplation**   There are meditators who feel absolutely wonderful as they meditate on the flame of a candle, an arrangement on a chosen altar, the sound and sight of a fountain or waterfall, the fascination of a lit fireplace, an exquisite flower or the aroma of burning incense. Mythology is full of marvellous symbols that lend themselves to fascinating contemplation. Consult the works of Joseph Campbell and Carl Jung's masterpiece, "Man and His Symbols" and similar literature.

OVERCOMING LIFESTYLE DIFFICULTIES

Some of the main reasons why people wishing to meditate find it hard to do so — and the suggested solutions are:

a. **Other People**   There may be those close to us who don't like to see us grow. They may voice opposing disagreeable opinions and even ridicule. The answer is to keep your own counsel; do not discuss your meditation with disagreeable persons. It is a private matter, and no one has the right to tell you not to follow your chosen path. Accept no human authority over you but be guided by the Higher Presence within you.

b. **Too Much Effort**   We are so accustomed to "push" ourselves in goal-directed, competitive living that we may want to hear the voice of intuition or feel the desired tranquillity before these have a chance to mature. The answer is to change your intent from goal- directed, horizon-directed to point-of-life or moment directed. When we dance, the objective is not to reach a spot on the floor but to enjoy the movement and spirit of it. So, let it be, relax and enjoy your peaceful time. Don't try to push to achieve something.

c. **Sense of Waste of Time**   Have you ever sat down to meditate and you kept thinking: This is a waste of valuable time, I could/should be doing such and such, etc.? The answer: if we think this, we need to think again: this **is** spending time in an infinitely valuable way to enhance and ennoble all aspects of your life. The work ethic is healthy but in it we require a proper balance as to what is important. Love yourself enough to meditate. If time pressure is the problem, re-read and apply the ideas outlined in chapter 9 of this book.

d. **Interruptions** Usually the culprits here are the telephone and other people "barging in." The answer: be firm in keeping your meditation time and place strictly private and off limits. Be absolutely consistent and insistent in this. Get a telephone answering device and activate it when you are in meditation. Take charge of your time/space!

e. **I'm Too Tired** In my own three decades of teaching meditation, one of the most frequently expressed problems is: I try to contemplate but I fall asleep because I'm so tired. Answer: don't be too hard on yourself if your relaxing results in healthy sleep. You must have needed that badly! Plan your life so you will not be so tired, perhaps more effective time management is your solution here too. Then, let it be, just try again.

OVERCOMING RELIGIOUS BARRIERS

The novice devotee of meditation practice frequently harbors an inner child that was subject to traditional religious doctrine, some of which may have been utterly opposed to the least suggestion of meditation. So, as the student practices thinking for her or himself, the old objections occasionally may "pop up." How to deal with them effectively?

a. **If Religious Terminology Bothers You** You are reading wisdom literature, perhaps the writings of Joel Goldsmith. You come across terms such as "god," "grace," "the Bible says," "Christ," etc. which remind you of a time when you were made to feel like an insignificant sinner, subject to fear, guilt and damnation, even though these terms mean something entirely different and mystical in the book you now are reading. The most helpful answer here is, in the Master Jesus' words "not to resist evil," that is, don't fight it or give consent to conflict in your mind. Rather, either leave that book alone for now or consciously replace the "offending" word(s) with acceptable substitutes. For "god" we can substitute Infinite Intelligence, or the Cosmic Spirit or the Wisdom of the Universe or the Higher Power. Adapt terminology to your own meaningful use. That way you won't be "turned off" or bothered.

b. **Meditation is "of the devil"** Fundamentalist Christian theology believes in an active evil spirit that rules the world together with their male god. Realize this is just someone's opinion and has no rational basis for truth or evidence. Meditation is, on the whole, a way of getting rid of evil and destructive thoughts and becoming increasingly aware of the presence of the one and only spirit of life. The harm that has been done by fundamentalism in all world religions is obvious and for all to see. But the fear of hell and damnation is still a powerful motivation for the converted who are convinced of their irrational destructive cause. Be sure you cleanse your mind once and for all of all superstition. If it enters the sacred silence of your soul meditation, it ruins everything and causes no end to strife and inner conflict. My friend, the late author Joseph Murphy, used to say that all the water in the ocean cannot sink the ship unless it gets on the inside. So it is with destructive thinking. Don't allow it to happen to you.

OVERCOMING INNER RESISTANCE

Let us be honest, there are those times when we are our own worst enemy, when we ourselves are sowing weeds in our garden of tranquillity. Here are a few of the most common species and their antidotes:

a. **"I Don't Have Enough Understanding"** See this opinion for what it is: nonsense. It just isn't true. If you will just **use** the understanding and awareness you now have, you will be guided to the next steps. Continue to practice what you know and study the meditation and wisdom literature. In this way you'll continually expand your mystical horizons and gain self confidence that makes you feel adequate.

b. **Interfering of Other Thoughts** If the stream of consciousness that comes into your awareness keeps on coming despite all your efforts to stop it, again choose not to resist evil. Pretend it is a parade you are watching on some festive occasion and watch it with intense interest. Like discovering the content and meaning of your dreams (chapter 5) you'll discover something valuable about the activity in your unconscious THAT YOU MAY WELL NEED TO BECOME AWARE OF.

So, watch the parade, be aware, draw your conclusions and watch the end of the parade which will surely come. Now you are at peace, at last.

c. **Fear of psychic happenings** Many of us have picked up all kinds of irrational beliefs connected with meditation, that may still frighten us, such as the appearance of ghosts and demons, the loss of control over oneself, the movement of familiar objects etc. The answer simply is: do not anticipate harmful, fearful effects and they won't occur. Remember, your subconscious tends to deliver what has been suggested to it, so don't suggest anything negative. Any such ideas are based on a basic misunderstanding of what meditation really is. When we comprehend that we, as individuals, are in reality becoming aware of the one Presence within us, which is Spirit, Love, Beauty, Truth, Light, Intelligence, Energy and Wisdom, all fear disappears and any superstition to the contrary, no matter how long it may have been believed, is remembered no more. Think of what happens to the darkness, when you turn on the light in your room. It no longer holds any power or influence for it was merely the absence of light. When consciousness becomes enlightened it does not fear the previous errors because it now perceives right answers and the pathway of growth and development of the soul is assured.

The garden of tranquillity is a delightful place. You are joined here by the mystics of all time who have become endowed with the Wisdom of the Ages. Can we think of another place in consciousness we would rather be? With Virginia Woolf we would do well to be satisfied with peace . . .

Bibliography & Recommended Further Reading

Spalding, Baird T: Life and Teaching of the Masters of the Far East
Marina del Rey, Calif: DeVorss & Co., 1964 Volumes I through V

Sohl, Robert and Carr, Audrey eds.: The Gospel According to Zen
N.Y.: Mentor, 1970

Stryk, Lucien & Ikemoto, Takashi: Zen Poems Prayers Sermons Anecdotes Interviews
N.Y.: Anchor, Doubleday, 1965

Kapleau, Philip ed.: The Three Pillars of Zen
Boston: Beacon, 1967

Suzuki, D.T.: Zen Buddhism
N.Y.: Doubleday, Anchor, 1956

Suzuki, D.T.: Manual of Zen Buddhism
N.Y.: Grove, 1960

Suzuki, D.T.: Mysticism, Christian & Buddhist
N.Y.: Perennial, Harper & Row, 1971

Suzuki, D.T.: The Field of Zen
N.Y.: Perennial, Harper & Row, 1970

Watts, Alan W.: The Spirit of Zen
London: John Murray, 1958

Watts, Alan W.: Does it Matter?
N.Y.: Vintage, Random House, 1970

Watts, Alan W.: Out of the Trap
South Bend, Indiana: And Books, 1985

Watts, Alan W.: The Supreme Identity
N.Y.: Vintage, Random House, 1972

Swearer, Donald K.: Secrets of the Lotus; Studies in Buddhist Meditation N.Y.: Macmillan Co., 1971

Khan, Hazrat Inayat: The Unity of Religious Ideals
Deventer, Holland: N. Kluwer, 1949

U.G./Arms, Rodney, ed.: The Mystique of Enlightenment
Bangalore, India: Akshaya Publ., 1992

CHAPTER 19

UNLIMIT YOUR THINKING

"Do you grieve when a light bulb burns out? It's the light, the energy behind it, not the bulb that counts."

A Fire in the Mind
Joseph Campbell (1904-1987)

When the great French composer Camille Saint-Saëns (1835–1921) began publishing one marvellously universal concerto after another, incorporating the total sweep of the keyboard with an almost infinite range of sounds, his envious critics accused him of "borrowing from Bach to Offenbach." Saint-Saëns' answer was: "Of course, my music has the sounds of every genius that preceded us, why don't you just sit back and enjoy it?"

Those of us who have really gotten deeply into the art of contemplation experience it as a most enjoyable activity. Because of its universal, cosmic dimension, it gives us the feeling, not only of transcendence, but also, of letting go of limitations, barriers and restrictions of all kinds. This is an essentially freeing experience, which, to some, can be frightening, as anything we don't know much about may invite a response of fear. Likewise, many people who would like to expand their knowledge and practise of meditation don't succeed because they are so used to thinking in terms of limitations.

This deserves our attention because I don't know of any person who is NOT subject to and accustomed to the habit of thinking in terms of limitations, hence we carry the habit into our contemplative life as well. Our everyday life and activity is completely, almost without exception, defined by boundaries. We drive a car and everywhere we are faced with and bounded by limitations and restrictions: a certain lane to stay in, limits to the speed we're allowed to travel, lights that tell us when we're permitted to proceed and when not; other signs tell us to yield, or slow down, or stop or turn etc. When you reach your place of work everything you do there is also subject to human and technological limitations. Even the sport you pursue or the choir you sing in, or the instrument you play, or the letter you write and mail are all subject to precise restrictions.

A central fact of our life's experience is that from the moment we arrive as a living individual we are forced to think, image, speak, feel and behave in terms of limitation — measured by space, time, regulations and boundaries of all sorts. Now, we're becoming contemplative meditators and we are invited, by the cosmic, spiritual mystics before us, to let our minds pursue infinity, to think and become aware of unlimited, boundless oceans of life, to unlimit our thinking; the jump is so great, the culture shock so traumatic and the change so enormous that many find it impossible to walk this kind of path of thought and reflection. What to do? Simply put, how can we, "normal people," **unlimit** our thinking?

Here are major avenues of thought that lead to unlimiting one's thinking. The secret, as always in mastering an art as personal as contemplation, lies in the actual practising — go beyond mere reading and thinking about these to **doing** and the results will be more convincing than any advice any mentor could convey to you.

BECOME MORE AWARE OF MYSTICAL MOMENTS

The eminent contemporary American Humanist philosopher Corliss Lamont says that normal people under the impact of a great intellectual, emotional or spiritual experience can suddenly become aware of a profound new insight or adopt an entirely fresh way of life and thinking. Think about this for a moment. When did you, in the last little while, really "follow your bliss," as Joseph Campbell used to say and have a transcendent experience? Was it while listening to a beautiful song or symphony? Was it while looking at a glorious landscape at sunset? Was it while listening to some immortal lines from Shakespeare spoken by a brilliant actress? Was it while watching puppies frolic? Was it while you were "tuning in" to the soul of a loved one in perfect silence? Was it when you were desperately looking for a solution to a problem and that inner voice told you to enter this bookstore and open this particular book and "bingo!" — there was your answer?

We have all witnessed such ineffably beautiful moments of exaltation. They felt like transformations of our spirit and momentarily we were unaware of the usual limitations of our existence. Moreover, they were also moments in which we sensed that our lives have some meaning beyond the time-space-regulations existence. As we become more alert, aware, and expectant of the mystical, our awareness will report an increasing frequency of such moments.

The mystical and transcendental are not contained in a separate world which most of us rarely enter, but rather interpenetrate our ordinary world so that consciousness of the mystical is potentially present in every moment and under all circumstances — at least this is what the spiritual masters have said. For us then it would seem highly beneficial to live in an attitude of the expectation of the mystical at all times. Furthermore, we can allow ourselves the time and opportunity to be more often exposed to the sights and sounds of the sublime and the truly beautiful. Reverse the usual media attitude of looking for the worst and start looking for the best in all circumstances and more of it will appear to us. That is the way all great art has survived the critics and cynics.

DETERMINE WHAT INFINITY MEANS TO YOU

We have already frequently implied in this book that WORDS represent only that meaning which is identified by the consciousness of the perceiving individual. Quimby used to say: words are like nuts, some are full, some are empty. What determines which it will be? Our own understanding, of course. Hence, the word "god" may mean one thing to one person, and something entirely different to another. Does this matter? Sometimes, yes. A woman who had been severely abused by her alcoholic father in childhood attended a seminar in which the presenter referred to "God" as "father." This person had difficulty staying in the seminar, let alone, benefiting from its instruction. She identified with the term "father" on the basis of her own experience and subsequent belief, and the results were understandably unhappy. So, when we start contemplating the infinite aspects of being we need to be sure the words and terms we use are truly unlimiting to us and not another description of a restricted world.

In his profound book "The Art of Meditation" the late master of this art, Joel Goldsmith explains the process he had to go through in order for him to arrive at a satisfactory description for what he calls the "synonyms for God" and arrived at the term "Infinite Invisible." Why this one? "Because," he says, "the Infinite Invisible did not mean anything that I could understand." This approach is not unlike that of some Zen masters who broke through limited, rational thinking by posing irrational questions, such as: what is the sound of the clapping of one hand? And: what did your face look like one year before your were born?

There is, however, another approach that may appeal to you. It does not imply a chasm or contradiction between the rational and the mystical. This approach is eloquently represented by Phineas Parkhurst Quimby after a lifetime of investigation of consciousness from a psychosomatic point of view. The dynamics of therapy with thousands of persons convinced him of the inadequacy of the usually held concepts of God or a supreme being. To him "perfect wisdom embraces every idea in existence" and that deepest spiritual being which is also the highest is simply "an invisible Wisdom."

Now here we have an entirely different perception: "Wisdom" unlimits my thinking — I no longer have the "I and Thou" confrontation of philosopher Martin Buber. I no longer try to comprehend some sort of large person, a ghostlike entity that is sometimes here, sometimes not and that looks, as Emmet Fox used to say, a bit like an archbishop. No longer do we wonder about the impossible reconciliation between all the horrible evils of life and the unwillingness of a personal god to interfere and do something about it. No longer do we wonder if this god we speak of dwells in some part of our unconscious being and not in other parts. "Wisdom" we recognize as something else — we all have it, it is still "there" even if none of us were aware of it. This perception also recognizes the individual awareness of it as personal, warm and wonderful. We can never lose it but we can lose our awareness of it. Take it as the subject of your meditation and see what happens. Your thinking will become more and more free from the old barriers and contradictions and enjoy unlimited scope and vision.

We each have to find our own handle on the concept of infinity. Quimby found his and when we find our own, something may "click" and you are suddenly beyond traditional limited thinking about god.

VISUALIZE IMAGERY OF SUBSTANCE AND FORM UNIFIED

One way of achieving the "feel" of our cosmic oneness with all being is to allow our thinking to vividly imagine that oneness in symbols, which are material, while signifying, a spiritual truth. To clarify the relationship between the universal and the individual, meditators have for ages imaged the distinctness, yet also oneness of, all forms with their substance. We may think of the ocean, a popular imagery, wild and furious, noisy perhaps and expressing as waves — the universal and the individual distinct, yet one in an immense dynamic field of activity. We may even see its end, the horizon, but we know if we reached the horizon, there would yet be another horizon, and so on, into infinity. All here is boundless energy, alive and dynamic. Similarly, we may think about the gold in a ring. The form, individualized use of its substance, is not apart from that substance but one with it and yet there are no opposites, no mastery or exploitation on the part of one over the other. All is the manifestation of sublime harmony.

Or, think of the sun and the sunbeam. The source and the emanation are one, yet distinct. We appreciate both, one without the other could not be, one does not take away from the other, it is the energy, as Joseph Campbell points out, that matters. We contemplate to become aware of our true relationship with the primal energy of life. The master teacher Jesus referred to this vital relationship as that of the vine and its branches (Gospel of John, 15:5). The branches could do nothing without the nourishment of their source, the vine. "I am the vine" (the Universal Christ), "you are the branches" (the Individual Christ). We all have the Wisdom within us, yet it does not diminish, even though billions of us are aware of it and letting it express through us. This is, as Matthew Fox points out, "the coming of the Cosmic Christ."

MEDITATE ON BEING BEYOND SPACE AND TIME

Many regular and deeply contemplative meditators have found that when they wish to relax, a relaxation meditation can make them feel so tranquil that they have little or no sense of weight. Furthermore, we may find that we are no longer directly "limited by" and "attached to" our immediate environment but, as in our dreams, can "travel" in imagination in any direction to sense "infinity of space." Such seemingly strange experiences are really not strange at all but a normal phenomenon of the aware and awakened consciousness. Historically, mystics have known it in all cultures and various religious traditions.

Our own culture, having been familiar to some degree, with the Bible, knows the recognition of going beyond ordinary conceptions of space when contemplating a higher, cosmic spirit or mode. In Psalm 8:3-4 we read of a "frail mortal" realizing something of the awesome dimensions of the world of outer space as (s)he wonders if there is a consciousness that is "mindful" of her/him. In Psalm 139:7-11 the poet realizes there is no escape from the cosmic spirit or wisdom of life — it is everywhere even if we decide to make a hell out of our existence or find ourselves groping in the dark. Wisdom is not subject to the limiting concepts of darkness and light, of east and west, of up and down. The mystic recognizes it as "the presence."

There have always been those who, fascinated by psychic phenomena, wished to bring some fame to themselves or break through their daily boredom by experimenting with their ability to leave their bodies and have out-of-body travelling experiences. This promptly frightened others out of their wits and devout fundamentalists cried out that it was "of the devil." Anyone who masters some degree of efficiency in contemplative meditation knows that it is normal and natural to experience life as consciousness and that it is an enjoyable, even thrilling "thing" to consciously unlimit yourself by letting your consciousness travel outside of your physical boundaries.

Your imagination can take you right now beyond your chair, providing you are relaxed and not afraid, to any "place" you may choose to "go." I have practised this natural phenomenon many times in meditation classes and of course, it can be done by individuals alone. It would be a philosophical question to decide if the "trip is real" that is, do we see what's now "out there" when you allow your imaginative awareness to leave your building, float upward and look down on your town or city and beyond, even into outer space? I have witnessed the testimony of those who were in a coma in hospital for many days and having returned to ordinary consciousness reported events and conversations which actually took place, not in their rooms or near them, but distances away and which were verified to be accurate both as to persons and in time and place. If life is consciousness this should not surprise us and it is high time that this whole area becomes included in the natural study of the human experience rather than looked upon as "weird" and discarded as illusionary nonsense. These phenomena happen and they happen through normal people.

The philosophically inclined and meditative ancient author of the biblical book of Ecclesiastes provided our culture with a profound reflection on the value and role of **time** (chapters 1, 3). Time too may be experienced as consciousness and in meditation we can go "backward" and "forward" in time as we choose. You can meet your "inner child" as many contemporary and advanced therapists now suggest, and hug, love and heal that little kid inside you and make it feel better, thus letting go of repressed hurt feelings that may have prevented your sense of true self worth. Contemplation may thus be a healing experience but it is not, as we have observed, primarily intended as therapy.

When we let our imagination freely travel back over the events of our lifetime, from today to yesterday, to last week, to last month, last year and back through the preceding years into receding adolescence and childhood — we'll find this too can be an eventful, interesting and enjoyable experience and sometimes also insightful and revealing. Such contemplations may extend beyond personal memory and imagery back through the years before your own direct knowing, into history. We may even find ourselves, in our chosen contemplation present at "long gone" events, listening to the Buddha explaining enlightenment under a bo tree or to Jesus sharing his wisdom on the shore of a lake.

Everything that has ever happened is available to your imagination and the reality of each chosen contemplation experience will be of distinct value to you, far beyond a casual use of the time-space-event limited imagination to which we are accustomed. Unlimit your thinking: just move through the barriers you always assumed were there. One of the finest ways to describe this freedom is recorded by the biographers of Joseph Campbell's life, Stephen and Robin Larsen. Professor Campbell's friend Emile Durkheim said: "Myth can only be understood when one is transparent to the transcendent." This comes oh so close in conveying what we become aware of in contemplation when the traditional barriers are removed and we have our being in the infinite ocean of life itself.

FAMILIARIZE YOURSELF
WITH THE LITERATURE OF INFINITY

We may feel ignorant and sometimes frustrated on our quest but you, the devotees of the Infinite, are not without teachers or resources. Many of these have already been mentioned and many more are listed as references in our bibliographies with each chapter in this section..

Of particular interest to meditators who desire to "go beyond" limited thinking are the great scriptures of the world religions. In the Bible we may wish to direct our attention to the many transcendental visions in the Book of Psalms, the Book of Ecclesiastes and the Gospel of John, especially the mystical chapters 12 through 17. There is a great deal of inspiration in the writings and anthologies of the mystics of all cultures and ages as well as the wisdom of the metaphysical philosophers such as Plato, Socrates, Plotinus, Marcus Aurelius, Benedict de Spinoza, George Berkeley, Gottfried Leibnitz, Georg Hegel, Karl Jaspers and Ralph W. Emerson.

All the idealist thinkers are helpful resources here and this naturally applies to all authors, poets and essayists of this vision. Many Hindu and Buddhist classics are excellent aids in unlimiting one's thinking. The Hindu Vedic scriptures, the Upanishads and the Bhagavad Gita, the Buddhist Wisdom of the Buddha and the great masters of Zen as well as the many more recent exponents such as Paramahansa Yogananda and the universal J. Krisnamurti can be of priceless assistance to you in becoming more and more aware of the infinity of life and consciousness. There is great beauty, truth and wisdom here and it is all ours, it is our heritage but it does require your choice and your attention.

Abandon yourself regularly to the all encompassing infinity of Wisdom. Words may not be adequate to describe your heightened joy of new found insight and meaning . . . And there's yet more!

Bibliography & Recommended Further Reading

Larsen, Stephen and Robin: A Fire in the Mind - The Life of Joseph
    Campbell
    N.Y.: Doubleday, 1991
Capra, Fritjof and Steindl-Rast, David: Belonging to the Universe
    San Francisco: Harper, 1991
Foster, David: The Philosophical Scientists
    N.Y.:Dorset, 1985
Lloyd, Donna H.: The View from Olympus — A New Gnostic Gospel
    Sedona, Arizona: Deltaran, 1991
Yogananda, Paramahansa: Metaphysical Meditations
    L.A.: Self-Realization Fellowship, 1969
Alcyone: At the Feet of the Master
    Adyar, Madras, India: Theosophical Publ., 1960
Yogananda, Paramahansa: The Master Said
    L.A.: Self-Realization Fellowship, 1953
Davis, Roy Eugene: The Teachings of the Masters of Perfection
    Lakemont, Georgia, CSA Press, 1979
Krisnamurti, J.: From Darkness to Light
    San Francisco: Harper & Row, 1980
Krisnamurti, J.: The First and Last Freedom
    N.Y.: Harper & Bros., 1954
Krisnamurti, J.: Think on These Things
    N.Y.: Harper & Row, 1964
Krisnamurti, J.: Life Ahead
    N.Y.: Harper & Row, 1975
Krisnamurti, J.: The Flame of Attention
    N.Y.: Harper & Row, 1983
Krisnamurti, J.: Commentaries on Living - Series 1, 2 & 3
    Wheaton, Illinois: Theosophical Publ., 1970

CHAPTER 20

USING YOUR INTUITION

*"Man must continually demonstrate the mastery of the physical
by the metaphysical faculties with which he is endowed."*

Utopia or Oblivion
R. Buckminster Fuller (1895-1983)

What will sustain us in the pursuit of our enterprise when the going gets tough? We have all known people who try to meditate, perhaps take a course or read a book or two on it, but do not acquire the habit of daily meditation, let alone master the art of contemplation. Why should we persist where others fail? The practical answer of course is: the benefits. When we realize the tremendous personal benefits of this practise we shall see that these far outweigh the costs, the objections. In my observation, those who gave up did not learn the art in the first place, then felt they were wasting time. Not having generated the self-awareness and self-esteem necessary, they decided it was not for them. Often criticism from those around them as well as the "falling back into" old habits of negative and cynical thinking makes them throw in the towel. All the excuses in the arsenal of the quitter do not add up to the benefits we are going to be discussing in this chapter. The major one of these is the development of the faculty of intuition.

When discussing creative thinking in Chapter 10 we recognized that intuition is important. Now we shall see that this is true not just in terms of the isolated, spontaneous moments we have all experienced when we had a "hunch" but the faculty of intuition is widely considered to be as important and decisive as our ability to think and plan. Examples in the worlds of business, invention as well as art abound. The story of the successful evolution of the McDonald fast food chain is but one.

When the late Mr. Ray Kroc was negotiating purchasing the name McDonald in 1960 when the enterprise was relatively small, he was asked to pay $2.7 million for it. Kroc was furious, and his lawyer thought it was outrageous. What to do? Call the product a "Krocburger?" He closed his office door, cussed up and down, threw things out of the window and carried on in anger for some time. Mr. Kroc had to make a decision between his rational opinion (what a rip-off, it's ridiculously expensive!) and his hunch or intuition (do it, it's the chance of a lifetime!). He decided, as we all know, to listen to what he called his "funny bone" and pay the price. Within twenty years of that moment, Kroc's hamburger chain, system-wide recorded sales in excess of $4.5 billion! What a story to illustrate the principle of prosperity: you will reap, providing you sow, you will receive, providing you give. You will realize your dream, providing you are willing to follow your intuition and take the necessary risks.

Intuition and the awareness of intuition was the key. And it is a benefit of contemplative meditation. Naturally, there are others and we will take just a little time to remind ourselves of these, before moving to a practical implementation of the personal use of the faculty of intuition.

Self-Esteem. Contemplation heightens your sense of worthiness and eliminates self-loathing, the cause of destructive addictions. We can assume two attitudes when, in deeper meditative states, we are aware of "something" vastly greater than we are. For instance, you may be seeing the tremendously impressive Rocky Mountains or a gorgeous sunset oceanside. Either we say (or think): how insignificant I am, I am next to nothing, a (religious) worm in the dust. Or we say: how wonderful and divine my consciousness is to "behold" this, a Universe sharing itself with me, in me, through me. You sense your unique individuality, you feel a new inner strength, you become more yourself, you respect yourself.

In contemplation we become, on a daily basis, aware of a Wisdom far beyond our comprehension, yet we are one with It and It has made Its home in us. The healthy roots of self-esteem are right here. This sense of self worth cannot be shaken by events or disappointments, or by mistakes you may make, or by opinions of others. Build your self-esteem on this rock of contemplative awareness and you will always be able to go back to it, a sound and reliable base upon which to build your life.

Healing Energy is a benefit of meditation, much of which will go unnoticed. Experts on the causation of disease ranging from Phineas Parkhurst Quimby to Carl Simonton and Bernie Siegel point out again and again how achieving peace within helps to reduce stress and anxiety, we get our minds on the inner wisdom and off worry and other negatives that interfere with the normal natural state of energy in your physical being, namely health. Meditation, as intended here, allows us to feel one with the Infinite, the source of health and energy, and to most of us who practise this awareness, we'll never know how much trouble we have prevented. It first becomes apparent in experiencing fewer colds, attacks of the flu, etc. Your new reaction to pressing upsetting circumstances is now relaxation instead of "cussing and pacing"   — how different, strangely more energetic and enjoyable life now is.

Cosmic Consciousness is probably the most fitting description of the other spiritual and more intangible benefits that come to the meditator. What is this "cosmic consciousness?"   Richard Bucke in his book by that title, tells of the wonderful feeling those who have been touched by it experience. He even includes "moral elevation". Once we've realized a sense of infinite love, a love that is able to dissolve inner discords, we no longer feel separated from life. To Jesus, the fulfilment of all the laws and restrictions on human behavior was summed up in the word love. But so many people don't feel this love — all they can see is trouble, injustice, crime, violence and all the negative, destructive phenomena dished up daily by their television set and newspaper. On the other hand, the person who takes up spiritual meditation and contemplation is able to transcend the physical world picture of the media and taste a different, superior world in which we feel the pulse of the love behind all there is in an infinite universe. Then the practitioner, and only then, feels something of that spiritual love now being imparted through her/him. Afterwards we find it difficult to judge, to resent and to hate anyone. With a realization of this cosmic consciousness we find it easier to live, we are easier to live with and we are naturally far more peaceful and serene. Cosmic consciousness is a process transforming our whole personality; we begin to love and care more because we understand and know more. We become more efficient, worry less, see the larger picture in issues and look for the best in circumstances and people too. The struggle and the striving cease and we are in the spiritual company of the great mystics, we feel something of what they felt. (See also Chapter 16)

Perhaps the summit or crowning glory of the cultivation of the art of contemplative meditation is the discovery, development and application of our inner faculty of . . .

Intuition. Everything we've been attempting to communicate in the preceding four chapters as well as the foregoing comments, demonstrates itself supremely in the hunches, guidance, direct knowing, synchronicity and intuitive awareness that is now open to us. Although not necessarily all who use intuition successfully are contemplative meditators, personal contemplation without a doubt enhances the intuitive faculty, deepens and perfects it.

All creative persons know this "intuitively." Read the lives of the great novelists, composers, inventors, social developers and artists — as well as C.E.O.'s (Chief Executive Officers) of successful corporate enterprises and you'll find people aware of and using their intuition. Some of the greatest benefactors of civilized life place it central in their personal achievement. Dr. Jonas Salk, the discover of the polio vaccine says of intuition: "I work with it, and rely upon it. It's my partner." Intuition has enabled people to predict accurately later technological developments: Leonardo da Vinci produced detailed drawings of a flying machine unheard of in his time. Robert Fulton, inventor of the steamboat and Samuel Morse, inventor of the telegraph started out as artists but their intuition led them to transform the lives of those in the society around them, who themselves had no such vision.

I had the distinct privilege of meeting the creative genius Dr. R. Buckminster Fuller, quoted above, with his wonderful wife Anne (both passed away within two days of each other after being together for sixty-six years, in July, 1983). "Bucky," as he was called, created the geodesic dome; he had developed the Dymaxion car in 1934, loaded with innovations that were not introduced in commercial automobiles for decades. What was the secret of his genius? Said he: "Inventors do not need a licence to invent. The Wright brothers did not have a licence from society to invent an airplane." Creative thinkers are far ahead of what he called "society's inertias and ignorant opposition." They follow their intuition and their inventions "are gradually conveying humanity from failure to success." When asked about the nature of intuition, Bucky answered: "I call intuition cosmic fishing. You feel a nibble, then you've got to hook the fish." He added that too many people get a hunch, then light up a cigarette and forget about it . . .

We know of numerous stories where people have intuitively known some vital truth, creating something completely new and novel no one had thought of, or we know of C.E.O.'s and others who could almost smell an impending failure or disaster and knew what to do to prevent it. Exciting stuff to be sure. The question for the meditator is: I may not have much of a sense or feel of this "cosmic fishing," how can I further develop my intuitive capacities through the use of contemplation?

The "process" of intuition, if we may take the liberty of calling it process (because intuition sometimes just "pops up" into awareness without a seeming process) appears to have five stages or phases.

PREPARATION: Creativity favors the prepared mind. In other words: do your homework, know all the facts there are to know about the question or project on which you seek guidance. Practitioners of the ancient Chinese I Ching or Book of Changes are fully familiar with all the various aspects, interpretations and possible applications of the materials they are using and no coherent conclusion can be reached without that knowledge and familiarity. Sometimes we meet people who think that intuition (and the whole world of metaphysical, mystical and spiritual thinking with its methods) can be used as a "shortcut" to success so the lazy mind is frequently attracted to the seeming promise of instant results. Nothing could be further from the profound truth that every inventor, writer, speaker, artist and leader who uses intuition for her/his benefit HAS FIRST DONE HER/HIS HOMEWORK, usually involving a great many hours of Winston Churchill's "blood, sweat and tears." We are not in the easy-get-rich-quick world of the cultist and the motivational schemer. So, for starters, if we are serious about obtaining an intuitive solution to a problem or challenge, gather all the facts, talk to the experts, do everything you know needs to be done to get the information available. Then define, in the end, exactly, in writing that is clear and to the point, what you want to know. And take your time.

AFFIRMATIVE CONTEMPLATION Now, in your meditation time (probably at the end of your day, for you wish to be absolutely private and not subject to time restraints or interruptions) let your mind, after having attained relaxation, gently "play" with the meaning of the question you have defined. Look at it, you now have in front of you the question you wish to have answered; you seriously seek guidance from the fountain of wisdom within you.

We do well to contemplate a little deeper what this really means. In the Upanishads, the Breath of the Eternal scripture of the Hindu mystics, the question appears: "At whose behest does the mind think? Who bids the body live? Who makes the tongue speak?" The "breath of the eternal," the cosmic wisdom of all mystic awareness is now PRESENT with you and what's more, you know it. You are now enveloped in this dynamic spiritual silence, with which you are already familiar because you experience it at the conclusion of each of your contemplative meditation sessions.

Now, the moment has come to affirm the statement you intuitively know to be true of you: "I am in the presence of Infinite Wisdom and it guides me, reveals and conveys the answer to me," using words that are **your words**. Remember Jesus advice, call no man your "spiritual father" or master or guru. You are your own authority, one is your source, the cosmic spirit is within you and "there is none other."

Remain in this contemplative mood until you feel your affirmation has "sunk into" your subconscious and has met with an as yet unconscious response from its deepest level. How do you know this for sure? Well, you just know. There is not a bit of doubt, uncertainty or worry in your mind. All is well, all feels good, you just "know." And you let it "be" at that.

INCUBATION We're now at the conclusion of our meditation; now what? If it is your habit to meditate immediately prior to going to sleep, that is likely what you will do in this case as well, but remember, there is a level of conscious intensity not usually present in contemplation, so it wouldn't be surprising if we were wide awake, wondering (and perhaps doubting too) if this were going to work. The rational mind may say: so where's our answer? If our meditation time was at any other time of the day or night, the same question may arise. All of this is normal but the energy is not flowing where we want it to go. We need to put our project into incubation as you would put a prepared dish on the backburner or into the oven of your stove.

Releasing and "letting go" expectantly does not mean forgetting or withdrawal of validity but knowing that the right answer will be revealed to you at the right time by the activity of your unconscious that knows infinitely more than our conscious mind how and when to bring about the desired response or solution.

Above all, when we "release it," we will lose our tension and have no anxiety about it. Just remain in an optimistic, quietly expectant attitude and let no one know what you are doing, unless your confidant is as tuned in to intuition and contemplation as you are. Repeat your affirmative meditation as you feel guided.

ILLUMINATION Now we come to the obviously unplanned stage, which nevertheless needs preparation. This is what in the ancient Greek world was know as Archimedes' Eureka experience. Arche means origin or beginning and here we have the mythological moment of truth, the revelation of revelation, the buoyancy principle: you KNOW you have the answer you were looking for. You may wake up in the middle of the night exclaiming (or at least thinking) loudly: I've got it, this is it! The answer may come in a dream, a "vision of the night," in reading a book you were led to open to a particular page, a remark you overheard, a lecture you attended on a hunch, a conversation as a result of a feeling you had about a chance meeting. Whatever the method, this is, for you the way of the guiding inner spirit and you know it. It works and you also know that. Now what?

VERIFICATION Now the time has come to test the idea. The inventor returns to the lab and works with what came to him/her. The painter returns to the easel, the composer to the keyboard and the novelist to the typewriter. The C.E.O. calls a meeting and throws the idea out for discussion, for follow-up, for verification of all aspects. This is the process of confirmation, perhaps also modification, and eventually application of the idea. Every practitioner of the intuitive way knows what to do. The drawing board of the mind takes on many forms but the point is, we never blindly act on an idea, we make sure within ourselves first, then by testing and working it out that what we are doing is sound. This does not mean we "back off" because of risk, nor do we reject because we have thought about it and it just seems foolish or "too far out." By verification we mean testing the truth of it, to make doubly sure what came to us is indeed the result of genuine intuition.

Intuition is a wonderful (full of wonder) part of authentic living we all really desire and deserve. The art of contemplation makes it possible and you will find that even if you do not consciously proceed with the five steps outlined above, your intuitive faculty will be gently sharpened and become more active and effective. This is a natural outcome and by-product of regular, contemplative practise. A life lived in this way becomes more and more guided, innovative, exciting and capable of what was previously thought of as impossible. This is a good thing because we'll be needing that capacity in substantial measure as we embark on the adventure of our journey into authenticity, the formation of an adequate philosophy of life and the discovery of meaning — yes, the meaning of it all . . .

Bibliography & Recommended Further Reading

Fuller, R. Buckminster: Utopia or Oblivion: The Prospects of Humanity
    N.Y.: Bantam, 1969

Hatch, Alden: Buckminster Fuller: At Home in the Universe
    N.Y.: Crown, 1974

Seymour-Smith, Martin (ed): Novels and Novelists
    N.Y.: St. Martin's Press, 1980

Betts, Glynne Robinson: Writers in Residence
    N.Y.: Viking Press, 1981

Sinkler, Lorraine: The Spiritual Journey of Joel S. Goldsmith, Modern
    Mystic   N.Y.:Harper & Row, 1973

Sadhu, Mouni: Meditation, An Outline for Practical Study
    N. Hollywood, CA: Wilshire, 1967

Wilhelm, Richard & Baynes, C.F. (transl.) The I Ching
    N.Y.: Bollingen Foundn., 1978

Wilhelm, Richard: The Secret of the Golden Flower
    N.Y.: Causeway, 1975

Murphy, Joseph: Secrets of the I Ching
    West Nyack, N.Y.: Parker Publ., 1976

Old, Walter Gorn: The Simple Way, Laotze
    Philadelphia: David McKay Co., 1939

Lao Tsu: Tao Te Ching
    N.Y.: Vintage Random House, 1972

Chuang Tsu: Inner Chapters
    N.Y.: Vintage Random House, 1974

Prabhavananda, Swami & Manchester, Frederick (transl.): The
    Upanishads — Breath of the Eternal
    N.Y.: Mentor, 1957

Prabhavananda, Swami & Isherwood, Christopher (transl.): The Song of
    God: Bhagavad-Gita   N.Y.: Mentor, 1954

Singer, Milton (ed): Krishna: Myths, Rites and Attitudes
    Chicago: University of Chicago Press, 1971

PART FIVE

THE ART OF REFLECTION
YOUR KEY TO MEANING

*"Guided by philosophical methods, I gain
awareness of authentic being. . ."*

Way to Wisdom
Karl Jaspers (1883–1969

CHAPTER 21

THE WORLD OF SYNCHRONICITY

"Synchronicity and seriality are modern derivatives of the archetypal belief in the fundamental unity of all things, transcending mechanical causality"

The Roots of Coincidence
Arthur Koestler (1905–1983)

Do you ever wonder if your life (your existence and being here) has any meaning? If and when you do, and you think and ponder, perhaps discuss and research the question and its possible answers, you are reflecting and philosophizing. The statement that "the unexamined life is not worth living," attributed to Socrates in ancient Greece some 2,400 years ago, still holds true for intelligent and aware persons today, in all walks of life and at all ages too. Perhaps it is not an exaggeration to say that in our culture, around the world today, the vast majority of people could care less. But there are those who feel this existential question stirring again and again in their consciousness and if you are one of them, chances are it won't leave you alone even if you are not in any great need.

For some, formal philosophy is a professional academic pursuit which expresses in teaching and writing. For others, the idea of philosophizing conjures up an image of pondering deep questions in an armchair by the fireplace. For this writer, reflecting, philosophizing and the need for finding the meaning in and of life has more traumatic roots. And if it is true, as most lovers of literature and art and music would agree, that we get more from a creation when we know where the auth is coming from, perhaps a personal note here is not out of place.

Strange and unlikely as it may seem, my own search for meaning started around age five or six, and particularly in more zi-ways, at age fifteen. You see, I was a youngster growing up occupied Holland during World War II. So, at an early a whole acquainted with suffering, violence, war, grief, hunger world world of fear and trembling. Witnessing this frightening are we made me think over and over again: "What's life all a

here? Why doesn't God, if there is a God, stop this holocaust?"
After my dear mother died as a result of the war and its aftermath, I
began questioning everything the Church was saying, as it made no sense
to me. Karl Jaspers, one of the great existential thinkers of our 20th
Century says that our quest for meaning, our need for philosophy starts
in three ways:

Wonder and curiosity As very young children we start asking
"why?" Why is the sky blue, why am I different from another person,
why was I born this way, why is there war, what is death? Or similar
questions. As for Plato, Aristotle and all the other great philosophers we
know about throughout recorded history, philosophizing has its source in
curiosity.

Doubt As we grow into adolescence we discover that much of
what we are being told is not true, reliable or complete. We begin to
doubt the statements, suggestions and opinions we hear around us and
want to find the truth for ourselves: how can we be **sure** of something?

Inadequacy Growing up in a world not of our own making and
regulated by persons and forces we do not control, as well as being
subjected to suggestions of smallness and insignificance, we seek to have
more **mastery** over our lives. **We** wish control of our destiny, so we seek
to understand and harness the forces of life and nature and our inner
selves to accomplish this. Our quest is based on our own sense of
weakness and inadequacy.

All of these sources were certainly alive and valid for me but I
would like to add that for me, the urgency of the quest was closer to
being rooted in despair and a sense of the absurd, than in the more
cely worded areas above. You may have had to face a crisis in your
life, perhaps your own philosophy of life is inadequate to handle
you are facing in your world of circumstances or your inner world
tion and reason. On the other hand, your search may be an
ng to a need for meaning that philosophers have also for twenty-
ries observed in THINKING individuals. Where do we turn for
disnd reliable answers? We have a choice of **two approaches** or
e either submit to an authoritarian regime or institution or

we choose to become free thinkers who independently pursue the pathway of truth and meaning.

If you choose — because of insecurity and a feeling of inadequacy of knowledge and resources, or out of fear or whatever outer suggestion or pressure — the authoritarian road, that is to accept without any or much questioning, a religious/social/political system of thought and behavior, you certainly wouldn't be alone. There are an estimated twelve hundred different religious denominations on the North American Continent alone, which are ready to shape your soul and control your behavior, not to speak of other social, cultural, political and commercial institutions which could function in a similar role in your life. But if we choose this path, we are not philosophizing and we close the door to the free development of our own thinking and the chances of reaching a truly authentic conclusion and way of being are greatly diminished.

But what does it take to choose the alternative, the pathway of free, independent, authentic and existential thinking? **Two ideas** may help us here: The **first** one is that by choosing this path you will become really yourself, not a "someone" designed and dictated by someone else. You will grow into a mature, independent thinker who doesn't attract or wear a label and you will know that **you** have really examined your own life and the life of the world and universe in which you exist. Whatever reality there is for you, it will be **your own**, not borrowed or copied. There will be no fixed creed but you will feel that your life **is** the journey and **your mind will be open** and unbiased, contemporary and **FREE**.

Secondly, you'll find you are not alone on your journey; we have the Wisdom of the Ages and we have as a vital, dynamic part of it, some outstanding 20th Century philosophers with whom we can identify because they too have lived in the midst of an acute awareness of the historical reality of our time. The existentialists in particular seem to have that awareness and it pays to dip into their writings. Although it may not always be easy to follow their enquiries and observations, the attempt to understand them will inevitably enrich our lives. Existentialist philosophers are usually independent thinkers and we cannot classify them as we would persons belonging to a club or movement.

A few of the better known existentialists, all European but

accessible in translation are: Karl Jaspers (1883–1969), Jean-Paul Sartre (1905–1980), Simone de Beauvior (1908–1986), Martin Heidegger (1889–1976), Albert Camus (1913–1960) and Paul Tillich (1886–1965). The roots of their philosophies may be traced back to three 19th Century thinkers: Soren Kierkegaard (1813–1855), Friedrich Nietzsche (1844–1900) and Fyodor Dostoyevsky (1821–1881). We are certainly not alone in our quest and our comrades here are brilliant and challenging: they do make you **THINK**! But what do we find? How shall our need for meaning be satisfied? Where do we start?

The wise and careful observer of life and behavior, a great thinker of our Century, Carl Jung (1875–1961) observed that there are **two principles** we will discover in our study of life, that convey meaning. An understanding of both of them functioning in our own individual life's scenario will add considerable meaning to our perception of life. The first principle, so commonly known that it requires little elaboration, is **causality** or the assertion that there is a necessary connection between cause and effect. Plato taught that meaning can be given to things by finding the laws of their beings and the purposes and goals of their activity. You hold a carrot seed in your hand in springtime, you proceed to plant it, nurture and care for it in accordance with the "laws of gardening" and by fall you may harvest a carrot for your own nutrition. So we might say that the meaning in the seed is the carrot and your own and others' nourishment. The meaning of the cause is thus determined by the usefulness of the effect.

Aristotle meant something like this when he wrote that all movement implies specific fulfillment. Causality plays that role in our own decision making, followed by effort: you earned that diploma, built that model railroad, worried yourself into an ulcer. Cause and effect are not always easily detected, as any medical researcher will tell you, but we always assume the connection is there, somewhere, to be uncovered. In nature, the weather warms, ice melts, grass turns green, it rains and the desert blooms and markets are eventually filled with fruits and vegetables.

All science and its application, technology, is based on the causality principle. In society's life, a government decides to collect a new sales tax and we who live in that society, have to pay it. Cause and effect governs much of our observable world, even internally as the relationship between thought and emotion as cause and health, mood, attitude, relationships and success as result. Causality seems everywhere present but does that explain the meaning of my existence and the events, people, circumstances and destiny of my life?

To pursue this question further we now turn our attention to the second principle: **synchronicity.** Coined by Jung, it is a combination of the Greek words sync (= together) and chronus (= time). Jung thought of this principle as acausal, not caused, but expressing itself in "the arrangement of events" that appears to us as meaningful. Another way of saying this is that we may notice meaningful coincidences in our lives, which do not appear to have been set in motion by us or anyone (anything) else, yet there they are, clearly happening and affecting us — perhaps causing us to refer to them in terms of good or bad luck.

During World War II, in October 1944, my sister and I were hiding in the cellar of our home one afternoon because another of those terrible air raids was being inflicted on our home town. We could hear by the whistle of the falling bombs how close or how far away they were hitting the ground. Then we heard one terrifying sharp whistle and we knew this bomb was so close it could hit us at any moment. An awful thud, everything shook, we could hear glass breaking, debris flying — but no explosion. By "coincidence" the bomb did not detonate, it had dug a big hole in our back yard and it stuck out like an upside-down boat. Had it exploded, it is highly unlikely that I would be sitting here sharing this story with you. It is the kind of "acausal" synchronicity one doesn't easily forget.

Other instances of this principle-in-action are less dramatic, sometimes an almost daily occurrence. You think of someone, the phone rings and this same person is on the line. You look for a quotation and, after meditating, you know what book to go to, to find it. You need a parking spot in a certain busy city district, you think of it being there for you and the moment you arrive at your destination, someone pulls out making room for you to park.

As cause-and-effect thinkers we have trouble with this principle: it is not predictable and it usually cannot be repeated. The logical, scientific mind doesn't like this — and, as with every great discovery, the traditional community does not readily welcome this strange intruder. But we had better get used to it, for the simple reason that it's there operating in our lives, affects us and adds, sometimes significantly, to the meaning and destiny of our existence. In the Bible we find several instances of synchronicity — in the life of Joseph (of the Book of Genesis) who was sold as a slave by his brothers only to become their "master" in a coincidental situation that developed years later. In the story of the nativity the wise men are coincidentally told in a dream for their journey home to avoid the destructive King Herod. A similar saving dream occurs again in our own experience.

A friend of mine was offered a lucrative position in Honolulu, Hawaii in the fall of 1941, when he lived on the U.S. mainland. In a dream he saw newspaper headlines announcing the Japanese attack on Pearl Harbor. He decided not to accept that position. A few short weeks after he had the dream the Japanese airforce actually did attack Pearl Harbor, drawing the United States of America into World War II. Call it coincidence, synchronicity or good luck — whatever it is and whatever brings it about, it undoubtedly is there.

The story is told of young Abraham Lincoln who had great aspirations for a legal career but had neither money nor influence. An impoverished traveler offers him a barrel of odds and ends for a dollar — a sizeable sum at the time. Lincoln was a generous, kindhearted man and bought the barrel, contents unseen. Later on, when he opened it he discovered a set of books known as Blackstone's Commentaries — enabling him to study law and eventually fulfilling his career dreams.

Sometimes, synchronicity appears as quite harmless and humorous too, yet so poignant: In the early seventies I was on the Island of St. Croix doing research work on the original writings of psychosomatics pioneer Phineas Parkhurst Quimby (1802–1866). I was the guest and colleague of the late scholar Ervin Seale who resided there with his wife Elva at the time. In the cool evening we would have our supper on the veranda of their home which was located in a rather remote area adjacent to the "jungle" where wildlife made their habitat. Among the smaller species found there was the calico cat, a lean, multi-colored, beautiful little animal. These calico cats would naturally be looking for a food handout; however, like birds, they were careful not to get caught or be touched by humans. One little cat, obviously about to become a mother, was a regular visitor night after night. Ervin and Elva told me that their daughter, who had visited with them a few weeks earlier, had named this little mother-to-be "Mini-Ma" — an appropriate name, we all agreed. That night we drove to the island's shopping mall which was called the Mini-Mall. As we approached the shopping centre, (it was dark by now) we noticed that the last two letters of the bright neon sign on top of the roof of the mall had apparently burnt out, so that now it read in blazing letters: Mini-Ma!!

How do we add meaning to our own lives by becoming more aware of this Synchronicity principle? Here are five ways to do this:

STUDY SYNCHRONICITY. Peruse the autobiographies and biographies of eminent persons in whom you have an interest. Ask yourself what coincidental events in their lives played a significant role in determining what happened next. The principle is always there. Study specific books on the subject by authors such as Carl Jung, Jean Shinoda Bolen and Ira Progoff. (see bibliography which follows this chapter.)

RETROSPECTING. Take a closer look at major events in your own life, including the more unpleasant happenings and especially those which seemed puzzling at the time. Ask yourself what might have happened if that particular event had not taken place? Does meaning present itself well after the event? And what about your "significant other"? What were the circumstances surrounding your meeting her/him? Did you or she/he "cause" your initial meeting to take place, or was that meeting a (sheer) coincidence, which neither one of you could have predicted? Look at the ways other opportunities came your way. Detect the operation of synchronicity in your own life events. It's fascinating!

RECORD COINCIDENCES. This is an additional way of becoming AWARE of the principle-in-action. As with your dream log, this can become a fascinating enterprise. You may wish to maintain it for a few weeks or months. Write down the circumstances of every coincidence that comes to your attention, including the seemingly trivial ones and the ones reported to you by friends, relatives and associates. Include also those that involve your inner life, dreams and verification, inner feeling and outer happenings, hunches of future events and coincidences for which there is no causal or rational explanation.

EXPECTANT ATTITUDE. This means be on "the alert" for synchronistic events. You will find that the more attention you pay to this phenomenon, the more evidence will present itself. Researcher-author Marcus Bach calls these events expressions of "serendipity" — that is, the occurance of fortunate discoveries when not in search of them. Jean Shinoda Bolen writes of synchronicity as a possible "matchmaker." Be on the expectant look-out for that synchronicity principle to alert you to that great idea or that vital bit of information which may otherwise elude you.

CONTEMPLATIVE MEDITATION. As conveyed in The Art of Contemplation section of this book, when we master this skill, we know ourselves to be touch with what appears to be a greater intelligence and higher wisdom, the source of intuition. It is here, coincidentally, we obtain insight and guidance that the causality principle of conscious rational thinking could not deliver. Meditators constantly are amazed by the surprising, unexpected nature of their intuitions.

Having established the phenomenon and ascertained five ways of becoming familiar with it, just what makes synchronicity what it is? Is it the evidence of a sort of invisible network of meaning that envelopes us all the time? Is it, in Arthur Koestler's terms, an indication of the fundamental unity of all things — something along the lines of the unified field theory Albert Einstein was looking for, encompassing the dynamics of the entire universe?

Perhaps when we take a closer look at so-called man-made "technological coincidences" we'll get a clue. Take, for instance, a happening with which we are all familiar a you visit to the grocery store. As you approach the super-market, the door that is labelled "IN," suddenly opens, just at the moment you were about to push it. What is this phenomenon? A miracle? No, but it would appear to be to the person who just arrived from a completely non-technological society. A coincidence? No, but it would appear to be to the rare person who was not familiar with automatic doors and similar devices. Philosophically speaking, as you approach that door, you know that an "ordering mind" (or minds or system) preceded you with beneficial intent in that situation and that is why you would not describe it as an acausal event or coincidence.

Similarly, we are familiar with the synchronization of traffic lights. If the traffic flows smoothly, at a preset speed, (that would actually be some sort of miracle in the larger cities I know) your car approaches the light and presto, it turns green. No need to hit the brakes or wait — we may proceed as conveniently and efficiently as possible toward our destination, because when we approach the next traffic light, that one too turns green just in time and so on along that route that is synchronized. Now we know that this is not a miracle or a coincidence, but a pre-arranged system that your city's traffic department designed for your and other motorists' benefit. Incidentally, the system is **not** imposed on us — we may choose to slow down or speed up, to turn right or stop altogether. It is there to be utilized or not, at our choosing.

Causality presupposes order and reliability in those processes where we are able to understand and apply the principle, and much of our civilization has been built on it. Synchronicity presupposes intelligent activity, the source of which is largely a mystery, although we may theorize and arrive at all kinds of assumptions. Both are dynamic, active principles, both carry meaning to those affected by their processes.

Naturally, our next question would have to be: What is the nature of the Intelligence of the Cosmos that apparently makes these two principles possible? Is there an "Infinite Presence?" Our next chapter is devoted to catching glimpses of the answer to these questions.

Bibliography & Recommended Further Reading

Jaspers, Karl: Way to Wisdom: An Introduction to Philosophy
    New Haven: Yale Univ. Press, 1975
Jaspers, Karl: Philosophy, Vols. I, II & III
    Chicago: Univ. of Chicago Press, 1969
Jaspers, Karl: Reason and Existence
    N.Y.: Noonday Press, 1966
Jaspers, Karl: Philosophy of Existence
    Philadelphia: Univ. of Pennsylvania Press, 1971
Jaspers, Karl: The Future of Mankind
    Chicago: Univ. of Chicago Press, 1973
Jaspers, Karl: Man in the Modern Age
    N.Y.: Doubleday, 1957
Koestler, Arthur: The Roots of Coincidence
    London: Pan Books, 1974
Jung, Carl G.: Synchronicity — An Acausal Connecting Principle
    Princeton, N.J.: Princeton Univ. Press, 1973
Progoff, Ira: Jung, Synchronicity & Human Destiny
    N.Y.: Dell Publ., 1975
Bolen, Jean Shinoda: The Tao of Psychology — Synchronicity and the
    Self   N.Y.: Harper & Row, 1979
Vaughan, Alan: Incredible Coincidence. The Baffling World of
    Synchronicity   N.Y.: Signet New American Library, 1979
VonFranz, Marie-Louise: On Divination and Synchronicity. The
    Psychology of Meaningful Chance
    Toronto: Inner City Books, 1980
Koestler, Arthur: Janus, A Summing Up
    London: Hutchinson, 1978
Durant, Will: The Story of Philosophy
    N.Y.:Pocket Books, 1956

CHAPTER 22

GLIMPSES INTO THE INFINITE

"The appeal to reason is the appeal to that ultimate judge,
universal and yet individual to each, to which all
authority must bow"

Adventures of Ideas
Alfred North Whitehead (1861–1947)

At the start of this book we suggested that the most important question we could ask is likely: How can I change my life for the better? We have now arrived at that point in our adventure where we realize that we are unable to change our life for the better unless we live in a Universe that supports and encourages such progress. In his visionary book, THE COMING OF THE COSMIC CHRIST, Matthew Fox reports that Albert Einstein was once asked "What is the most important question you can ask in life?" He answered: "Is the Universe a friendly place or not?"

What would you answer? If you were visiting with me right now, I would invite you to join me on a short walk to the nearest shopping center where a small successful tailoring shop is owned and managed by a capable lady whose birthplace is Vietnam. A few years ago she escaped that Asian country in a small boat overloaded with refugees like herself. She is one of the few survivors who was rescued by an American ship whose crew picked her out of the South China sea. How would she answer Einstein's momentous question? How would those who didn't make it?

Another lady we could see came to this continent of North America after fleeing Czechoslovakia at the time of the uprising against the communist regime in 1968. She's originally from Hungary, where for years she and her relatives plotted and pondered to find a way to freedom. She now manages a fine ladies' fashion store. What would her answer be? Not long ago I visited the great U.S. war museum THE INTREPID in the harbor of New York City. I spent a day conversing

with two veterans of D-Day - 6 June 1944 - and the Allied campaign of
'44-'45 to end World War II in Europe. To these warriors I owe my life.
Their experiences are almost impossible to adequately describe. They too
survived. Millions did not. How would they answer Einstein's challenge?
Is the Universe friendly — or not?

For as long as there has been human memory, recorded or not,
there has been the overwhelming awareness of the evils of war, crime,
poverty, slavery, despair, exploitation, disease, disasters and suffering of
all kinds. No wonder humans throughout the ages have cried out for
SOMEONE TO SAVE US! The world's historical religions have
suggested many answers and the one we in the Western Hemisphere are
most familiar with is the conventional, traditional, orthodox, evangelical,
fundamentalist Christian theology that says: Jesus is our Savior and he
will return to this planet in person, defeat all evil and those who accept
the doctrine will then live happily ever after, while those who do not will
find their sufferings never end.

Let's reflect on this, still only too prevalent belief. Despite the
promise of a literal return of Jesus "very soon," he has not returned for
some two thousand years. "God," in this theology, becomes an absentee
landlord and the gospel a life insurance policy that over two millenia has
not paid off. Meanwhile, the suffering of millions continues. During
World War I hundreds of thousands of the best of the world's youth
perished in Flanders' mud, both sides praying to this same Christian
"God" for victory. The victims of the Nazi monsters begged and
beseeched the "God" in vain in the concentration camps of World War
II. What a sad, irrational, cruel religion! Our desire for the wish-
fulfillment of salvation has been so strong that we've overlooked the fatal
flaws of our culture's traditional Christianity. The great mystics and rare
visionaries have always known it. "Park" Quimby wrote in 1861: "The
Christian's God is a tyrant of the worst kind — God is the name of
man's belief." And we suffer from our beliefs until we find the truth. If
you mistake the rope on the path ahead of you for a snake, you'll
respond in fear until you realize your mistaken belief. It is time we asked
the question clearly of traditional Christianity: **What really is the truth?**

Let's start with the life and teachings of Jesus. Theologians whose
task it is to apologize on behalf of their "God" would say: Jesus taught

the doctrine, therefore it must be true. But let's pursue this statement. Did Jesus teach world-transformation through supernatural apocalypse? Many Bible scholars say: "No, but St. Paul and other persecuted early Christian leaders did." This view is supported by the seventy-three scholars of the Jesus Seminar who translated the five gospels (including the Gospel of Thomas, rediscovered in Egypt in 1945). Their volume, "THE FIVE GOSPELS - WHAT DID JESUS REALLY SAY?" (published in 1993) explores the authenticity of the known 1500 sayings of Jesus and their findings suggest that only 18% of these sayings may be considered reliable. The NEW "SCHOLARS' VERSION" is a shocking document indeed. Unless we've studied the origin of the New Testament.

The beginnings of what would be accepted by the Roman Catholic church for authority in doctrine and scripture are found in the Church Council of Nicea, 325 AD. This Council was ordered by Emperor Constantine I, the first Christian Roman Emperor. Three hundred and eighteen male bishops met under direction of the Emperor to decide on how the nature of Christ was to be expressed in sacred creed. Also a study was begun, which was to continue over centuries, to declare which of the scriptures were to be "canonized," that is, become the accepted rule of the church. But the central point is, that it was from this momentous, historical occasion that the authority of the Church, implemented by the state, now declared what people must believe.

What happened to a believer's fate was becoming decided, not from one's personal faith, but rather **from the outside**. Some scriptures whose message apparently did not support the agreement between the Roman state and the Christian church were in process of being rejected from the Bible's canon while others would be added. A censorship was being imposed by church **and state** which would make non-canonical writings illegal; to read and share them would be at the risk of one's life. What happened to the truth in all this? The physical Second Coming, promised to each successive generation by the Church, never materialized. Is there any "appeal to reason" here?

What is the alternative to the viewpoint of a literal, material second coming of Jesus? The answer is found in the mystical view. It asserts, with many of the Christians of the first century, that what we look for is **the awareness that the Christ** or god-in-Jesus **can be in each**

of us. When we realize this, we **personally** experience the Second Coming. Today, this concept is known as the coming of the Cosmic Christ. Did Jesus believe in it?

In Luke 17:21 (Scholars' Version) Jesus says that we won't be able to observe the coming of "God's imperial rule" because it is "right there in your presence." We find the same teaching in the Gospel of John 15, and in Thomas 3, 51 and 113. The spiritual transformation of individual PEOPLE has not been waiting for one apocalyptic event, but has been occurring over and over again from the days of the ministry of Jesus Christ through every century and is continuing to happen in our current times. This awareness of the entire human race as "of God," is bringing about a corresponding transformation of our global community; this is the Second Coming to the the human family.

Before this can happen, and the signs of it are evident all around us, we need to become aware of the glimpses of the presence of the Infinite already accessible to us — while we're on our way to "becoming mystics." To me, reflecting on a few of these "glimpses" brings us ever so much closer to an authentic answer to Einstein's question: "Is the Universe a friendly place — or not?"

GALAXIES OF INFINITY - One of the best and most rational ways of getting the feel of infinity is to recognize the physical immensity of the cosmos. Study Stephen W. Hawking's "A BRIEF HISTORY OF TIME" or a similar volume. Our galaxy, we are told by scientists, is 100,000 light years across, containing some 100,000 million stars and our galaxy is but one of some 100,000 million galaxies. Can we imagine what this cosmos of ours is really like? From the closed, tiny, flawed world of conventional theology, we enter the infinity of cosmological scientific fact — the ocean of incredible truths where the limits of our knowledge are pushed further outward every time a new discovery is made.

ENDLESS PROCESS IN NATURE - Next we discover that what seemed lifeless, fixed matter is in reality dynamic energy, forever forming itself anew and into novel forms through organic and inorganic modes of life. Study the Process Philosophy of Alfred North Whitehead and other great thinkers in the Process field (see bibliography). Add to this our experience of awe, reverence, beauty, and the glory of form and sound and taste and touch. I have met many persons, especially men, who have shared the experience that they felt what to them was "God" by communing with nature, in the woods, the mountains, on the shores of lake, river and ocean. My own mystical experiences have frequently been facilitated by being alone in the wilderness, often close to wildlife. Matthew Fox calls this "radical amazement."

UNUSUAL STRENGTH - We've all heard of, or perhaps experienced, unexpected endurance, courage, power to handle a situation that seemed impossible to overcome. To me, to be given the strength to endure the war experience referred to in the previous chapter is quite beyond my ability to explain. War veterans and others who have survived near insurmountable crises know the same feeling. Something infinite is added to our finite being. Study the biographies of those who describe such incredible life experiences and we get the "feel" of it, again and again.

INTUITIVE GUIDANCE - When from the spiritual depth of your soul you receive the exact answer to your life's question, the solution to a tough problem or a hunch that throws light on a puzzling situation, you've been in touch with the Infinite Presence within you. We've already discussed the wonderful ways of intuition open to each of us, in chapter 20. Synchronicity is an expression of this same guidance.

SOUL DEVELOPMENT - The dire need for true spirituality, instead of dogmatic formalism and tradition, is beginning to make itself felt more and more in a society that has left people so unfulfilled and lonely in the midst of technological advancement and social prosperity. The 21st Century will see a breakthrough away from the grip of traditional patriarchy that has ruled since Constantine I. Other cultures witness similar trends. You and I are participants in a current spiritual revolution that has its roots in **individual, direct mystical experience of the Infinite Presence within.**

      We now deepen our spiritual life by reflecting on the phenomenon of No-Thing-Ness in our next chapter.

Bibliography & Recommended Further Reading
Whitehead, Alfred North: Adventures of Ideas
        London: Penguin, 1948
Whitehead, Alfred North: A Philosopher Looks at Science
        N.Y.:Philosophical Library, 1965
Whitehead, Alfred North: Religion in the Making
        N.Y.:New American Library, 1974
Whitehead, Alfred North: Modes of Thought   N.Y.:Free Press, 1968
Whitehead, Alfred North: Process and Reality, An Essay in Cosmology
        N.Y.:Free Press, 1979
Ford, Lewis S.: The Emergence of Whitehead's Metaphysics
        Albany, N.Y.:State University of N.Y. Press, 1984
Anderson, C. Alan: The Problem is God
        Walpole, New Hampshire: Stillpoint Publ., 1984
Lowe, Victor: Alfred North Whitehead, The Man and His Work, Vol. I & II
        Baltimore, MD: Johns Hopkins Univ. Press, 1990
Flew, Antony: A Dictionary of Philosophy
        N.Y.: St. Martin's Press, 1984
Flew, Antony: An Introduction to Western Philosophy
        N.Y.: Bobbs-Merrill Co., 1971
Solomon, Robert C.: The Big Questions, A Short Introduction to Philosophy
        N.Y.: Harcourt Brace Jovanovich, 1982
Angeles, Peter A.: Dictionary of Philosophy
        N.Y.:Barnes & Noble, 1981
Adler, Mortimer J.: How To Think About God
        N.Y.: Macmillan Publ. Co., 1980
Edwards, Paul (Ed.): The Encyclopedia of Philosophy, Vols. I through VIII
        N.Y.: Macmillan Publ., 1972
Hartshorne, Charles: Insights and Oversights of Great Thinkers
        Albany, N.Y.: State Univ. of N.Y. Press, 1983
Heidegger, Martin: Being and Time, Transl.: John Macquarrie & Edward Robinson
        N.Y.: Harper & Row, 1962
Funk, Robert W., Hoover, Roy W. and the Jesus Seminar: The Five Gospels "The
        Scholars' Version" - What Did Jesus Really Say? N.Y.: Macmillan Publ., 1993
Fox, Matthew: The Coming of the Cosmic Christ
        San Francisco: Harper & Row, 1988
Redfield, James: The Celestine Prophecy   N.Y.: Warner Books, 1993
Winterhalter, Robert:The Fifth Gospel   San Francisco: Harper 1988

CHAPTER 23

THE POWER OF NO-THING-NESS

"Certainly one can describe being in terms of non-being, and one can justify such a description
by pointing to the astonishing prerational fact that there is something and not nothing"

The Courage To Be
Paul Tillich (1886–1965)

The 21st Century is almost here and to the aware and awake observer it is obvious that the transition into the new Century is more than the turning of the diary page, the clock and the calendar. There is also a definitive turning, an evolution, a transformation of human consciousness, the dawning of an entirely new way of seeing things. This is the progressive development envisioned in the futuristic writings of Pierre Teilhard de Chardin (1881–1955). It is what is now often called the New Spirituality, the fulfillment of the soul hunger of modern centuries, and it is here now.

Reflection, as a fifth part of the practice of the Art of Authentic Living brings us closer and closer to that new, dynamic lifestyle which may also become the long-awaited solution to the many social horrors of the 20th Century. For as Margaret Mead (1901–1978) used to say: "Never doubt that a small group of thoughtful, committed citizens can change the world. Indeed, it's the only thing that ever has."

How can you and I become part of such a change? What is this new spirituality and transformation all about? Let's try to discover the essence of it. We have already seen that contemplative meditation can carry our souls into a higher dimension of living, the mystical awareness. In Chapter 19 it was suggested how we can "unlimit our thinking" and that "there is yet more" Here we'll move right into that "more" and it promises to be a most unusual journey!

The more we reflect along truly authentic, unconditioned lines, the more introspective we become; and the more the ordinary world of physical beings, things and beliefs becomes transformed into a new reality: everything is subject to change and becomes potentially final.

As new truths emerge, traditional cherished beliefs may crumble, if they are not based on an authority we can trust. We will have to be prepared to have "the courage to be" the person to accept that premise. Even if it means we may have to admit our beliefs were flawed, perhaps entirely mistaken. In my experience, this proves to be the most difficult barrier to overcome. We noted an example of this in Chapter 22: The origins of the Bible, on the interpretation of which so much of our western society's beliefs are based. Who dares to place a question mark, where Church authority was for so long the final word? David Hume (1711–1776) did: he tied the question of truth to the credibility of witnesses — to their conditioning, their vested interest, their trustworthiness.

But it is not enough to place question marks, to introduce doubt. We can see this as just the beginning of Renaissance humanism. More than 200 years after Hume we wake up to the fact that our own consciousness, rather than ANY outside authority, now is becoming the central arena for our spiritual quest. The "outside world" becomes subject to a new soul power with which we interpret that world and evaluate all our experiences. What happens when we let go of all the old "security blankets" and proceed to think in this way? Let's follow this path. . .

We reflected on Einstein's question "Is the Universe friendly or not?" But, going deeper, philosophers have pondered if we shouldn't really ask these questions first: Why is there a universe in the first place? Why the "Big Bang?" Why life? Why is there something and not nothing? Why existence? Why consciousness? Why "being?"

One possible answer comes to us from the profound thought of the 20th Century theologian-philosopher Paul Tillich (1886–1965) whose mission was to unite philosophy and religion in our time. He was not a distant ivory-tower-academic, as we so often imagine about professional philosophers. Tillich served as a chaplain on the battlefields of Flanders in World War I. Here was this brilliant mind, at age thirty confronted with massive destruction and death, with human ceasing-to-be, with non-being. . . Years later he speaks of "the power of being which makes itself felt through despair." The existential despair is often coupled with the feeling of inevitability, it cannot be helped or changed. As Samuel

Beckett (1906–1989) wrote in the opening lines of his novel "MURPHY"
"The sun shone, having no alternative, on the nothing new."
Just when things seem pretty hopeless, with the exposure of traditional
religion so clear, the reflections of Tillich lead us through it all to his
mystic "striving for union with Ultimate reality."

To accomplish that in THIS WORLD we need to bring everything
we know and experience into our consciousness in its totality and
therefore this must include what we know as non-being or nothingness.
Hence, Tillich speaks of the "qualities of non-being."

So, Nothingness now becomes our subject of reflection, not as a
strange abstraction, but as a transforming power that allows us to finally
transcend the old dualism and to instead include all of life in our
philosophy. This would mean our ultimate freedom, if it can be done. It
would satisfy Jean-Paul Sartre's objective when he wrote in his "WAR
DIARIES," "My ambition is . . . to know the world. . . as a totality." The
question is: how can we know and apply this Power of No-Thing-Ness?

Unlike those who simply accept religious or politcal authority, the
mystic does not follow or blindly believe, but cuts her or his own path
through the jungle of life's situations. My own contemplative-reflection
path, which to be sure is highly personal, has made me become aware of
Five Modes of nothingness that secrete real meaning into the 21st
Century's New Spirituality experience; in this we now join Sartre, when
he said: "I'm not at ease, except in Nothingness" (War Diaries).

EXPECTATION - Our conscious mind is full of it - we think
constantly of what is not there, what we suppose, hope, anticipate will be,
or should be there. In his major work "BEING AND NOTHINGNESS,"
Jean-Paul Sartre (1905–1980) illustrates this marvelously in the chapter
on "The Origin of Negation." Imagine, if you will, that you have an
appointment with your friend Pierre in a Parisian café at 4 o'clock. You
arrive 15 minutes late. "Pierre is always punctual." Will he have waited
for you? You look around the café. Pierre is not there. Did he leave?
Has he not arrived yet? Has he forgotten? WHERE IS HE? In the café
are many interesting people, there's fine food, the decor is artistic, the
band plays great music — but you don't notice any of these. All you can
think of is WHAT'S NOT THERE, Pierre, who is a "Nothingness."

Think of how Nothingness pre-occupies your thinking and emotions every day and night!

Marcel Proust (1871–1922) wrote that the only true paradise is always the paradise that's not here now, the "lost one." Mahatma Gandhi (1869–1948) said that "to the hungry, food is god." Think of the power of the Not-yet in your own life. . .

UN-CONSCIOUS-NESS - Nothingness also manifests as what-we-thought-is-not-there. Aurelius (St.) Augustine (354–430) reflected that an individual is "for the most part unknown, even to him (her) self." It may seem irrational to say that what isn't there is there just the same. Yet, I had this proven to myself distinctly for fifteen years following my experiences in World War II. In wartime, night after night, and often during the daytime as well, airplanes, bombers and their accompanying protection aircraft would drone over our heads. Sirens would announce their approaching our town and we became conditioned to the "ALERT! DANGER!" scenario every time the drone was heard and of course, we hurried for shelter. The war ended, liberation came, the danger was over; nevertheless, every time an airplane flew over our home, at nighttime, I would wake up with a start. Even after I moved half way around the world, the same phenomenon occurred with regularity. Only following my first mystical experience in August 1960 did it disappear.

What isn't there obviously has power; it persists in governing our experiences and conduct. Carl Jung (1875–1961) in this context may be appreciated when he wrote at the end of his long career that the significance of his life had to do with his encounters with the Unconscious — the power and dynamics of what appears not to be there. . . the No-Longer, the seemingly disappeared. . .

NON-BEING - Nothingness takes on the form of a threat — or a promise, depending on one's viewpoint — when we think of ourself as not being, not existing at all. In Zen the question is pondered: What was your face like before your parents were born? Can you imagine yourself as not being? Are we potentially final, as the beings we are now?

William Barrett whose work on contemporary Existentialism is widely acknowledged writes in "Irrational Man" about the French philosopher Blaise Pascal (1623–1662) who encountered Nothingness when his carriage, while driving by the Seine in Paris, suddenly swerved; the door was flung open and he almost "catapulted down the embankment to his death." Nothingness suddenly and arbitrarily reveals itself. The Norwegian artist Edvard Munch (1863–1944) created a furor with his symbolic painting "The Scream" which reflects the "angst" of non-being. His imagery has become so well known that we find it on pillows and other reproductions. The drive of sex as the striving for the possibility of pushing being out of non-being is evident in our society everywhere, even if we do not consciously recognize it.

Every night we repeat the cosmic play or dance of life: we sink from being into non-being and out of nothingness we once more emerge in the morning. For many years, while searching for ultimate answers, a dream would present itself with unbelievable clarity to my unconsciousness — to be remembered upon awakening with riveting reality: I was on the very edge of an enormous bowl, the size of planet Earth — about to slide down into nothingness — but it never happened. Ludwig Wittgenstein (1889–1951) once remarked that our difficulty is to say "no more than we know." Do we emerge out of nothingness without a cause — and then disappear in the same manner? Chapter 25 attempts to throw some light on the answer to this question of Nothingness.

SILENCE AND SOLITUDE - To prove to yourself yet another manifestation of this power of Nothingness, allow yourself to withdraw into solitude for a few days, or just to be silent for a day. In the opening lines of the first chapter of the Gospel of John in the Bible's New Testament (Scholars' Version) it is suggested that "In the beginning there was the divine word and wisdom...and it was what God was." In the complete silence all things after a while seem to melt into no-thing-ness and pure ideas, words and wisdom, become more real than the "physical sounds" of everday communication.

Novelists May Sarton in "JOURNAL OF A SOLITUDE" and Doris Grumbach in "FIFTY DAYS OF SOLITUDE" describe the direct link between experience and reflection; and then, the break-up of that link. In silence and solitude we gain a wholesome, nourishing nothingness that has gotten rid of unnecessary conversation, radio and television and all the other noisy debris of our culture. Again, we find power in the nothingness that we allow to emerge. . .

MASTERY over self and life. My friend Larry Morris of Albuquerque, New Mexico, author of "EASY DOES IT" tells of a bomber veteran of the Vietnam war who experienced nightmares years afterwards, in which once more he was dropping lethal cargo from his aircraft. Larry, himself a veteran, suggested he visualize, before sleep, the same scene, except replacing the bombs with flowers. In time, this Vietnam vet was healed of his nightmares. We have the capacity to apply the power of Nothingness to any mental-emotional image.

During a recent healing meditation which I conducted, an ill woman in the audience who was greatly disturbed by a personal hurt, applied the suggestion of seeing any harm being dissolved into nothingness in her mind. A warm glow came over her, her sinuses, plugged for weeks, instantly cleared, all her pains disappeared and she felt herself radiantly well. She was using the power that says: This is nothing to me, it has "no power" over me!

Plato proposed a world of no-thing-ness where all perfect ideas and ideals dwell and of which our physical everyday world is but a dim reflection. No-thing-ness has incredible spiritual power. Imagine again Sartre's café where Pierre is absent. Now, instead of thinking of Pierre, let's imagine dissolving more of the café's interior into nothingness. Visualize the scene with all the feeling and intensity you can create. Then, tell the band to go. No music. Now let the staff go home, empty the kitchen, no food. The patrons leave also and soon there's only the furnishings left. That too goes and next we make the entire café disappear. Follow that up by dissolving a whole city block, then the blocks with parks, traffic, buildings, persons, animals around it. Now we make the whole of Paris, with the Seine go away. Next follows the countryside and we gradually erase all of Europe from our mind map, then all the other continents, one by one, until we let the whole planet slide into nothingness. How very close we are now in our realization of what it means to be a spiritual being! Just "the Divine Word and Wisdom" and your own consciousness. . .

With this realization now comes a new sense of what it means to be really free. No-Thing-Ness endows us with brand new power.

Bibliography & Recommended Further Reading
Beckett, Samuel: Murphy   London: Pan Books, 1983
Teilhard de Chardin, Pierre: Let Me Explain   N.Y.: Harper & Row, 1966
Teilhard de Chardin, Pierre: How I Believe   N.Y.: Harper & Row, 1969
Teilhard de Chardin, Pierre: The Future of Man
        N.Y.: Collins, Harper & Row, 1964
Teilhard de Chardin, Pierre: Man's Place in Nature
        N.Y.: Collins, Harper & Row, 1966
Teilhard de Chardin, Pierre: The Phenomenon of Man
        N.Y.: Collins, Harper & Row, 1966
Delfgaauw, Bernard: Evolution, The Theory of Teilhard de Chardin
        N.Y.: Collins, Harper & Row, 1974
Camus, Albert: The Myth of Sisyphus
        N.Y.: Vintage Books, 1955
Hume, David: An Enquiry Concerning Human Understanding
        LaSalle, Illinois: Open Court, 1966
Adler, Mortimer J.: Ten Philosophical Mistakes
        N.Y.: Macmillan Publ., 1985
Adler, Mortimer J.: Six Great Ideas: Truth, Goodness, Beauty, Liberty, Equality,
        Justice   N.Y.: Macmillan Publ., 1981
Kung, Hans: Does God Exist? An Answer for Today   N.Y.: Doubleday, 1980
Korzybski, Alfred: Science and Sanity
        Lakeville, Connecticut: Instit. Gen. Semantics, 1950
Lamont, Corliss: The Philosophy of Humanism
        N.Y.: Frederick Ungar Publ., 1986
Tillich, Paul: The Courage to Be   New Haven: Yale Univ. Press, 1959
Tillich, Paul: Systematic Theology, Vols. I, II & III
        Chicago, Ill: Univ. of Chicago Press, 1967
Grumbach, Doris: Fifty Days of Solitude
        Boston: Beacon Press, 1994
Gilbert, Martin: First World War   London, UK: Weidenfeld & Nicolson, 1994
Shapin, Steven: A Social History of Truth
        Chicago, Ill: Univ. of Chicago Press, 1994
Morris, Larry: Easy Does It
        Albuquerque, New Mexico: Hillside Community Church, 1993
Sartre, Jean-Paul: The War Diaries of Jean-Paul Sartre
        N.Y: Pantheon Books, 1984, Translation by Quintin Hoare
Barrett, William: Irrational Man   N.Y.: Doubleday Anchor, 1962
Gaarder, Jostein: Sophie's World
        N.Y.: Farrar, Straus & Giroux, 1994, Translation by Paulette Moller

CHAPTER 24

ESCAPE TO FREEDOM

"I am a very wild bird and like liberty"

Recollections of a Happy Life
Marianne North (1830-1890)
(British artist & world traveler)

Every once in a while when travelling along a highway we may notice a stalled car. Something went wrong and the vehicle no longer moves. Sometimes we discover why. The driver, rather sheepishly, is walking back to the car with a can of gas — he or she had just forgotten to fill up. . . It's relatively easy to solve such a problem — it may happen to any of us.

Far more frequently do we witness human lives who seem to have come to a virtual standstill, they too may have run out of fuel to live, to try, to persist, to move ahead. And the trouble may not be motivation, for a person may be motivated and have great goals and the best of intentions and yet "tread water." Many of us are stalled on the highway of life and the trouble is that we've run out of the fuel that is basic to the smooth and healthy running of a civilized, global society as well as to the functioning of an individual, namely liberty or freedom.

We may have a tremendous potential to become highly productive and creative, we may live in a free society that provides both the means and the opportunity to develop that potential, we may even believe in our capacity to become successful and yet not proceed — because we think we lack the freedom to do so.

Reflecting on this consideration, it may seem to be far-fetched, irrational, exaggerated. But the benefit of pursuing the Art of Reflection is that, as Friedrich August von Hayek (1899–1992) points out in his monumental work "The Constitution of Liberty," we begin to become more aware of what civilization's functioning and continued existence depend upon. Part of this awareness is generated within us when, despite much earlier promise, we all too often see the tragedy of personal failure.

A woman I knew all my life was, as a student, by her peers

considered as "one most likely to become a success." Growing up in a middle class European family, she had the chance to become a professional person and responded by studying hard, as well as being smart, and all her family and friends rejoiced when she graduated as a teacher. She then found a good job, developed and applied her skills and became a star educator for some years, widely recognized and honored, and she was a happy person. Until she fell in love and got married. Her husband, a conservative, traditional Christian, influenced her to give up her teaching career; soon she was pregnant, and a few years later she found herself doing what her husband wanted her to do: manage his grocery store, as well as raise a family. He then bought another store and the two competed for the greatest profits to be realized.

She began to resent her situation thoroughly — she knew what she really loved and wanted to do, go back to teaching. Traditional church doctrine where "the man is the king of the castle" prevented this "good Christian wife" from escaping to freedom and instead her antagonism and resulting depression grew and she began to eat more and more. Obesity became obvious and while loving and caring relatives and friends as well as her medical advisors urged her to change her eating habits, her reply was: "What else is there?" Food had become her consolation and at age forty-nine she suffered three strokes, leaving her an invalid. This got her out of the grocery business and eventually into a care center. She lost all capacity for physical, mental and emotional quality of life. After some seventeen years in this greatly disabled state, she passed away.

When we don't fill up with the fuel of Freedom, we stall and wither and tragedy is our life story. So, it pays to reflect on exactly what the dynamics of Freedom are, both collectively and personally. History has may idealists who have attempted to help civilization take another step forward by appealing to this right, this precious value called liberty. In our time few, if any, have put it more clearly than Simone de Beauvoir in her "The Ethics of Ambiguity": "Freedom is the source from which all significations and all values spring. It is the original condition of all justification of existence." She adds that we, who seek meaning and justification of our own lives "must want freedom itself absolutely and above everything else."

How do we move from the grand philosophical stance to its

practical application? For we all have areas in our everyday existence where we feel restricted, hung-up, obstructed, stalled. We are all in some ways like the little boy who decided to run away from home and was spotted standing a block away, at the crosswalk. A neighbor who'd been watching him asked: "Why don't you cross the street?" The little tyke replied, "But I'm not allowed to cross the street!"

When we reflect on it, Freedom appears to make its presence felt in five ways which may lead to specific paths for attaining genuine liberty:

EMOTIONAL FREEDOM We tend to think that the limitations placed on us are always caused by outside forces — by a society and by associations, such as family and church, which prohibit the free development of our soul. Yet, what hinders us may be self-created, caused by some unresolved inner conflict, the need to feel continually deserving punishment and the inability to free oneself from a belief in fate. Sigmund Freud sighed, after counselling countless number of sufferers in this area, that half the world's population is masochistic. Just how does this affliction get its grip on us and how can we free ourselves?

My mentor, the late William M. Graham (1904–1984) of Portland, Oregon, was well known for his uncanny ability to resolve traumatic emotional disturbances. He was once consulted, in the years following the end of World War II in the Pacific hemisphere (August 1945), in the case of a member of the bombing crew who had carried out the atomic bomb assignment over Japan. The officer in question was confined to an institution where he refused to speak and could barely be kept alive as he made every effort to end his life. Graham was able to break his silence by asking him repeatedly: "What is it that you really wanted to do as a boy?" The man unexpectedly responded by describing his boyhood dreams. Subsequently, he was able to pursue an educational path that made his dreams come true and he was completely healed.

We can become emotionally free if we can by-pass the guilt barrier that holds us prisoner. It helps to realize, we always did the best we could at the time. It also helps, on the basis of this realization, to forgive ourselves. It helps to understand that we have suffered enough and need not continue to punish ourselves.

A woman, who told me her story of emotional confinement, had divorced her husband, who subsequently died of cancer. She thought of herself as having caused the man's demise and since then turned down every synchronistic opportunity to further her career or gain intimate happiness and fulfillment. The escape to freedom comes in the Buddha's guidelines for the meditation of serenity: rise above love and hate, tyranny and thralldom, wealth and want. See yourself as not involved any more.

POLITICAL FREEDOM It has been said that we don't appreciate the freedom we enjoy in our democratic, constitutional societies, until we lose it. I know, and I'm sure many of my readers do too, what it means to have one's homeland trampled underfoot by tyrants and thugs. The entire titanic struggle for political liberty of World Wars I and II, of the Korean and Vietnam conflicts, and many other wars of our 20th Century was about people wanting and deserving to be FREE. To me, each child in our schools needs to be well informed of this struggle and so learn to appreciate and maintain the foremost value that makes it possible for that child to have a promising future.

Every time I have the opportunity to see the imposing Statue of Liberty at the entrance of the Hudson River, I have an emotional experience quite difficult to describe. Freedom fighters in every repressed society, from Eastern Europe to much of Asia, Africa, Central America and everywhere else where people were, or are, held in slavery have but one primary desire: to be FREE!

PHILOSOPHICAL FREEDOM Are we really personally free in our consciousness to make authentic choices? Some thinkers, known as "determinists" have argued that given our upbringing, conditioning and circumstances, most people's choices can be predicted and are inevitable. That may be so, but at the same time, is it a "given," is it necessary? In practice we **do** have choices.

The ancient Greek mythologist Aesop (c. 470 BC) tells of a half-starved wolf who meets a fat and healthy dog, who explains that his good fortune is due to his position as watchdog at a farmhouse. The wolf is about to apply for a similar position when he notices an ugly scar on the dog's neck and discovers that it is caused by the chain the dog is on, as part of the job. In the end the wolf decides: "I'm not going to be chained up for anyone day or night!" "You are free, choose." writes J. P. Sartre, commenting on the freedom we have in our minds. And, if we don't, adds Simone de Beauvoir, we shall forever remain children.

So, with freedom comes responsibility and as we have seen, this in turn is an essential ingredient for personal success. The greatest of spiritual sages history has known have emphasized our philosophical freedom. Gotama, the Buddha, said that "just as the great oceans have but one taste, the taste of salt," so there is but one taste to all the true teachings of the Way, the taste of freedom. Jesus taught that we can "know the truth, and the truth will make you free."

ARTISTIC FREEDOM How we admire those who present us with great music and art, the expression of the freedom of the artists to be themselves! To be creative we need not be artists, but we do have to free ourselves from what Friedrich von Hayek called "coercion by the arbitrary will of another or others." Still, freedom doesn't mean: do whatever you like. . .

To fulfill our greatest potential destiny we need to be committed to the ethical life that is based on the Universal Principle that we will act toward others as we would like others to act toward us. If this "golden rule" was taught in all elementary and high schools, even simple self-interest would reduce criminal behavior dramatically, as has been proven in the application of character and values education. Justice and fairness are the inevitable results.

Given the ethical basis, our 21st Century civilization now has a global opportunity, never before present in all of known history, to encourage and develop individual creativity. We detect in the life of the great Albert Schweitzer (1875–1965) the embodiment of this ideal. This obviously means prejudices, patriarchy, religious repression, corporate and institutional tyranny, all manifestations of domination have to go. We who wish to build a genuinely free and content society in the 21st Century have our challenges cut out for us, for the forces of the status quo are evident everywhere.

We thrill at the thought of achieving, actually living, the idealism expressed by author Manly P. Hall (1901–1990): "We are not here to tell the Universe what to do; we are here to find out what the Universe wants us to do." But this can only happen if we free ourselves collectively and individually from all the beliefs that say, in effect: you're not allowed to cross the street of Liberty! What a revolution that will be!

ECONOMIC FREEDOM We live in a time when the national and regional governments of the world have accepted it as normal that their administrations be run on deficit budgets, resulting in enormous debts, which in turn necessitate a tax burden that restrains prosperity and discourages the entrepreneurial activity that generates full employment. The solution is quite simple: reduce government spending and bureaucratic interference and promote a free market while encouraging ethical education and social compassion.

Besides supporting those causes that seek to bring about such a society, how can the individual realize economic and financial freedom? The Art of Motivation section of this book tells the story of personal success in today's and tomorrow's society. What happens when we add the mystical-intuitive-function? Freedom here means managing our financial affairs and obligations in such as way that our strategy leaves our consciousness free from stress and worry. It means managing our purchases, our expenditures, it means studying and applying the laws of personal achievement until something "clicks" inside and you've found your economical equilibrium. It will balance your bank books too!

Escape to freedom in every department of your life! Perhaps the bottom line of liberty was best described by inspirational author and one of our century's great orators, Emmet Fox (1886–1951): "Your free will lies in the direction of your attention. Whatever you steadfastly direct your attention to, will come into your life. . ." Now, supposing we gave our steadfast attention to freedom. . . we shall then arrive at the front door of the House of the "Good Life," the subject of our exciting concluding chapter.

Bibliography & Recommended Further Reading
Schweitzer, Albert: The Light Within Us   N.Y.: Philosophical Libr.1959
Schweitzer, Albert: Out of My Life and Thought   N.Y.: Mentor, 1961
Schweitzer, Albert: The Essence of Faith, Philosophy of Religion
        N.Y.: Philosophical Library, 1966
Schweitzer, Albert: Indian Thought and Its Development
        Boston: Beacon Press, 1960
Schweitzer, Albert: Reverence for Life   N.Y.: Harper & Row, 1969
Bell, Linda A.: Sartre's Ethics of Authenticity
        Tuscaloosa & London: Univ. of Alabama Press, 1989
Barnes, Hazel E.: Existentialist Ethics
        Chicago & London: Univ. of Chicago Press, 1978
Mackie, J.L.: Ethics, Inventing Right and Wrong   N.Y.: Penguin, 1981
Lippman, Walter: A Preface to Morals   Boston: Beacon Press, 1960
Ponsonby, Laura: Marianne North at Kew Gardens
        Exeter, Devon, U.K.: Webb & Bower Publ., 1990
Hall, Manly Palmer: Pathways of Philosophy
        Los Angeles: Philosophical Research Society, 1947
Streller, Justus: To Freedom Condemned, Transl: Wade Baskin
        N.Y.: Philosophical Library, 1960
Hayek, Friedrich, A.: The Constitution of Liberty
        Chicago: Henry Regnery Co., 1960
Hazlitt, Henry: The Foundations of Morality   L.A.: Nash Publ., 1972
Camus, Albert:The Rebel. An Essay on Man in Revolt N.Y.:Vintage,1956
Cornforth, Maurice: The Theory of Knowledge
        N.Y.: International Publ., 1977
Munitz, Milton K. (ed.): A Modern Introduction to Ethics
        Glencoe, Illinois: Free Press, 1958
Dougherty, Kenneth F.: General Ethics
        N.Y.: Graymoor Press, 1959
Sartre, Jean-Paul: Being and Nothingness, Transl: Hazel E. Barnes
        N.Y.: Philosophical Library, 1956
Sartre, Jean-Paul: The Age of Reason, Transl: Eric Sutton Harmondsworth,
        Middlesex, UK: Penguin, 1966
Sartre, Jean-Paul: Notebooks for an Ethics Chicago: University of Chicago Press '92

CHAPTER 25

CHOOSING THE GOOD LIFE

"It is this idea of the good that gives value of its own to all knowledge."

Lectures on Philosophy
Simone Weil (1909–1943

If you have ever found yourself in a really "tight spot" — a life threatening situation, or perhaps a mental-emotional trap that held you prisoner, one thought, that like the constant flame of a blow torch, may have kept you alive was this: If ever I get out of this awful mess, I will DO SOMETHING worthwhile, meaningful, significant, GOOD with my life! What kept fearful, deprived, hungry, abused, tyrannized citizens in Nazi occupied Europe going during World War II was the noble motivation that once this horrific ordeal was over, they would have the opportunity to build a better world, a truly GOOD society. . . Allied prisoners-of-war, resistance fighters, children in underground schools all shared one common dream of a GOOD LIFE, a vision that enabled them to endure and persist.

Millions of folks left their homelands in Europe, Asia and elsewhere to move to a new country, in North America or Australia or wherever they thought and believed a GOOD LIFE could be found. In Canada and the United States of America it was the homesteaders and the pioneers, the peasants and the workers, who followed their dreams and ambitions for this good life, who settled two new, free nations.

We all desire a "good" life but may not be too sure exactly what it should be. To those in physically, mentally, emotionally, spiritually, socially and politically deprived conditions, their first and foremost desire would be to meet their immediate needs for food, shelter and the opportunity for free choices. For many however who were, as I was, looking forward to a "brave new world" hinted at in Aldous Huxley's (1894–1963) book (dated 1932), the years following the end of the Second World War were disappointing. The Good Society we wanted did not materialize and it became clear that, since our world community is shaped by the prevailing consciousness of the human beings who govern it, what was needed was a **transformation** of consciousness, a completely new orientation away from violence, selfishness, greed, dogma and all the other destructive forces that created the world we did not want.

Philosophers have known this throughout recorded history, in all cultures, but have not often found people who would both listen and enact the needed changes. In our time, we have a unique opportunity to build a truly GOOD new world. Enormous challenges in the Third World remain, the major countries burden themselves with huge military budgets and the ecological demands to save our planet are greater than ever. Yet, at the same time, the demise of Marxism, the global means of communication - allowing access to the masses of humanity, the availability of resources and the technology, are factors that hold the potential for a GOOD society for all. . .

But what does all of this mean for you and me, as individuals? What can we do to contribute to this GOOD world, thereby also building a GOOD life for ourselves and for the generations who share this planet and will follow us? Given the free will and choice we all seem to have to a large degree, what does it mean to "choose the Good Life?" Again, as with all the subjects we've been discussing, finding answers to this question requires thinking. Poet Erma Wells has written that "thinking is hard work, perhaps that's why so few do it." But hard work, like love, has had a bad press. Yes, it's easier to "take" your ideas from what television, radio and newspapers suggest, or what churches and other institutions teach. The "good life" may then, for those who so choose, be to never work again and drink cold beer for the rest of one's life; or prepare yourself like a worm in the dust, for an after-life where everything is perfect regardless of what we did with our lives here. Ideas that lie, de-motivate, insult and debase are plentiful and their powers of suggestion have built precisely the kind of society we do not want.

But the philosophically and spiritually aware person thinks and contemplates. She or he, associated with other seekers, discusses and deliberates. The answers that come, following this process, will be by their own nature, unique, personal. Your selection and emphasis may differ from mine. Yet, it would not surprise me, having followed this reflective philosophical process, if your preferences would not be close to, or similar to, the ones we have chosen here. Let your lifestyle be authentic. As you read and study these considerations may they assist you to do for yourself, what they have done for many. Here then is what CHOOSING THE GOOD LIFE means to me.

BEING A FREE THINKER

Millions of people have fought for and given their lives so we could live in freedom. Personal freedom is more than living in a democratic society — it means thinking for yourself, not being a prisoner of any institution, book or person. Albert Camus (1913–1960) himself a WWII resistance activist, put it beautifully: "Do not follow me, I may not lead. Do not lead me, I may not follow. Walk beside me and be my friend." Plato tried to wake people up to self-responsibility, to value the processes of our own thinking, to avoid anything that looks like a doctrine. Of course, those who could not live up to his teachings made a dogma out of them, as did many of the followers of the Buddha and Jesus.

Being a free thinker does not mean having no values or commitments — it means choosing your lifestyle freely, being truly yourself and changing as you grow. Karl Jaspers (1883–1969) calls philosophy "the school of . . . independence." He speaks of "rising from the chains that bind us to our emotions." This means breaking forever with any conditioning that limited us, and it implies an inner strength and resilience that reminds us of an ancient school of philosophers known as the stoics. ("Stoic" comes from "stoicus", Greek for "porch", which was the place where Zeno of Citium (336–264 BC), the founder of the school, lectured.)

To the stoics, the virtuous person finds happiness, contentment, in personal independence, regardless of stress from the external world. In other words, in your mind you are free. Realize this and you will have true freedom and dominion over your own thoughts and emotions. Your will must be your own. Accept what cannot be changed — a suggestion that has become a major guideline in any effective recovery program. Marcus Aurelius (121–180), still a popular author of stoic philosophy today, recommended that "contentment. . . comes of doing a few things. . . well" and that since most of what we say and do is not necessary we can become much happier people by letting go of the superfluous. Simplify your life. Be yourself. Don't expect more of other people than they can, by their conditioning and personality, deliver. Don't expect anything from a fig tree except figs, and then only in season.

The personal freedom Jean-Paul Sartre (1905–1980) wrote about in his main text "Being and Nothingness" is one side of life's coin. The other side is personal responsibility: humans are nothing else than what we make of ourselves. Existentialists insist on our finding a justification for our existence. Once we have largely overcome the influence of repressive institutions, sectarian denominationalism and churchianity we can then rightfully consider what this justification may mean.

In his hilariously funny, yet wise, book "Fables for Our Time," James Thurber (1894–1961) tells the story of "the fairly intelligent fly" who won't sit in a spider's net because there are no other flies present but lands happily on a flypaper because all the other flies there appear to be dancing. . . Be free. Be authentic. Be yourself.

DEVELOPING YOUR CREATIVE POTENTIAL
= (follow your dreams)

How many happy people do you know who do nothing with their constructive potential and who probably "hate" their jobs? As we have seen in THE ART OF MOTIVATION, pursuing the right individual goals is a key element in creating a good life for yourself and also makes life for those who know you well, more interesting, harmonious and rewarding. It was Abraham Maslow (1908—1970) who developed the idea that if individuals deliberately choose to be less than they can be, they will be unhappy for the rest of their lives. This thought was central to his developement of a comprehensive humanistic psychology, yet his idea is not new.

Aristotle (384-322 BC), student of Plato, thought that the good life, which would also become a happy life, is the result of fulfilling one's potentialities, talents, character and personality. Our function in life, according to this viewpoint, is to convert potential into actual, with moderation as guiding principle. Aristotle believed — and who would disagree? — that human behavior which is destructive (vandalism, crime, violence, addictions) is so because of frustration, of not being able or willing to fulfil one's potential. According to this teaching, our three-fold nature of physical (good health), emotional (good feelings and mood) and rational (good reason and intellect) being requires fulfillment and these are not options. As a consequence, our lifestyle will include the pursuit of such fields of human activity as music, art, philosophy, science and technology, compatible with the inclination, talent, interest and potential of the individual.

Wouldn't it make sense if we designed our educational systems with this principle as the dominant guideline? Wouldn't our economic world also change to suit this pursuit? And wouldn't all graduates of our educational institutions at all levels be much better motivated, more productive and happier as a result? And, incidentally, have fun at it as well? Be creative. Be what you can be. Be your best.

BEING COMMITTED TO ETHICAL LIVING

It was the great American philosopher Josiah Royce (1855–1916) who, upon lifelong study of what would constitute a good human life, concluded that the key element is loyalty to a worthy cause — and to develop such a spirit of loyalty and devotion is to become happy. Any volunteer would tell you that this statement is oh so true. I have worked with numerous volunteers for over a quarter of a century and have been a volunteer myself for most of my years. There is no greater satisfaction in life than to feel that you are contributing something (work, financial or other tangible support) to making this world a better, a safer, a more prosperous, a happier, a more equitable and a healthier place for everyone. To lessen suffering, to enhance love and compassion, to improve social, economic, cultural and political conditions, to help people in need — what more wonderful feeling is there deep down in your soul and heart than to know the spirit of compassion lives in you?

The opposite (and when philosophizing, assuming the opposite is a vital tool of evaluation) is selfishness, self-centeredness, egotism, stinginess and insensitivity. Who looks for friends (or relatives!) who display these negative characteristics? Who wants their company? What kind of society do we build when we omit character education and the promotion of good will and compassion from our schools' curricula and our homes' code of ethics?

One of the best known and loved tales of all time is Charles Dickens' (1812–1870) "A Christmas Carol." In one of the unforgettable episodes where the ghost of former company C.E.O. Jacob Marley appears to the current company president Ebenezer Scrooge, the latter excuses Marley's remorse, at having been so tightfisted in his lifetime here, by saying that he was, after all, "a good man of business." Whereupon the ghost, while wringing his hands in chained agony, cries out: "Mankind was my business! The common welfare was my business!" Be compassionate. Be ethical. Be generous.

FILLING YOUR LIFE WITH THE WISDOM OF THE AGES

Never before in human history have you and I been so fortunate in having access to so many treasures of civilization: the great thoughts, ideas and concepts, the finest arts and music, information on the greatest of all accomplishments; all is available to us, and at comparatively little cost and effort.

Our age is called the information and communication age — yet people are, generally speaking, ignorant of the most sublime of human achievements: the great ideas upon which a new and good civilization may be built. It was said of Socrates (470–399 BC) that he did not hand down wisdom but made others find it. The the filling of your home and life with the wisdom of the ages, the great philosophers and thinkers, the great creative geniuses of history, as well as the latest knowledge of our universe, of life amd ourselves, will make you feel fully alive and aware. It will not only bolster your self-esteem, make you more interesting and enable you to understand yourself, others and life better, it will do much more. By becoming familiar with the finest and deepest wisdom, beauty and knowledge you will participate in the best civilization has to offer, you become an insider on the stage of life and this helps you to feel at home in the universe.

Build your own library of great ideas and become friends with the minds that perceived the mythology, scriptures and philosophy that shaped all that is admirable in human history. You will not only never be bored or feel useless, but you will have your feet firmly planted on the pathway of wisdom, unveiling the mysteries of life that baffled you, becoming one with the best that was expressed throughout the ages.

Socrates felt that what we search for we already know; that when we are enlightened we sometimes feel as if we've uncovered some ancient memory. This is like Carl Jung's concept of the collective unconscious being revealed to the awakening individual's consciousness. As we surround ourselves with the greatness of history's legacy we find we are able to be helpful to a much wider circle of people. Be enlightened. Be informed. Be aware.

PRACTICING MYSTICAL AWARENESS

It is impossible to imagine anyone striving earnestly to generate a good, meaningful and happy life without the achievement of inner peace. The mastery of the Art of Contemplation is a "must" and absolutely vital to developing the good feeling and the personal contentment which, regardless of many circumstances, can be ours. In contemplative meditation we reflect on our oneness with all living things and we may achieve a genuine feeling of union with the Absolute, the spirit of life itself. The benefits of this practice exceed healing and inner peace for they also include guidance, intuition and an increased awareness of the meaning of your life, with insight into events past, present and future.

In the early seventies of our 20th Century serious research began, in various countries, into the phenomenon of near death experiences (NDE). One remarkable aspect of this experience is that there is an involuntary mystical awareness, a feeling that life is endless, that we are one with an encompassing Presence. The words and phrases such as seeing "a light so pure, powerful and overwhelming that it seems to pervade all being," are the same as those utilized by the mystics to convey their elevated spiritual experience. This knowledge about NDE is one of the most convincing confirmations of the validity of the mystical experience to be brought to public attention in all of human history.

Near Death Experiences have been documented by several scholars over a period of two decades. These records originate with persons who "die" for brief periods but are resuscitated to normal physical functioning and consciousness. They recall what happened while they were "dying" and "dead" and their reports are remarkably similar. All recall that the individual actually "floats out" of her/his body, signifying that **individual consciousness** has being or **exists independent of the physical body.**

There are portrayals of experiencing travelling through a tunnel, of being aware of a great light, of meeting loved ones who had passed on before, of seeing an inner "video tape" of their life's story in mere seconds of time, of great joy and anticipation of **a new dimension of life** where time and space (somewhat as in our dreams) are unlike what we are used to in this life. There is also a deep feeling of **universal love**. All these similar experiences are usually followed by remembering the sudden return to the physical body, and often the disappointment at having to do so.

Folks who have had these NDE's (and I know several individuals personally) do not fear death and dying any more than they would fear going on a trip to a distant city, as Quimby remarked just before passing January 16, 1866. NDEers also have a feeling that they have been transformed in some vitally significant way in relation to the purpose and meaning of life. They feel that we are here to love and to learn, and that life is a precious gift of the all-givingness of the Universal Spirit whose light, life, energy and intelligence manifests in us as wisdom and love. NDEers usually report, as do the Mystics, that our language is inadequate to express the intensity and enormity of the encompassing light and love of the Universe they have experienced. Many of them subsequently devoted themselves to helping those who are facing the end of their earthly lives in hospices and hospitals.

I mention this phenomenon first of all because it clearly shows that there is no need to fear the experience of dying. This dissolves one of the greatest stumbling blocks to the "good life" we've been discussing, namely the fear of death caused by the superstitious belief in heaven, purgatory, limbo and hell, as taught by conservative, fundamentalist theology. This fear has held and still holds millions of basically good and decent folks, especially senior citizens, in its grip — destroying and preventing the wonderful peace of mind and serenity to which they are entitled. The NDE research is a major step in our time, toward the liberation of the human soul and authentic living.

The second reason the NDE phenomenon is of vital importance, as noted earlier, is that it validates the mystical awareness that may already be ours in contemplative meditation. To the busy "westerner," so involved in our material world, it usually does not occur to us that a beautiful, peaceful, love-filled spiritual life is available in the here and now and that this spiritual life can become the foundation of and empowerment for a truly authentic life.

It is interesting to note that the NDE with the mystical experience and spiritual awareness is the subject of the meaning of much of history's mythologies in all cultures. The Bible, interpreted from a mythological, metaphysical and metaphorical point of view abounds in wisdom describing our journey, the meaning of our lives and our destiny.

We are used to hearing a "quip" in everyday language, originating in the early "nineteen nineties" that goes like this: "Oh, get a life!" or: "Why don't you get a life!" Tragically, most people don't have a clue how to get an authentic life. They are bogged down by superstition, conditioning and destructive suggestions that have caused them to become a totally different person from what once was their dream — and perhaps deep inside still is. They have become victims of false belief, actors living someone else's script. They hate and despise themselves and their self-loathing motivates substance abuse and destructive, often violent behavior. Others, caught in their own introverted consciousness, lead, in Henry David Thoreau's (1817–1862) words, "lives of quiet desperation." And misery and illness. They stay in relationships that are a living hell and in jobs that bore them to tears, so that their weekends are the temporary relief of a dreadful existence, in which retirement becomes life's objective. It's bad news.

The good news is that any destructive beliefs can be changed, that true liberation from negative conditioning is possible.

The pathway to accomplish this is called here Authentic Living. It offers freedom from the past, empowerment to live today, the awareness that to live means to learn and to love, and the achievement of authentic selfhood whose destiny is unlimited. What is our part in this process? It probably couldn't be better expressed than in the words of existentialist philosopher Jean-Paul Sartre: **YOU ARE FREE. . . CHOOSE!**

Bibliography and Recommended Further Reading

Weil, Simone: Lectures on Philosophy
    N.Y.:Cambridge Univ. Press, 1978
Weil, Simone: Waiting on God   London: Fontana, 1959
Weil, Simone: Formative Writings (1929–1941)
    Boston: Univ. of Massachusetts Press, 1987
Coles, Robert: Simone Weil, A Modern Pilgrimage
    Reading, Mass: Addison-Wesley, 1987
Jaspers, Karl and Bultmann, Rudolf: Myth and Christianity
    N.Y.: Noonday Press, 1971
Jaspers, Karl: Kant   N.Y.: Harcourt, Brace & World, 1962
Jaspers, Karl: Plato and Augustine
    N.Y.: Harcourt Brace Jovanovich, 1962
Jaspers, Karl: Socrates, Buddha, Confucius, Jesus
    N.Y.: Harcourt, Brace & World, 1962
Jaspers, Karl: Spinoza   N.Y.: Harcourt Brace Jovanovich, 1966
Jaspers, Karl: Anselm and Nicholas of Cusa
    N.Y.: Harcourt Brace Jovanovich, 1966
Kornfield, Jack: A Path With Heart   N.Y.: Bantam, 1993

Books that have reference to Near Death Experiences (NDE):
Anderson, C. Alan: More Than Mortal?
    Canton, Mass: Squantum Press, 1991
Harpur, Tom: Life After Death   Toronto: McClelland & Stewart, 1991
Moody, R.A.: Life After Life   N.Y.: Bantam, 1975
Moody, R.A.: Reflections on Life After Life   N.Y.: Bantam, 1977
Rinpoche, Sogyal: The Tibetan Book of Living and Dying
    N.Y.: Harper San Francisco, 1992
Blackmore, Susan: Dying to Live - NDE Experiences
    Buffalo, N.Y.: Prometheus Books, 1993
Eadie, Betty J. with Curtis Taylor: Embraced by the Light
    Placerville, CA: Gold Leaf Press, 1992

AFTERWORD

Today, more and more persons find it helpful to center their lives and their thoughts by using an affirmation that reflects the state of consciousness they wish to attain.

As a public speaker this writer has found that the following statement, presented here in the first person, present tense, is popular both as an affirmation of self-empowerment and as a reflection of the philosophy of authentic living. It may be used as a personal affirmation and as a subject for deeper meditation.

As you read and think these thoughts, and ponder their meaning, the feeling that will follow will allow your consciousness to become an active center of that meaning, and the expression in every day life will inevitably be yours as well.

AUTHENTIC LIVING CONTEMPLATION

As I relax, I now become aware that the Universe has unlimited possibilities for me to experience love, happiness, health and success. As an expression of the Universal Life Spirit I now realize that I am entitled to the best that the universe has to offer.

I now accept responsibility for my own life and I commit myself to think for myself and to be myself. I now choose to express and radiate love, happiness, health and success.

The higher Wisdom and Intelligence of the Universe is now guiding me to the right place, the right persons and circumstances, at the right time. I feel the presence of Infinite Love indwelling and surrounding me and giving me the strength and confidence to become the fascinating, creative person I can be.

In this infinite ocean of love and wisdom, I live and move and have my being. I accept this for myself. Therefore, love and wisdom flow from me to others and our planet Earth. I am a center of compassion, of sharing and caring.

From the Source of Life, the meaning of my life is being revealed to me. I give thanks for the dynamic activity of the Cosmic Wisdom in me and I remain serene in the conviction that the highest and best are now being done.

And that's the way it is!

- Herman Jan Aaftink

Recommended Further Reading

Addington, Jack Ensign: The Secret of Healing
    N.Y.: Dodd, Mead & Co., 1979
Anderson, C. Alan: Healing Hypotheses. Horatio W. Dresser and the
    Philosophy of New Thought
    N.Y.: Garland Publ., 1993
Collie, Errol Stafford: Quimby's Science of Happiness. A Non-Medical
    Scientific Explanation of the Cause and Cure of Disease
    Marina Del Rey, Ca: DeVorss & Co., 1980
Cousins, Norman: Anatomy of an Illness as Perceived by the Patient
    N.Y., London: W.W.Norton & Co., 1979
Evans, Warren Felt: The Mental Cure, Illustrating the Influence of Mind
    on the Body.
    Boston: Banner of Light Publ., 1869
Goldsmith, Joel S.: The Art of Spiritual Healing
    N.Y.: Harper & Row, 1959
James, William: The Varieties of Religious Experience. A Study in
    Human Nature N.Y.: Random House, 1929
Moyers, Bill: Healing and the Mind
    N.Y.: Doubleday, 1993
Quimby, Phineas Parkhurst: The Complete Writings ed: Ervin Seale with
    Herman J. Aaftink, C. Alan Anderson, Errol S. Collie, Isabel Price,
Elva Seale, Kathryn and W.B.Wier Vols. I, II & III
    Marina Del Rey,CA: DeVorss & Co., 1988
Seale, Ervin: Mingling Minds, Some Commentary on the Philosophy and
    Practice of Phineas Parkhurst Quimby
    Linden, N.J.: Tide Press, 1986
Siegel, Bernie S.: Love, Medicine & Miracles
    N.Y.: Harper & Row, 1988
Siegel, Bernie S.: Peace, Love & Healing
    N.Y.: Harper & Row, 1989
Simonton, O. Carl: Getting Well Again
    N.Y.: St. Martin's Press, 1978

ACKNOWLEDGMENTS

It's Thanksgiving Day every day for this book!

Grateful acknowledgment is made to all those whose wisdom has contributed to the making of this book. Their names and sources are stated in each instance.

There are three special persons, without whom this book could not have been produced: my editor, **George W. Fisk**, whose tireless efforts reflect infinite care.

Beverly Shea, who prepared the manuscript for diskette with incredible excellence.

Last, but not least, my significant other, **Diana North**, whose love, devotion, encouragement and sense of humor are without measure.

Thank you so much, one and all!

hja